PORTRAIT OF AN OBSESSION

PORTRAIT
OF AN
OBSESSION

HOW ENGLAND'S GREATEST PRIVATE LIBRARY WAS BUILT FROM THE RUINS OF EUROPE'S MONASTERIES

KELSEY JACKSON WILLIAMS

OXFORD
UNIVERSITY PRESS

OXFORD
UNIVERSITY PRESS

Great Clarendon Street, Oxford, OX2 6DP,
United Kingdom

Oxford University Press is a department of the University of Oxford.
It furthers the University's objective of excellence in research, scholarship,
and education by publishing worldwide. Oxford is a registered trade mark of
Oxford University Press in the UK and in certain other countries.

Published in the United States of America by Oxford University Press
546 Fifth Avenue, New York, NY 10036, United States of America

British Library Cataloguing in Publication Data
Data available

Library of Congress Control Number: 2026933788

ISBN 9780198879053

DOI: 10.1093/oso/9780198879053.001.0001

Printed and bound by
CPI Group (UK) Ltd., Croydon, CR0 4YY

MIX
Paper | Supporting
responsible forestry
FSC
www.fsc.org
FSC® C013604

The manufacturer's authorized representative in the EU for product safety is
Oxford University Press España S.A. of Parque Empresarial San Fernando de Henares,
Avenida de Castilla, 2 – 28830 Madrid (www.oup.es/en or product.safety@oup.com).
OUP España S.A. also acts as importer into Spain of products made by the manufacturer.

For Bill Zachs
Friend and mentor in bibliomania

Books ought always to be bought.

—Richard de Bury, *Philobiblon* (*c.*1345)[1]

What wild desires, what restless torments seize,
The hapless man, who feels the book-disease.

—John Ferriar, *The Bibliomania* (1809)[2]

Contents

Acknowledgements

It is a pleasure to acknowledge the many individuals and institutions who have made this book possible. The University of Stirling was my institutional home throughout its composition and I am grateful both to the Eighteenth-Century Writing Group for camaraderie and feedback as well as to the Division of Literature and Languages for granting me research leave during the final completion of the manuscript. In the latter stages of writing, Blackie House Library and Museum provided me with a much-loved second institutional base whose good bibliography, good fellowship, and good food did much for the genesis of this volume.

The staff of the John Rylands Library in Manchester, home to Spencer's library, and the British Library, home to his papers, have been unfailingly helpful throughout and I am particularly grateful to the John Rylands for permitting the reproduction of the many images from their collections which appear here. I owe similar debts for the reproduction of images to the National Portrait Gallery, London, the Masters and Fellows of University College, Oxford, Blackie House Library and Museum, Edinburgh, and the Earl Spencer. Ségolène Gence was the best research assistant one could hope for at the British Library, while Sofie Pedley at Althorp was invaluable in securing the reproduction of a key portrait of Spencer.

I have discussed the contents of this book with more people than I can easily remember and I fear the following list is far from exhaustive. Michelle Craig, Daryl Green, Katherine Halsey, Dawn Hollis, Emma Macleod, David Pearson, Ed Potten, Angus Vine, and Eric White have all offered thoughtful comments on various aspects of the text. John Gandy gave me invaluable tips and suggestions over regular coffees in Manchester during my trips there to work with Spencer's books. William Zachs, to whom this book is dedicated, was an always sympathetic ear and an unflagging friend in bibliomania.

At Oxford University Press, I am indebted to Matthew Cotton who commissioned this volume as well as to the conscientous and sympathetic anonymous readers. As this work has moved into production, Rachel Ruisard and Thomas Stottor have provided consistent encouragement and aid.

Finally, Vera Jackson-Hollis, who was there from the beginning, and Sorley Jackson-Hollis, who arrived in the middle, have been sources of welcome distraction and much love throughout. I hope they might one day read "daddy's boring book".

Cellardyke, Fife
April 2026

List of Illustrations

A Note on Prices

I have not attempted to give modern equivalents for the many prices—of books and other commodities—referenced in this work. This is for good reason: it is very difficult to attach a meaningful modern value to a purchase price from two hundred years ago. Not only has the international economy changed beyond recognition, but the relative values of different types of good and service have altered radically, as have average incomes, and the cost of what constitutes a "normal" quality of life.

Accordingly, we cannot reduce a historic price to an "X = Y" equation. What we can do, however, is think in more specific terms about different types of possible equivalence and, using those collectively, build up a sense of the historic value of an item. Take, as an example, a book: the 1471 edition of the Latin orator Quintilian printed in Venice by Nicolaus Jenson, which Earl Spencer bought from the London bookseller James Edwards on 16 March 1801 for £20.[3] We could consider this in terms of "real price", a metric linked to the Retail Price Index, which measures the relative values of a representative sample of basic goods and services. If we did, we could say that the present "value" of that £20 is £1,925.[4] Alternatively, we could tie our calculation to wage indices, which would lead us to conclude that the "labour value" of that £20 is the much more substantial £28,140. Or again, we could link it to a multiple of the average income and conclude that the "income value" is the slightly more modest £25,030. Finally, we might consider the book's value in relation to the GDP of Britain as a whole and suggest that its modern worth in terms of "economic share" is a staggering £147,700.

Clearly, there is a huge discrepancy in these calculations. A useful reality check, however, can be offered by considering the present-day prices which the same book currently fetches. In 2018 Lambeth Palace Library acquired a copy of the Jenson Quintilian for £50,000, though this copy was made more desirable by its association with John Morton, Archbishop of Canterbury (*d.* 1500).[5] In 2021 a pleasingly illuminated but essentially unremarkable copy of the same edition fetched $37,500 at Christie's (about £27,000 at the time).[6] This might lead us to suppose that labour or income value is a reliable metric, but this only holds true if we assume that the rise in the cost of incunables has been entirely proportional with larger changes in value. This is doubtful at best and we would not be amiss to presume that, as they have grown scarcer, their absolute value, as well as their relative value, has increased. As such, I do not believe that any of the possible metrics I have outlined above fully capture relative worth for the items discussed here, but I encourage interested readers to make use of the tools available and reach their own conclusions.

PROLOGUE

The Book Fool

In 1509 the Scottish priest Alexander Barclay wrote a long poem, part translation of, part improvisation on, Sebastian Brant's *Das Narrenschiff*, the *Ship of Fools* (1494). Both Brant's original and Barclay's Anglicisation are half-funny, half-gloomy depictions of a gallimaufry of human idiocy divided by types: everything from negligent students to people who talk in church. First of all, however, comes the Book Fool. *Das Narrenschiff* became famous in large part because of the woodcuts accompanying each fool—many are by Albrecht Dürer—and the Book Fool does not disappoint (see Figure 0.1). Dressed in a scholar's gown and fool's caps and bells, he wears thick spectacles and carries a feather duster (all the better to keep his tomes clean with). He sits in front of a late medieval lectern covered with books. More are on the shelves behind and he is leafing through a particularly large volume open in front of him.

Who is this man? Barclay ventriloquises for him in the accompanying text (which I have here lightly modernised from its Middle English original):

> Still am I busy book assembling
> For to have plenty it is a pleasant thing
> In my conceit and to have them ay in hand,
> But what they mean I do not understand.
>
> But yet I have them in great reverence
> And honour, saving them from filth and ordure
> By often brushing and much diligence
> Full goodly bound in pleasant coverture
> Of damask satin or else of velvet pure.
> I keep them sure, fearing lest they should be lost,
> For in them is the cunning wherein I me boast.

Figure 0.1 The Book Fool, from Sebastian Brant, *The Shyp of Folys of the Worlde*, tr. Alexander Barclay (London: Richard Pynson, 1509), fol. XIIIr, John Rylands 15412.

But the Book Fool, though he may love his books, not only does he not understand them, he does not even read them:

> But few I read and fewer understand.
> I follow not their doctrine nor their lore;
> It is enough to bear a book in hand.
> ...
> I am content on the fair covering to look.

Whenever I read this description of a fifteenth-century book collector, I am always surprised anew at how little this stereotype has changed.

When we think of modern Book Fools, crowded out of their homes by obsessively purchased volumes, we censure them in much the same terms. They can't possibly have read them all, can they? And even if they have, surely they're somehow doing the wrong thing—prioritising the book as an object rather than for the knowledge it contains? Maybe they just like looking at the covers?

These are deeply-held beliefs on the part of many intelligent, reasonable people when faced with a book collector. And the larger and finer the collection, the more intensely these beliefs are held by onlookers. I am in a good position to comment on this, being myself the owner of a few thousand books. When confronted with them, friends and visitors usually make some polite, faintly embarrassed comment, often followed by the ever-green query, "and have you read them all?" What I say in response depends on my mood—sometimes, "yes, many of them twice"—but the real answer, as everyone involved knows, is "no". After a certain point, one stops buying books simply to read them and enters the strange land of the collector, where ownership is justified by any number of clever self-deceptions: "it might be useful", "it will be handy as a reference", "I'm sure I'll read it some day", "it makes sense to have X if I have Y", and so forth, none of which really gets to the root of the matter.

What *is* the root of the matter? Many people have tried to answer this question—I will be discussing some of their theories later in this book—but the urge to collect is a difficult, slippery thing. Non-collectors like to belittle it, it makes them uncomfortable somehow, and even collectors find it an awkward topic; they collect because they *must*, but explaining why they must is almost impossible. Nonetheless, it is a conundrum which has occupied my thoughts, as a collector, as an academic, and, latterly, as a librarian in an independent research library, and while we may not be able to discover the psychological well-springs of the collecting instinct, we can certainly watch it in action, like a naturalist observing a wild animal or, more accurately, like a biographer watching a life play out according to its own obscure but ineluctable logic.

One of the conclusions I have reached in the course of these deeply self-interested observations is that, much as book collecting might seem to be an inward-looking, private activity, it very rarely is. Instead, the collector sits in the midst of a cat's cradle of connections, with booksellers, libraries, other collectors, and with each book acquired that tangled web becomes denser, more multi-layered, more encompassing. Every library is made up of the detritus of other libraries and every collector is re-collecting books which had been sought out long before he or she was born.

We might be tempted to view this web of connections as essentially benign, perhaps of merely antiquarian interest to anyone except the collector. But I am not convinced it is always—or even often—so. The problem is the books themselves, old books anyway. I recall one senior colleague saying that "any truly good book has been stolen at least once" and while this is probably an over-statement, it is nonetheless true that there is something about books which arouses cupidity, on the part of individuals, but also of states. Perhaps it is because they are both small and valuable, easily moved and easily *re*moved. And even when an old book has not been stolen *per se*—and I think, on the whole, most probably have not—there are ways short of theft to make someone part with a rare volume, arguments from exigency, from threat, from an awareness that fate is catching up with the owner and ready money will be more useful than an old book.

Nowhere has this been more evident in the past half millennium than in the case of monastic libraries. Once the great keepers of Western Civilisation's written sense of itself, since the Reformation they have become easy targets for reformers, governments, and private citizens, all of whom have felt, at one time or another, that they had a much better right to the books there than the monks who inconveniently owned them. It is an awkward fact for modern librarians and scholars of the book that most very early printed books were once in monastic libraries and most no longer are.

What happened? There are many answers to that question, depending on time and place, but one great turning point occurred during the course of the Napoleonic Wars, the almost universal conflict which gripped Europe for nearly three decades at the end of the eighteenth and beginning of the nineteenth centuries. Never, before or since, have so many monasteries and nunneries been pillaged, so many books sold under duress, confiscated, or simply destroyed, both by the French armies and their opponents. Suddenly, the book market was flooded with previously unobtainable old volumes and a generation of collectors rose to the challenge, assembling what were probably the best private libraries ever formed, before or since, private libraries which, as often as not, now form the basis of the major research libraries of the western world.

This is a book about one of those libraries and about the man who formed it: George John Spencer, 2nd Earl Spencer (1758–1834). It is also a book about the effect of wealth in an unsettled and violent time, occasionally a lament for the lost world of the monastic library, and, perhaps more than anything, an attempt to understand the Book Fool. How does he pursue his obsession? What is at stake? What are the potential rewards? What, in the end, is he trying to *do*?

Each Book Fool is his own island, driven by his own passions and obsessions in a way obscure, at bottom, to the rest of us. But we have every advantage when confronted with this particular Book Fool. We have his library, his correspondence, his receipts, even the very detritus of his desk drawers. We also have the ripples of his wake: the empty shelves, the rubbed out inscriptions of previous owners, the attempts, too often successful, to obscure the undeniable fact that these books had once, in another lifetime, been owned by people, sometimes different from, sometimes surprisingly similar to, the Book Fool himself.

This is not a story which has been told in full before, though its result—the Spencer library—has been the subject of awe and admiration for near two hundred years.[1] The culture of book collecting during the Napoleonic era has been explored by a number of distinguished scholars, notably Kristian Jensen, David McKitterick, and Eric Marshall White, to whose works I owe a great debt, but Spencer's career has been at best one case study amongst many, at worst a footnote.[2] His immense manuscript archive in the British Library has been cherry-picked for information on the book trade before now, but never studied intensively, and his books in the John Rylands Library have often been consulted, but not with the intent of recovering their owner's collecting practices. Perhaps most importantly, the psychological and moral implications of Spencer's collecting have remained carefully untouched.

I too am a Book Fool, I confess it freely, so do not expect any baffled condemnation in these pages. Condemnation there is, but weighed carefully and given, on the whole, reluctantly. Instead, what follows is, I hope, not simply a narrative of how a great library was formed at the expense of many a smaller one, but a story about the love of books, and of how two men (our first Book Fool and myself, the late-come second) have responded to some of the oldest and most beautiful printed books in the world. It is also, inevitably, a story about those books themselves and how the art of printing spread from one shop in Mainz to transform the world of Renaissance Europe in a few short decades. And, above all, it is a story about desire: its roots, its actions, its costs, and, sometimes, its rewards.

ONE

An unexpected offer

It was the spring of 1789 and a storm was brewing over Europe. After a dry summer and rising food prices there came "a winter of such severe cold, as was without example in the memory of man".[1] The mercury dipped below freezing for eighty-six days at Paris, reaching −21.8 degrees centigrade on New Year's Eve.[2] The Thames froze at London and ships were diverted to Portsmouth. In the face of mounting unrest in France, the Estates General were called, opening their convention on 5 May. The storming of the Bastille was only months away.

In London, the hard winter was gradually giving way to a wet spring. Rain fell on the gentlemen and ladies hurrying across Hanover Square. It dripped down the neo-classical facade of St. George's, the church where the best society prayed and married (when they remembered to do either). It was churned into mud by carriage wheels and ran through the railings to pool and puddle at the foundations of fashionable town houses. Running down from the square into Conduit Street, water splashed on the steps of Trinity Chapel—privately owned by the bookseller James Robson—and was tracked into the "Great Room", the auction house opposite, by a group of men, some richly dressed, some shabby, who crowded into its doorway just after noon one damp, late spring morning.[3]

The occasion: the sale of an ancient Venetian library. For two hundred years, the Pinelli family had been *stampatori ducale*, printers to the Doge and Republic of Venice. Their last scion, Maffeo Pinelli, had died comparatively young in 1785, leaving an unparalleled collection of early printing. "The Books fill three or four Rooms compleatly", one contemporary witness wrote, and "they are indeed curious & valuable... scarcely ever more of [the first printed books] were collected by one man, & in excellent preservation".[4] Such treasures did not lack for interested buyers and in the summer of 1787 a group of hungry English booksellers—James Edwards, James Robson, Robert Faulder, and Peter Molini—met with the library's then proprietor, Signor Lanchi, and agreed to buy the lot for something amounting to about £7,000, which "the Executors and Trustees found it [in] their Interest to accept".[5] Even for a consortium of established men of business this was an enormous sum, and even once obtained, getting the books home to London was no easy matter. It was not until the following winter that they could be boxed up and placed on ships destined for England and even then their arrival was further delayed by the harsh conditions; they only reached Portsmouth in early January 1789.[6]

By April, the boxes had been unloaded, the books transported to Robson's auction rooms, a catalogue hastily prepared, and the sale had begun.[7] Bidding was fierce on that first day, with early editions of the Bible fetching record prices—14 guineas, £25, even £30—and continued strong. It was a sale that changed the face of the European book trade; from now on, its centre was London.[8]

But we are less concerned with the Pinelli sale—a triumph of publicity, a revolution in taste, and something of a failure in actual financial terms—than with a small interaction which took place on its side lines. Let me draw your attention to two men at the edge of the auction room, speaking quietly between themselves as the lots are hawked from the auctioneer's podium. One is tall, very well dressed, in the prime of his life—he is halfway through his thirty-first year—with close-cropped, already receding red hair (see Figure 1.1). He is not particularly prepossessing in his appearance, though nor is he ugly as such. With a long, beaky nose, a wavering chin, already inclining towards fleshiness, thin lips, and a heavy furrowed brow which gives him a perpetual air of severe concern, he is, in so many ways, a characteristic specimen of the English aristocracy. Yes, it is our Book Fool. His names are George John Spencer and six years before he had succeeded his father as the 2nd Earl Spencer,

Figure 1.1 John Singleton Copley, *George John, 2nd Earl Spencer* (*c.*1800), National Portrait Gallery 1487.

inheriting fifty estates and about as many mortgages.[9] He is currently in the process of relieving himself of one, so that he might be relieved of the other.

His companion offers a striking contrast. A neat, older, foreign gentleman—he is fifty-two to Spencer's thirty—he has an indefinable air of distant lands about him and a polished poise which would have been envied in any court in Europe. Lacking a portrait, we can only guess at the details of his physiognomy. This is the Hungarian-born Count Károly Imre Reviczky de Revisnye (1737–1793), envoy extraordinary from his Imperial Majesty, the Holy Roman Emperor Josef II, to the court of Great Britain, a man "ingenious as he is faint-hearted".[10]

As we watch them talking, we see Reviczky take a comfortably pocket-sized book out of his tailcoat and "slily" proffer it to Spencer.[11] It is a vellum Aldine, a little octavo bound in blue morocco—the Pindar of 1513—but to understand the temptation such an object might hold for men like the two we are observing, we must pause for a moment and define our terms: octavo, morocco, vellum, Aldine.[12]

* * *

Let's begin with the easiest: octavo. Books from the first age of printing exist in different formats depending on the number of times the sheet of paper laid on the press was subsequently folded. If you took a single sheet of paper and printed two pages on each side, then folded it once, you got a large, rather tall book called a folio. But if you printed four pages on each side and folded it twice, you got a smaller, square book called a quarto. If you kept going, printing eight pages on each side and folding your sheet three times, you got an octavo, like the Pindar we see here. This can go on to absurd lengths, with duodecimos (12mos), 16mos, 18mos, 24mos, and even 32mos, possible, but we will mostly be encountering folios, the preferred format for much very early printing, and the occasional quarto and octavo.[13]

Most books in the first centuries of printing were bound in some sort of leather, the product of unfortunate sheep, cows, goats, or pigs, which was tanned, died, stamped, and tooled into more or less elegant, more or less functional, bindings to protect the pages within. By the late eighteenth century, a distinct hierarchy of luxury had emerged with paper and other more or less ephemeral bindings at the bottom and "morocco" at the top.

What was morocco? It was goat skin, but not, usually, a product of North Africa. Instead, it was sourced from across the eastern Mediterranean, in this period principally from the dominions of the Ottoman Empire in and around Istanbul, in Anatolia, and sometimes from as far north as the Crimea.[14] The raw skins were steeped in stagnant water for several days, pared, aged in lime pits for as much as a month at a time, then washed, the remaining hair removed, limed and scraped and washed again, several times over, then stamped and stretched while still wet and finally allowed to dry.[15] This exhausting, noisome process was lengthy, physically demanding, and foul, with one traditional method requiring the skins to be soaked in dog's excrement. Only after it was complete were the skins ready to be dyed.

Goat skin, in comparison to calf or sheep, takes and retains dye very well, but the traditional processes remained closely guarded secrets within the fraternities of Anatolian and Crimean dyers until well into the eighteenth century. It was not until the end of the century that dyeing began to take place in Europe as well as Asia, with European merchants in Istanbul purchasing substantial quantities of both dyed and undyed skins for western markets.[16]

Used for everything from slippers to furniture, morocco was the luxury binding of choice for books. From a comparative rarity in the seventeenth century, it had become an essential part of high-end bookbinding in the eighteenth, though compared to other skins it was difficult to work, tending to easily stain and tear if not handled with skill.[17] The natural grain of the goat skin could also be subjected to further alteration or refinement at this stage. Most of the goat skins used were pebbly, with a noticeably high grain in their natural state. This could be accentuated by rolling and rubbing, reduced by pummelling (creating "crushed" morocco) or stretched out into long vertical or horizontal ridges, called "straight grained" morocco, through repeated passes with a grooved ball of boxwood.[18] Only then was the skin ready to be applied to the book itself, laid onto boards and tooled with the rich blind or gold designs which made bindings of this period so sumptuous. Suffice it to say, the exterior of Reviczky's Pindar was the product of a long process, extending across continents and months, if not years, which saw it transformed from rough animal hide to collector's gem.

When I first held this engaging little volume on a cool October afternoon, sitting in the reading room of the John Rylands Library in Manchester—where Spencer's library now resides—I did not see the binding in which it would have been bound in 1789. Earl Spencer, its eventual owner, commissioned one of his favourite bookbinders, Charles Hering, to rebind it in a high and tactile straight-grained olive morocco, lavishly blind-tooled in a heavy geometric pattern with Spencer's arms gold-tooled in the centre of each board and a spine that can only be described as encrusted with tooling, blind and gold. Opening it, you find wide inner dentelles—overlapping leather surrounding the edges of the inner boards—also lavishly gold-tooled and golden moire silk endpapers. The entire production is so gem-like that it has been encased in a slightly more modest blue straight-grained morocco book box. When I first opened it I was caught off-guard by a stark reminder of the perishability of colour: the inside of the case is a bright, almost royal blue, compared to the darker, yellowish exterior.

I confess, I regret the loss of the earlier binding. Spencer's sometime client, librarian, and friend Thomas Frognall Dibdin might have described Hering's rebinding as having "redeemed" the Pindar "from the choking thraldom and tawdry taste of its previous condition", but I find it too heavy, almost overwhelming on this delicate volume.[19] For delicate it is, once you fight your way past its imposing exterior. It is, in fact, one of the most tactile books I've ever held.

Medieval manuscripts were overwhelmingly written on vellum, sheep's or calves' skins scraped thin and prepared to receive ink, with paper only slowly gaining ground in the fifteenth century. The process is not unlike that for goat. The skins are washed, soaked in lime, scraped, stretched, and beaten into shape until they are fine and smooth enough to take ink. The finest are finished with pumice powder or a similar abrasive material to produce a silky smooth surface.[20]

Unsurprisingly, when Gutenberg first printed his Bible, he printed copies on both vellum and paper and printing on vellum remained an important aspect of early book culture. Rapidly, however, it became clear that the cost of the skins together with the comparative difficulty of making them receive a good impression from the type made paper by far the more economical choice and consigned vellum to occasional presentation copies or works of fine printing.[21] By the period in which we are concerned, very little vellum printing was undertaken and that, by contemporary consensus, was distinctly inferior to what had been done in earlier centuries, owing, one critic opined, rather to "the preparation of the vellum than…the execution of the press-work".[22] Giambattista Bodoni (1740–1813), the Italian printer, appears to have attempted to overcome this by printing on vellum made, not from sheep, but from aborted calf foetuses, which was, his contemporaries thought, "more white and delicate".[23]

Had I known this last fact during my introduction to the Reviczky Pindar it might have somewhat cooled my enthusiasm, but as it was I could uncomplicatedly enjoy the pleasure of a new discovery. I had never worked closely with a vellum book before and had wondered, more than once, what made them so highly prized by collectors? It makes no sense if you see only a digital surrogate: the quality of the printing is about the same—maybe even a little worse as vellum is tricky to work with—and the page itself looks like slightly yellowed, rather unremarkable paper. But only touch a vellum page and you instantly understand. The material under your fingertips is infinitely soft and tactile, like tissue paper made of velvet, but is surprisingly durable and turns—at least the pages of the Pindar turned—with a soft, mesmerising swish altogether unlike the rustle and crackle of old paper (see Figure 1.2).

I was entranced. My Greek is, I admit, inadequate for reading Pindar without the aid of a facing-page translation (or at least a good dictionary), but I happily puzzled my way through the volume just for the feel of its pages. Even such an exceptional example of vellum printing, however, was not without the faults that inevitably go with it. On one page I came across a small hole in the vellum—always a risk during the scraping process which pares it down from its initial rugged thickness to that of a printed page—which had been delicately patched with a thin piece of paper, perhaps once the same colour as the vellum but now standing out against its pearly backdrop.[24]

But the Aldine Pindar is more than just a beautiful binding and tactile pages; it is a monument to and an epoch in the history of printing. The Venetian printer Aldo Manuzio had established his press in 1494 and produced his first book the year after. His printing was good, he had access to many important classical manuscripts, and he was working in a city which had rapidly emerged as a centre of the growing book trade. But that was not what made Manuzio—better known by the Latinised form of his name, Aldus Manutius—remarkable. Instead, it was the innovations he brought to his craft. First, he commissioned the cutting of elegant italic types, the first to be used, modelled on the humanist handwriting of the period. Then, he eschewed the larger, heavier formats so common to early printing in favour of the *enchiridion*—Greek for a

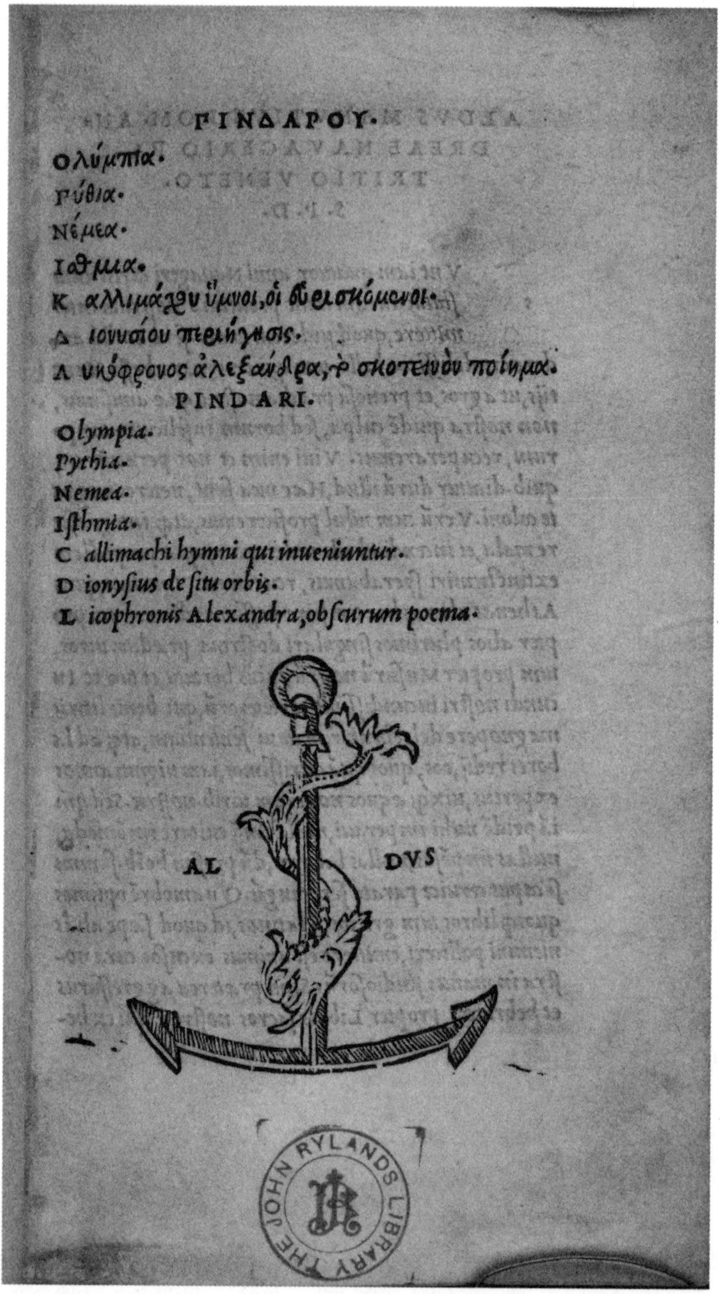

Figure 1.2 Pindar, *[Works]* (Venice: Aldo Manuzio, 1513), title page, the vellum presentation copy to Andrea Navagero, John Rylands 3205.

hand-held weapon—a book one could carry about, slip into one's pocket, pick up, and read at ease. These elegantly printed pocket editions of the Greek and Latin classics defined later printing and are, by distant and winding routes, the ancestors of the modern paperback.

Besides these technical and commercial innovations, Manuzio had an intellectual agenda: quite simply, he wanted to print Greek books. At the end of the fifteenth century, Greek was far less universally known than Latin, though it was gaining ground, and many important Greek texts remained accessible only in manuscript. Manuzio wanted to change that and over his career he printed dozens of works in Greek, many of them for the first time.[25] These *editiones principes—editio princeps* being Latin for what we would call a "first edition", i.e. the first time a work appeared in print—became legendary as, indeed, all of the output of his press did in succeeding centuries. Collecting Aldines, especially Aldine *editiones principes*, was already an established practice when Reviczky showed this volume to Spencer.[26]

According to Dibdin, who will serve as our *cicerone* to Spencer's growing library long before he figures in this book as a player in his own right, "a more lovely vellum Aldus can with difficulty be conceived" and the Pindar is, by any standards, a stunningly beautiful volume.[27] Nor is this just any Aldine Pindar. It is, quite literally, *the* Aldine Pindar: the dedication copy which Manuzio presented to his friend and patron Andrea Navagero in 1513. From there it found its way through the magnificent libraries of the historian Jacques-Auguste de Thou and the collector Jean-Jacques Charron, marquis de Menars, to Prince Charles de Rohan-Soubise, whose library was sold in Paris under the storm clouds of February 1789. Reviczky was on the ground and made short work of any competition; *the* Aldine Pindar was his.[28] Holding it over two centuries later, I can understand his enthusiasm. This is one of the most perfectly restrained, elegant, beautiful—leaving aside the Hering binding—books I've ever held.

* * *

Reviczky proffered the Pindar to Spencer; the younger man, as attentive and as eager as might be fitting in a properly languorous member of the aristocracy, received it. At this stage it is doubtful whether any sale was intended. Most likely Reviczky, with his air of ultimate connoisseurship, was simply showing the younger man the difference between the *good* things in the Pinelli sale and the truly *excellent* things to be had by those in the know. This quickly changed. One day in June 1789, Reviczky and Spencer met in the fashionable Pall Mall premises of the bookseller James Edwards (1757–1816), one of the partners in the Pinelli sale and one of the leading London dealers who catered to the bibliophilically-minded aristocracy. Spencer was there, so the story goes, to give various commissions to Edwards, then about to depart for the continent and, seeing Reviczky, could not help but ruefully lament that, "no expense or pains will ever enable me to form so complete a collection as you".

"Will you buy my collection?" Reviczky asked.

"Yes, and I will refer the price to Edwards", Spencer replied.

Reviczky hesitated at the earl's eagerness, retiring and saying that he "must consider of it".[29] It was one thing to tempt Spencer that perhaps, just perhaps, he might quite like to purchase, not merely Reviczky's Pindar, but his entire collection, altogether another to have that offer accepted so eagerly.

The prospect was given sudden urgency later that day. "On returning home", Reviczky wrote to Spencer, "I found letters from Vienna which confirmed my recall from here, and my new destination for Naples, which in view of the difficulty of taking my whole Library from here, made my proposal…for which you have shown some inclination" both more pressing and more realistic.[30] Selling a library like Reviczky's, however, was not something to be done hastily and the count carefully outlined his initial terms in a letter written a few days after their meeting. Afflicted though he was, he protested, at the thought that his library might "become the share of some idiotic heir" and eventually be sold, he had to be practical. After all, "According to the estimate of several local Booksellers, my Library, taken collectively, has been valued at ten thousand pounds sterling and you know yourself, my lord, what it has already cost you to begin to form one like it."[31]

And so, Reviczky proposed a truly unusual deal. "My favourite plan", he wrote, "has always been to convince some Prince or Sovereign to assure himself during my lifetime of a public and permanent Library, by giving me annually about £300 sterling [*sic*, but £600 is the sum named later in the letter and in the rest of the correspondence] to be able to continue to enrich it with new acquisitions, and by getting the free use of it for the rest of my life. This may well be your case too, my lord…"[32]

Spencer responded almost instantly once he had received the count's letter. It had, he wrote, "created two sensations in my mind of very different kinds": the sadness that their recent acquaintance should soon be interrupted by Reviczky's departure for the continent and the "no less sincere delight, that by the very candid & handsome offer you make me, I shall now have an opportunity of doing that at once, which it might have cost me many years of trouble & expense to do perhaps but imperfectly at last". "I am", he concluded, "very ready to become the Possessor of your Library upon the terms you propose."[33] The £600 life annuity would be arranged and the library obtained.

While the particulars of the annuity proved awkward to set up due to Reviczky's status as an alien, the deal had been accomplished. The count, in his evident elation, could not resist reminding Spencer of just what a catch his collection was. "To give you an idea of the acquisition you are about to make," he wrote, "I will observe that, in addition to the complete collection of ancient Greek editions, the Latin ones are there in such great number that Pinelli's Library, so vaunted in the world, compared to mine, will appear to you very poor, not to mention the difference in the condition of the copies, and their binding."[34] What might initially seem to be pardonable exaggeration was nothing less than the truth: Reviczky really did have one of the best classical libraries in Europe, a collection assembled over a lifetime and not easily surpassed.

Five years before, he had printed a catalogue of his collection, entitled *Bibliotheca Graeca et Latina*, and issued under the pseudonym of "Periergus Deltophilus" (Greek for "Pernickety Booklover"—Reviczky had a good sense of humour). In the elegant French preface to the work, addressed as a letter to his friend the historian Abbé Carlo Giovanni Maria Denina, he expanded upon his method:

> Confined within the narrow bounds of a simple curiosity, I have given my principal attention to the beauty of the copies, always seeking them as they came from the hand of the artist, and when one of these first

> typographical productions of the fifteenth century seemed to me to have preserved all the freshness and cleanliness of a book which has just left the press, I thought it best to acquire it. I also confess that a copy printed on vellum has great attractions for me, and that I am not insensitive either to the attractions of large paper, early bindings, and other frivolities of this kind, so highly disdained by the great scholars.[35]

In other words, he was participating, not just in the collection of classical texts, but the collections of *editiones principes* and editions from the very earliest decades of the printing press's history. Incunables, books printed in the cradle (Latin *incunabula*), that is to say the earliest stages of printing—a period generally taken to mean from Gutenberg to 1500—had already become desirable objects in their own right for several generations and prices were rising with dizzying speed. Reviczky had had the advantage of assembling much of his collection as the obsession with early printing was only beginning to gather steam and so had already gathered together works which would soon become, at the least, unaffordable, more often, unobtainable, to the next generation of collectors. His professed love of vellum, large paper copies (i.e. books printed on a larger paper size than was standard for the edition, a common way of producing volumes targeted to the collecting market), and "other frivolities of this kind" was a careful move setting himself apart from the mere practical classical scholar, whose library must, inevitably, be assembled with use rather than beauty in mind. This was the library of a connoisseur.

Part of being a connoisseur meant not taking oneself too seriously. "Men are only too happy to have some madness which amuses them agreeably", Reviczky wrote. "After all, what does it matter how one obtains this advantage, if it is by chasing butterflies, or by gathering shells, by arranging one's medals, or by completing one's authors."[36] The wealthy amateur collector, he was implying, was a harmless, amusing specimen, provided, of course, "that those who devote themselves to such collections take care not to value them beyond their fair price".[37]

The 1784 catalogue already listed a remarkable library of early editions, but Reviczky had not been idle since then and his manuscript catalogue from the time of his sale—now amongst Spencer's papers in the British Library—shows that, despite his claims to lazy gentility, he had been collecting with a passionate obsession in the later 1780s, taking every advantage to add to his collection.[38] He was discretely expressionless in a letter he wrote to Spencer on 15 July in which he recorded that "careful to fulfil my commitments", he had sent to Spencer's town house, "all the Boxes containing the Books of my Library, of which you have acquired the property, and which consist of eight large boxes, and three locked chests".[39] Was there a pang, however slight, at this parting? Of course, the terms of the sale ensured his access to the collection for the remainder of his life, but access is not ownership and it is hard to imagine that a collector as consumed by his passion as Reviczky would not have suffered at the loss of the latter. Perhaps it was not this moment which provoked it, but the sending of the now-completed manuscript catalogue a month later, "by means of which all will be in order relative to this Library, of which I wish you, my lord, a long enjoyment, with the same pleasure that it has always caused me".[40] Here Reviczky, who normally hid behind a careful gloss of worldly politeness and irony, bared his heart to Spencer, and to us. That pleasure was no longer his.

* * *

While the heavy boxes and chests of books were being hauled up the steps of Spencer House overlooking Green Park, amidst the shouting of porters and servants, and Reviczky, whether with melancholy or satisfaction or both, was putting the finishing touches on the catalogue of a collection no longer his, across the Channel an enraged mob was storming the Bastille and shaking the French monarchy to its foundations. The French Revolution had begun. Before it was over, Spencer's life and Europe's libraries would be forever transformed.

TWO

The making of a young nobleman

Before we follow Spencer into his London town house and watch him unpacking his first great acquisition, we might ask ourselves the question, "why?" Why did this young aristocrat enter into what, by any standards, was a financially demanding bargain with his diplomatic acquaintance? What made him so desperate to own a few chests full of old books? To answer these questions we need to become better acquainted with our young nobleman and to explore what is known of the psychology of collecting.

George John Spencer was born on 1 September 1758 to a wealthy MP named John Spencer—later 1st Earl Spencer—and his wife Georgiana, née Poyntz. He was his parents' second child, a circumstance which profoundly affected his childhood. Writing a month after the birth, Georgiana Spencer wrote to her friend Thea Cowper that she was "so partial" to her eldest child, Georgiana, "that I think I never shall love another so well".[1] George's younger sister Harriet, born just under three years later in 1761 was, in her mother's opinion "a little ugly girl" with "no beauty to brag of".[2] From the outset, the two younger siblings were distant seconds to their favoured elder sister.

George's father, who was only twenty-three when his son was born, was "a rather private person, generally quite shy and withdrawn", who had been saddled with the dubious blessing of a great inheritance, courtesy of his great-grandmother, Sarah Churchill, Duchess of Marlborough, and the proviso that he was to accept no crown office lest the inheritance pass to his next heir.[3] Effectively excluded from a public career, while at the same time being in possession of an enormous fortune, John Spencer began a round of extravagant and largely undirected spending which would only end with his death. He had already inherited a fine collection of art from his father—over four hundred paintings—and a substantial gentleman's library.[4] From the moment of his majority he began to expand both and to seek out spaces in which his collections could be suitably displayed. In the autumn of 1755 he commissioned George Gray to be his architectural advisor for a massive building project which would see the Neo-Palladian Spencer House emerge on the edge of Green Park.[5] In 1756 he purchased the 5,000-volume library of William George, Dean of Lincoln.[6] But he excelled himself as a collector of visual art more than anything, buying heavily in Old Masters throughout this period, most notably in the year in which George was born.[7] As his grandson would later recall, John Spencer "never put any restraint upon himself" and exhibited a "total absence of all self-command", in spending as in other avenues of life.[8]

George's mother, twenty-one at her son's birth, shared her husband's "love of the fine and decorative arts".[9] The daughter of a career diplomat, she was highly educated, obsessive, and addicted to charity and gambling in equal measure.[10] We owe much of our knowledge of her children's youth to her habit of compulsively saving and organising her correspondence and other papers. Both she and her husband were slight, dark, sharp-nosed and reticent—images of fragile, obsessive excess.[11]

We know little of George's first five years. He and his siblings seem to have followed their parents between their various estates: Althorp, their ancestral seat, Wimbledon Park, their suburban London residence, Holywell, near St. Albans, and others.[12] Althorp, a beautiful seventeenth-century manor house in the depths of the Northamptonshire countryside, was their favourite home and there George would have grown up surrounded by Renaissance paintings—including works by Holbein, Rubens, Rembrandt, and Michelangelo, among many others—and decorative art as well as the family's now expansive library.[13] His parents entertained themselves with hunting and gambling, two shared passions, at Althorp and elsewhere; what the infant heir did is not recorded.[14]

Attempting to recover the emotional timbre of a life lived two hundred and fifty years ago is an uncertain business. Was little George happy in those years? We cannot say. He was at least in the vicinity of his parents, whatever warmth they could or could not give him. What we can say with more certainty is that any stability he may have enjoyed in those first years came to an abrupt end in early 1763—he would have been four and a half—when his parents left on the Grand Tour, taking their favourite Georgiana and leaving George and Harriet behind. They were away for a year and a half.[15]

The proximate cause of this was his father's ill health. A melancholy hypochondriac by temperament—one fellow traveller on the Grand Tour recalled that he had "an unhappy disposition to look always on the worst side of things, and if he does not find a subject for fretting to make one"—he spent most of his life crippled by real or imagined illnesses.[16] On this first of many flights to the continent, he was "ill the whole time" according to his acquaintance Viscount Palmerston. "It is a thousand pities he has not a better constitution," Palmerston added, for "he seems to be a man whose value few people know. The bright side of his character appears in private and the dark side in public."[17] Having dispensed even with Georgiana partway through their travels, the children's parents wandered through Italy, Austria, and Germany before finally returning to England in July 1764. Their exhausted travelling companion William Arden wrote to Palmerston on 15 July that "I sit down with great satisfaction to tell you that our journey is over", John Spencer's difficult temperament having "rendered both himself and his company insensible to much of the satisfaction which the circumstances of our journey might have occasioned to us".[18] Soon after, and £50,000 later, the family moved into the now-completed Spencer House.

What effect did all this have on the younger Spencer? We do not directly know, but there can be little doubt—even if, as was the norm in an eighteenth-century aristocratic family, relations between the parents and their young children were limited and distant—that what must have felt like his abandonment in England while his older sister followed their parents to the continent would have left deep scars. Infant sureties had been proven wrong and parents, whatever they may have seemed before, unreliable. George's life would never be quite the same again.

* * *

If his parents' sudden departure had marked one epoch in the life of young George—who, with his contemporaries, we might now know by his courtesy title of Viscount Althorp—the next was surely the appointment of a nineteen-year-old Oxford student as his tutor: William Jones. Young as he was, Jones, who would go on to become the discoverer of the Proto-Indo-European language and founding father of the modern study of ancient India, was already well known to be brilliant. Nicknamed "the Great Scholar" at Harrow, he had won a scholarship to University College, Oxford, and was busy improving his Arabic when the offer of tutoring Althorp came in 1765.[19] Jones and the Spencers had never met when he was offered the post, but upon meeting his future charge the undergraduate was instantly charmed with the boy and happily rose to the challenge given him by Georgiana Spencer to "make him, if you can, like yourself".[20] Indeed, Jones was charmed with Georgiana herself, now twenty-eight, and with their aristocratic milieu. He rapidly sought naturalisation into the latter, taking secret dancing lessons from Harriet's Italian dancing master and generally doing what he could to refashion himself in the Spencers' mould.[21] A copy of a portrait of Jones by Joshua Reynolds which must date from this time or a little later shows a plump-faced, sharp-eyed youth with heavy, dark eyebrows, graceful hands and an expressive, open countenance. He is not classically beautiful, but a puckish humour and razor-sharp wit, together with an intense striving to achieve, are barely contained within his small frame (see Figure 2.1).

Before Jones, George had been tutored by the same William Arden who had accompanied his parents on their first, fateful Grand Tour. Arden, a King's Scholar at Eton and then a Fellow of King's College, Cambridge, was a clever and, by all accounts, mischievously funny, young man who had met the Spencers and the famous actor David Garrick in

Figure 2.1 John Linnell (after Joshua Reynolds), *Sir William Jones*, University College, Oxford 58. Reproduced courtesy of the Masters and Fellows of University College, Oxford.

quick succession whilst on the continent in 1763–1764.[22] A talented amateur actor, he particularly showed to effect in the role of Falstaff, exciting the great Garrick's unqualified admiration.[23] On the strength of their new friendship Spencer had presented him to the rectory of Brampton Ash, twenty miles away from Althorp, and it was presumably sometime between 1764 and 1766 that he briefly tutored the young George. When Jones took over, Arden provided him with a "favourable [written] account of Lord Althorp's disposition".[24]

Jones rattled between Oxford and the family's various residences, pupil (mostly) in tow over the following years. He seems to have taken pleasure in his improved dancing, which he had the opportunity to show off at Althorp in the winter of 1766–1767, and interspersed his new skill with German lessons when John Spencer's hypochondria took them to Spa in the spring of the following year.[25] It is not until the summer of

1768 that his and his tutee's lives come into focus, however, for it was in that year that Jones began a voluminous, ardent correspondence with George's mother. He was profuse in his praise of his situation, desiring "to convince your Ladyship that my most romantic wishes could not have formed even an idea of a situation so entirely agreeable to me as that which I have enjoyed for more than two years, and which I shall always consider as the glory of my life", but the meat of the correspondence, at least in this first stage, was news of young Althorp.[26] In August Jones, Althorp, and young Georgiana were "amus[ing] ourselves with playing at chess and reading Shakespeare".[27] In September he wrote proudly that Althorp "has such a quickness in learning about Greek and Latin, and makes such striking observations upon what he reads, that I have not a doubt of his becoming one of the first scholars of the age", adding, with the pomposity of learned youth, that "the vulgar notion that a little learning is sufficient for a gentleman, is extremely absurd".[28]

Entirely absent from Jones's jolly letters was any mention of the event which must have overshadowed all others for the family in the autumn of 1768: William Arden's suicide. Arden had married in July and been subsequently overtaken by "a lurking melancholy", due to an unhappy love affair, according to one source, or the rigours of "humble domestic life" for one who had previously "been connected with the excitements of society at the most splendid tables", according to another.[29] Whatever the cause, the young clergyman, recently made a prebendary of Worcester Cathedral, shot himself in his garden at the Brampton Rectory on 25 October, devastating both Garrick and the elder Spencer.[30]

Althorp's parents were now "travel[ling] obsessively", as they would for the remainder of John Spencer's life, and Jones was more than ever *in loco parentis* to his charge, who he cajoled into cold-water bathing and continued to educate as a classical scholar.[31] In November he wrote from his Oxford college to George that "when I come to town we will apply ourselves diligently to parsing Greek & Latin to verse, and to Latin composition, and then, away we go to the land of play, I mean, school".[32] For a great change was about to come to George's life. On 8 June 1769, aged ten years and nine months, he arrived at Harrow, some miles north-west of London, one of the ancient public schools and a nursery for the British political elite.[33] He arrived there, one later commentator wrote, "with a suite and attendance of such state as even at that time [was] considered an intrusion upon the uniformity of school life", though the anonymous writer was quick to add that he nonetheless "grew up in unaffected simplicity".[34]

The truth was inevitably more complex, but the forced jollity of Jones's letters to Lady Spencer makes it difficult to get at the bottom of what really occurred. All started well in the first week, when Jones wrote that:

> I wish your Ladyship could look through the wonderful glass in the Arabian Tales, and see the satisfaction and content that are marked upon Lord Althorp's face at this moment. He is so well acquainted with the boys, and so perfectly accommodated to the customs of the school that if I had not come with him myself last Thursday, I should think he had been here five months instead of five days.[35]

In July "My little hero" continued to be "as happy as possible, and in higher health than I ever remember him".[36] This caveat is significant, for there seems to have been an unspecified concern over Althorp's health which had initially led him to be educated at home by Jones and only later sent to school. In the event, this concern was only too fully justified. Come August, Althorp was ill with a respiratory ailment, apparently a serious one, which lasted for most of the month.[37] This illness precipitated his parents removing him from school (though not into their own care as they were busy holidaying at Nice). By March 1770, Jones hoped that they had dropped any "thoughts of keeping [Althorp] at home in the summer", arguing that Harrow was perfectly healthy in that season, but evidently he did not return, instead joining his parents, first in France, then in Germany.[38]

Jones was becoming increasingly impatient. Was his charge to stay at home? Was he to go back to Harrow? On 28 September he wrote to Lady Spencer with considerable asperity, that "Lord Althorp seems to himself, and to me to be very well. It were much to be wished that his Education were as settled as his health seems to be. At present he is as much to be pitied as he is amiable; which is, surely, saying a great deal."[39] Jones was evidently trading on the friendship which had sprung up between him and the young noblewoman, but this was too much. She must have responded sharply—her side of the correspondence does not survive—and he met it with a letter in turns indignant and pleading, begging her to make a decision about Althorp's education, begging her to let him continue as Althorp's tutor, and violently rejecting what seems to have been an offer of a living in the Spencer's patronage.[40]

This was the beginning of the end. Further letters passed, but it was clear as the autumn of 1770 dragged on that the Spencers wished Jones out of their service. In his dudgeon, Jones wrote to Earl Spencer on 22 October that:

> As to Lord Althorp I most heartily love him and ever shall. The step I take at present proves my affection for him; I knew, or at least thought, his education defective and irregular; I made an useless attempt to rectify it, and finding my good intentions vain, I resign a charge which most men would have continued for motives which I disdain.[41]

Somewhat surprisingly, this breach ultimately proved to be an amicable one, though it still removed Jones from the immediate ambit of the family. He continued to write, regularly, voluminously, didactically, and, on the whole, with immense affection, to Althorp throughout the following decade in tones that read much more like those of a kindly father or older brother than any used by Althorp's own family.

He also continued to write to Lady Spencer. There is a tension in their correspondence, never articulated, but which comes closest to the surface in a letter from late December 1774 which Jones sent along with a copy of his *Poems Consisting Chiefly of Translations from the Asiatick Languages*. "[I] cannot refrain", Jones wrote, "from acquainting you with a plain truth, that the first of them, called Solima, would never have been written, if I had never had the honour of knowing your Ladyship."[42] The titular Solima is a princess in an eastern fantasy, described in Jones's poem as an angelic benefactress, "radiant as the star of day" who willingly listens to the "plaintive tale[s]" of the bereaved and oppressed.

"And as they mourn, she steals a tender sigh, whilst all her soul sits melting in her eye."[43] Lady Spencer, née Georgiana Poyntz, who would have been thirty-one to Jones's twenty-two when the poem was written, was clearly an object of idolisation, and quite probably one of romantic adoration, awkwardly concealed beneath the over-enthusiastic but donnish demeanour of his letters. There is no indication that she returned his sentiments, much less that those sentiments were ever explicitly declared. Nonetheless, we might pause to consider the situation in which George Althorp found himself as he reached puberty: the favourite student of a teacher who was far more a father to him than his own and who, moreover, seems to have nursed an unrequited passion for his mother. The air must have lain thick at Althorp and Wimbledon in those years and it is difficult to suppose that this febrile psychological environment would not have left its mark on the young man.

* * *

Althorp eventually returned to Harrow, remaining there until 1775.[44] On 13 February 1776, aged seventeen, he was admitted to Trinity College, Cambridge, proceeding M.A. in 1778.[45] What can we say of this young man at the end of his second decade? His childhood had been defined, we may speculate, by three moments of sudden loss: his parents' departure to the continent when he was four, leaving him and his younger sister in England, his former tutor Arden's suicide when he was ten, and his mentor Jones's precipitate departure from the Spencer household when he was twelve.

Something of Spencer as he was then is caught in a penetrating 1774 portrait (see Figure 2.2) of the three siblings by Angelica Kauffman (1741–1807), the Swiss-born Neoclassical painter who was busy making her name as portraitiste to London's great and good.[46] Georgiana would have been about seventeen when the portrait was painted, George about fifteen, and Harriet about thirteen, though to our modern eyes they look a touch older than those ages, characteristic of the greater responsibility already weighing on their shoulders. Georgiana, the beauty, looks calmly and determinedly out at the viewer while Harriet clutches her sister's

Figure 2.2 Angelica Kauffmann, *Lady Georgiana, Lady Henrietta Frances and George John Spencer, Viscount Althorp* (1774), Althorp.

hand and leans in to her and away from Althorp, upon whom she is gazing with an ambiguous expression. Concern, perhaps? Dislike? Fear?

For his part, Althorp, who is standing and dressed in a faintly ridiculous *fête galante* costume, looks every inch the awkward teenager. Legs crossed and one hand placed on a convenient stone balustrade, his pose apes that of a fashionable gentleman but it is stiff and awkward, his head with its profusion of ginger curls tilted uncomfortably down as he gazes at his sisters' clasped hands. A gently misty classical landscape behind them does nothing to ease the unnatural awkwardness of the painting.

The remainder of Spencer's youth passed in something of a blur. University was followed by an obligatory Grand Tour which has left a surprisingly faint footprint in his archive; if he was, as some were, transformed by his time on the continent, we have no evidence for it. Instead, he entered Georgian society, becoming engaged to Lavinia Bingham (1762–1831), the seventeen-year-old daughter of the Anglo-Irish Lord

Lucan (later Earl of Lucan), on 9 May 1780 and marrying her in her father's London town house on 6 March 1781.[47] William Jones wrote an epithalamium on the marriage (it is rather dull).[48]

Lavinia, Countess Spencer, was evidently beloved by her husband, which was a good thing, because she brought little wealth into the family and was almost universally disliked by everyone else. Her sister-in-law Georgiana, in particular, detested her and Georgiana's modern biographer has summed up this vision of Lavinia as "highly strung, vindictive, hypocritical, and a calm liar".[49] Henrietta also failed to take to her new sister-in-law, writing that "I respect her, I admire her cleverness (which term peculiarly suits her in every way)...but there is something in her Character and manners wholly repugnant to me...a coarseness of mind, as well as of expression, that scarce any talent makes up for".[50] How fair these judgements are is not clear. Lavinia was certainly spendthrift, sharp-tempered, and quick to judge, but these were far from being rare qualities in her time and class.

Spencer and Lavinia would ultimately have eight children, of whom two died young. The two eldest, John Charles (1782–1845), who would succeed his father as 3rd Earl Spencer, and Sarah (1787–1870), later Lady Lyttelton, will occasionally reappear in these pages, but by and large Spencer's library was not a family concern. Lavinia certainly took no interest and the children seemed to have regarded it with the detached amusement which is so often the reaction of family members to the obsessions of the collector. Though he may have been surrounded by wife and children after 1781, psychologically, at least so far as concerned his central passion, Spencer remained the same lonely, awkward youth we have seen in Kauffmann's portrait.

Psychologising the past is dangerous; applying universalising schema to individual experience even more so. And yet it is hard not to see in Spencer's childhood, defined by loss and the removal of the central people in his life one after another, the kind of childhood which the psychoanalyst Werner Muensterberger saw as the essential conditions for the development of the collecting instinct. Muensterberger saw objects, and the collecting of objects, as a response to a child's suffering and loss, a response which gradually became a dominant expression of the individual's pysche.[51] In modern academic psychology this already somewhat reductive interpretation has been further reduced into the language of "terror management theory", proposing that collecting is simply a "culturally approved activity [performed] in order to ward off the awareness of [the collector's] mortality".[52]

A different, though not necessarily contradictory, explanation of the nature of collecting was made by the bibliographer Thomas Tanselle who saw it as composed of four related aspects, "the creation of order, a fascination with chance, curiosity about the past, and a desire for understanding", which collectively sit within a larger "urge to tame the external world".[53] Just as Muensterberger's vision of collecting as a response to childhood trauma seems echoed in Spencer's early life, so we might see the reasons in that life which could lead to a desire for order and a taming of the external world, at least within the confines of a library.

And yet I do not think any of these schematic and totalising "theories" of collecting can adequately describe individual experience. Tanselle, with some frustration, poses the question neatly:

> There are other ways of passing the time, or securing fame, or satisfying a love of beauty, or feeding one's self-importance, or taking financial risks, or amassing wealth, or following fashion; and the most fundamental question in trying to understand collecting is to ask why it should be the path, rather than some other, that is chosen...[54]

In Spencer's case, all psychologising and theorising aside, we must accept that we ultimately cannot know "the reason" why he became a collector and that in accepting that lack of knowledge we are probably no more ignorant than Spencer himself. Currents of the human soul are not easily reducible to cut-and-dried explanations. Instead, I would point to two facts which are, or at least appear to be, pregnant with meaning and take from them what is no more than a fantasy, but perhaps such a fantasy as allows us to glimpse, however imperfectly, the complex and ambiguous truth of why a man's life should have become dedicated to the collecting of books.

The first fact is that William Jones loved old books almost as much as he loved the Greek and Roman classics. In a long letter to Althorp penned on New Year's Day 1774, when his former pupil was fifteen and still at Harrow, he wrote:

> I have just bought a charming edition of all Cicero's works by Elzevir [one of a family of Dutch printers whose works were a by-name for good seventeenth-century printing and which were widely collected] in ten small volumes; it is the finest copy I ever saw; I would rather a thousand times have it than Olivet's splendid edition: these ten volumes I shall carry almost *in sinu* [in my bosom], and shall make a rule to read them all diligently every year of my life...[55]

The desire, whether conscious or unconscious, to imitate the man who seems to have been more of a mentor and father-figure to Spencer than any other cannot have been entirely absent. The two men came to love each other through the medium of the ancient classics—in a way almost unimaginable now—and Jones's evident pleasure in a good Elzevir was a physical manifestation of that shared love which it would have been easy to copy.

The second fact is that, when Spencer stood chatting with Count Reviczky at the Pinelli sale, that nobleman was not unknown to him. Far from it. Amongst his many talents, Reviczky was an accomplished oriental philologist and translator of Persian poetry. In that capacity, he and Jones had been long-time correspondents since at least the late 1760s, offering each other advice on thorny problems of translation, discussing issues of prosody and metaphor, and explicating newly-discovered texts.[56] Reviczky was, indeed, the first of what would become a lengthy list of Jones's international correspondents and must have occupied a large place in the young scholar's mental world when he was tutoring Spencer. It seems vanishingly unlikely, then, that the boy would not have been privy to his tutor's enthusiasm for Reviczky and his scholarship. The opportunity, many years later, when Jones was a world away in Calcutta undertaking the work that would make him famous as the discoverer of Indo-European linguistics, to buy Reviczky's library, a library sanctified both by its contents and its personal connection to his sometime mentor, must have been impossible to resist.

And so I fantasise that the genesis of Spencer's collecting lay in fond memories of his relationship with Jones, intertwined with his evident love of and aptitude for classical learning, perhaps precipitated or given focus by a childhood which, if hardly deprived, had more than its fair share of loss and uncertainty, even amidst the Old Masters and high ceilings of Althorp or Spencer House. That, I imagine, might account for the scattering of early purchases and the decision to acquire Reviczky's collection *en masse*. But childhood, whether figured as trauma or golden age, can never adequately account for a whole life and whatever may have first directed Spencer towards collecting, it was fundamentally transformed by his possession of Reviczky's library, a transformation we can still glimpse in the traces Spencer has left us and in the books themselves.

THREE

Unpacking a library

"I am unpacking my library. Yes, I am. The books are not yet on the shelves, not yet touched by the mild boredom of order."[1] So wrote Walter Benjamin in 1931 at the beginning of his famous essay on collecting and so might Spencer have written in 1789. But Benjamin was returning to books long-owned and long-beloved; Spencer was discovering the full extent of his new acquisitions. Let us imagine what Spencer saw and what he might have felt on opening the "eight large boxes, and three locked chests" delivered to him that summer.[2]

The opening would have taken place in Spencer House. Probably it happened in the library—a substantial room which Spencer had recently had remodelled and enlarged by his favourite architect, Henry Holland.[3] We can imagine the normal order of the library rudely disturbed by the arrival of its future contents. Boxes half-unpacked, books tumbling out on the floor. It is probably evening, probably late, after-dinner guests have gone home. Lady Spencer, who does not share her husband's interests, is elsewhere. Spencer, alone, is on his knees in front of his new treasures, almost at prayer before them. What he sees is much more than just a collection of beautiful books. It is the intertwined stories of the beginning of printing and Reviczky's own life-long obsession.

Printing with moveable lead type, as everybody knows, was first practised in the West by that ingenious Mainz patrician, Johannes Gensfleisch zur Laden zum Gutenberg. After slow starts in the 1440s, he began printing around 1450, entered into partnership with the goldsmith and financier Johann Fust and the latter's son-in-law Peter Schöffer, and in 1455 completed what is now known as the Gutenberg Bible: the first substantial printed book.[4] Reviczky had possessed no printing by Gutenberg, and Spencer could not know that his own Gutenberg Bible was only a year away. He did, however, have the next best thing. In 1456 the relationship between Gutenberg and Fust had gone sour and the latter, together with Schöffer, had set up their own, rather more financially successful, press in Mainz. It was there that they produced what was probably the first classical text ever printed: Cicero's *De officiis*, a handbook of moral precepts from the late Roman Republic, which was finished in 1465.

Spencer draws a small, neat folio out—I imagine—of one of the three locked chests.[5] It is bound in eighteenth-century red morocco, the colour of which is darker and less garish than its nineteenth-century equivalent. On one level it is quite plain, but the significance of the volume is never in doubt: "EDITIO PRIMARIA 1465" is tooled in large gold capitals on its spine. Opening it to the first leaf he sees a simple blue and red initial 'O' beneath a title in red characters. The fount still looks like that of a mid-century German manuscript; only its regularity betrays its printed origin. Although Spencer probably doesn't know to look for this yet, most of the leaves have tell-tale pinholes at the edges, traces of the pins which would have held each sheet of vellum—for this, like many of the earliest books is printed on vellum—in the press.

But wait, you may be asking: "a blue and red initial"? Did the earliest printers produce technicolor books? Not quite. The initial in question was, like many other details in this volume, added by hand after the main text was printed. This was a standard practice for books printed in the fifteenth century; they were produced to look like manuscripts; manuscripts had more or less lavishly illuminated (i.e. decorated with abstract patterns or pictorial illustrations in multiple colours, often incorporating gold leaf) or rubricated (i.e. written in a contrasting red or blue ink) initial letters, and so did they.[6] The hand finishing of books only gradually died out in the early sixteenth century as printers stopped leaving blank spaces for scribes to add their work and began printing elaborate woodcut initials instead. In a way, you could say that this Cicero, and the books of the incunable period more generally, were intermediate objects: both manuscript and print.

When I came to this volume in the John Rylands Library, a couple of centuries after Spencer but unpacking, in my own way, the same collection and with, I imagine, at least some of the same feelings, the Cicero was a little the worse for wear. The spine had been rebacked, that is to say, a new spine had been constructed, probably because the old one was falling apart, and the original spine's gold-tooled leather had been carefully laid on, i.e. pasted on top of the repair. Unfortunately, the laid-on sections are beginning to peel and will need to be repaired again soon. The text-block, the sewn sheets of vellum, now sits a little too tight in the binding, probably due to modern conservation work, and there are other traces of well-intentioned intervention throughout, a small hole in one leaf, for example, which was once sewn shut but which has now been unpicked and had a piece of eighteenth- or nineteenth-century paper pasted over it (the sewing would have looked nicer). On the final page is the famous woodcut of Fust and Schöffer's conjoined arms, printed in red and marking the conclusion of what would become one of the most famous books in typographical history.

I should say a word or two here about the Rylands, which I visited frequently while writing this book, taking the train down from Scotland to Manchester and impatiently waiting for 10 a.m. and opening time. It is an architectural peculiarity. A soot-stained Neo-Gothic wedding cake onto which has been welded—like a robotic prosthesis—an ultra-modern plate-glass extension. If you are a researcher, you pass through doors on the ground floor and ascend progressively narrower staircases up five levels until you reach the special collections reading room. There you must be buzzed through two layers of security (after the first you deposit your bag and have a chat with the librarian on duty) before entering the holy of holies, a medium-sized, light-filled reading room, full of pale wood and long, deep desks where scholars are at work, each pursuing their own obsessions. Books are delivered to you one at a time through a glass window, like that of an old-fashioned bank teller, and rest on the usual grey archival cushions, their pages held open with "snakes", lengths of white cheese cloth filled with lead weights. It is a peaceful space—quiet, cool, and untroubled save for the rustling and crackling of turning pages. Imagine it, if you will, as the background to my examinations of each book. I thought of them, not as examinations, but as *autopsies*, harking back to the Greek αὐτοψία, a seeing with one's own eyes, but not quite free of its modern meaning either. Maybe this says a little too much about me.

One of the many things I like about the Rylands is that they've preserved Spencer's accession numbers as the books' modern shelfmarks. Spencer's basic system was to provide each of his books a unique accession number which was given sequentially when he first acquired each volume or set of volumes. This number was, however, keyed to the edition, not the specific physical book, and if he discarded a book in favour of a better copy this new acquisition would be given the accession number of its predecessor. In other words, we can use these numbers as potential guides to when he bought a book (e.g. a book with an accession number in the 3000s should have been acquired about 1790 while one in the 17000s should have been acquired about 1819), with the caveat that the copy we're looking at may be a later acquisition. There is also the problem that he was perennially behind on cataloguing and didn't always give books their numbers in quite the order in which he purchased them. In addition, there seem to have been a good number of more modern books to which he never gave these numbers at all, making any calculation of the overall number of books in his collection difficult, if not impossible. Despite all of this, they still provide us with essential information about his collecting and are sometimes the only way we have of dating when he bought a book. I'm very glad the Rylands has kept them.

The Cicero is accession number 3140, just where it ought to be in the sequence. Reviczky had bought his copy for 1,450 livres tournois—roughly equivalent to a little over £100—at one of the most famous auctions of the eighteenth century, that of Louis César de La Baume Le Blanc, duc de La Vallière (1708–1780). Scion of an old aristocratic family, and with the portly figure and receding chin to prove it, La Vallière was one of the great book collectors of his age. With the assistance of his irascible librarian, the Abbé Jean-Joseph Rive, whom the duke referred to as his "bull-dog", La Vallière assembled what was certainly the greatest library in *ancien régime* France and quite possibly one of the greatest private libraries ever seen, if one measures not simply quantity but also quality of the books present.[7] There were manuscripts, including the Rohan Hours, one of the most beautiful and haunting productions of fifteenth-century French illumination, hundreds if not thousands of incunables, and a collection of early editions of the classics almost impossible to rival. When the duke died and his library was dispersed by his daughter, the Duchesse de Châtillon (who, incidentally, hated Rive and ensured he had nothing to do with the sale; he responded by writing a lengthy and rather rude book), it filled eleven volumes of catalogues and took five years to disperse.[8]

The Cicero was lot 2275 in the first part of this great sale and was sold in December 1783. Guillaume de Bure, the bookseller and bibliographer who compiled the catalogue, described it in all-caps—shouting at the reader, if you will—as the "FIRST EDITION. A SUPERB EXAMPLE PRINTED ON VELLUM" and the price Reviczky paid for it was accordingly steep.[9] The count neatly recorded its provenance on the flyleaf, noting the price and that it was "chez le Duc de la Vallière". Spencer had only been in his twenties at the time of the La Vallière sale and not yet a serious collector, but he would undoubtedly have known of it and would have recognised the illustrious provenance when he opened this volume.

* * *

Printing remained confined to Germany for the first decade of its existence, but by the time Fust and Schöffer had produced their Cicero in 1465 it was beginning to spread. A year before, the Cardinal-Abbot Juan de Torquemada had welcomed two unusual artisans to the ancient Benedictine abbey of Subiaco, south of Rome. The abbey clings to the face of Monte Taleo above the town and is immensely old, allegedly dating back to the time of St. Benedict himself in the early sixth century. Benedictines are scholars and it is not surprising that they were fascinated by the new technology; their guests: Conrad Sweynheym, possibly a sometime assistant of Gutenberg, and his partner the Prague-born Arnold Pannartz. They were the first printers in Italy and, sometime in the same year as Fust and Schöffer, they printed their own Cicero, the great orator's work on his profession, *De Oratore*.[10]

While the Fust and Schöffer Cicero has chronological precedence, there is something truly moving about the first classical text printed in Italy, not that many miles from where it had been written a millennium and a half before. When I first opened the anonymous grey card book-box in the Rylands and saw what was inside, I had to pause and, going back to the issue desk, asked the librarian on duty whether or not I ought to be under supervision while looking at it (we will find me being watched by the benign eye of a Rylands librarian later on). After investigation, it emerged that the Subiaco Cicero occupies an intermediate position as a "very special book", but not one requiring close supervision (beyond what I was already under by virtue of calling up some of the rarest and most expensive incunables in the world).

Both Spencer and I must have immediately noticed something striking about the Subiaco Cicero: its binding is identical to that of the Fust and Schöffer Cicero we have just been examining: the same wine-dark red morocco and the same delicately gold-tooled flowers on the spine. The reason for this unexpected coincidence becomes clear upon turning to the flyleaf: this is another of Reviczky's acquisitions at the La Vallière sale (lot 2253, "in the most beautiful condition" per De Bure, and a steal at 603 *livres tournois*).[11] Looking further, one might initially think that the printing in the two volumes is rather similar, but already changes are happening. The type used by Sweynheym and Pannartz at Subiaco is still a distinctly Gothic German, but it is slightly elongated and the capitals now echo those of an ancient Latin inscription rather than the lavish pen-strokes of a medieval scribe; printing, almost imperceptibly, is moving away from its hearty Germanic roots in the direction of an Italianate classicism.

Subiaco is lovely, but not the best place from which to sell books, and two years later Sweynheym and Pannartz moved to Rome. There, in 1467, they produced yet another volume of Cicero (have you noticed that he was a favourite author of the fifteenth-century Humanists?), this time his letters, the *Epistolae ad familiares*.[12] Perhaps, having seen the Subiaco volume, Spencer went hunting for its Roman successor. If he did, he would have fished out a rather hefty folio bound in faded blue-green crushed morocco—dyes in this spectrum tended to be rather unstable—with a heavily classicising design of gold-tooled foliage and urns on the spine. Spencer would have had at least some inkling of what he was going to see and I imagine him turning hurriedly to the opening leaf for comparison with the Subiaco volume.

There is always a moment of pure astonishment when you open a book printed by Sweynheym and Pannartz (see Figure 3.1). The widely-spaced, elegant layout of the page is as pleasing to the eye as any manuscript of the period and this particular volume has been additionally graced, not with the plain red and blue ink rubrication of the two Ciceros we have already seen, but with a richly-coloured, gold, green, blue, and purple cornucopia of flowers which flow out from the initial 'E' to cover three of the four page edges (conveniently leaving the outside edge free for turning with the fingers). If Spencer was like me, he must have paused, lingeringly, on this beautiful piece of illumination, turning the book under the library lights to make the gold sparkle.

He might also, like me, have taken a few moments to realise that what you see on this opening page is not entirely fifteenth century. The bottom quarter must have been damaged or lost at some stage and has been replaced, seemingly in the eighteenth century, with a very good but not quite perfect facsimile, cunningly pasted onto the bottom of the original fragmentary leaf. The colours of the replacement, especially the blue, are duller, not so unearthly and glowing as true Renaissance pigments, and the gold leaf has crackled while its fifteenth-century partner remains crisp and unblemished. The fix becomes more obvious on the verso where some humbler rubrication has been cut off without replacement.

Another surprise: the page edges are gilt, standard on a lavishly bound book, but when you gently riffle them you perceive an underlayer of marbling, what is called a fore-edge painting. There is something delightful

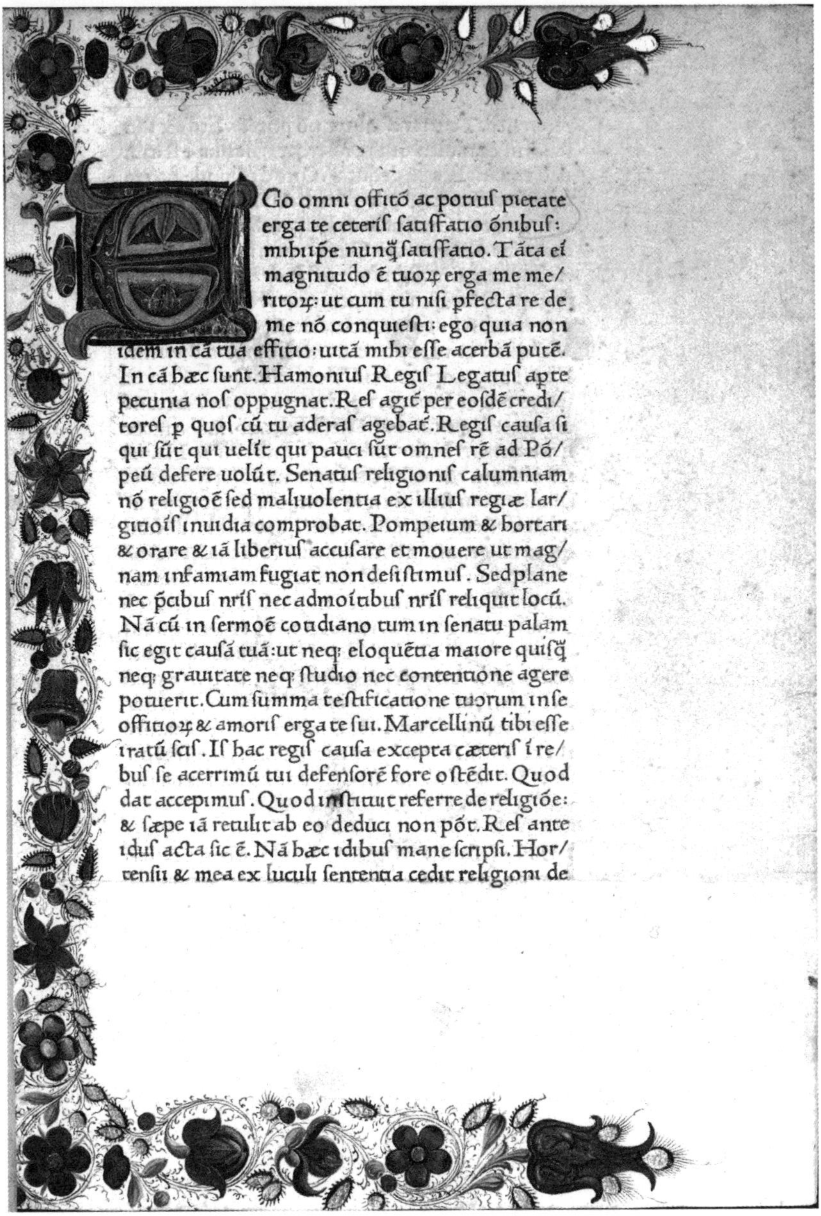

Go omni offitĩo ac potiuſ pietate
erga te ceteriſ ſatiſſatio õnibuſ:
mihiipſe nunq̃ ſatiſſatio. Tãta eſ
magnitudo ẽ tuoꝝ erga me me/
ritoꝝ: ut cum tu niſi pfecta re de
me nõ conquieſti: ego quia non
idem in cã tua effitio: uitã mihi eſſe acerbã putẽ.
In cã hæc ſunt. Hamoniuſ Regiſ Legatuſ apte
pecunia noſ oppugnat. Reſ agit per eoſdẽ credi/
toreſ p quoſ cũ tu aderaſ agebat. Regiſ cauſa ſi
qui ſũt qui uelĩt qui pauci ſũt omneſ rẽ ad Põ/
peũ defere uolũt. Senatuſ religioniſ calumniam
nõ religioẽ ſed maliuolentia ex illiuſ regiæ lar/
gitioĩſ inuidia comprobat. Pompeium & hortari
& orare & iã liberiuſ accuſare et mouere ut mag/
nam infamiam fugiat non deſiſtimuſ. Sed plane
nec p̃cibuſ nrĩſ nec admoĩtibuſ nrĩſ reliquit locũ.
Nã cũ in ſermoẽ cotidiano tum in ſenatu palam
ſic egit cauſã tuã: ut neq; eloquẽtia maiore quiſq̃
neq; grauitate neq; ſtudio nec contentione agere
potuerit. Cum ſumma teſtificatione tuorum inſe
offitioꝝ & amoriſ erga te ſui. Marcellinũ tibi eſſe
iratũ ſciſ. Iſ hac regiſ cauſa excepta cæteriſ ĩ re/
buſ ſe acerrimũ tui defenſorẽ fore oſtẽdit. Quod
dat accepimuſ. Quod inſtituit referre de religiõe:
& ſæpe iã retulit ab eo deduci non põt. Reſ ante
iduſ acta ſic ẽ. Nã hæc idibuſ mane ſcripſi. Hor/
tenſii & mea ex luculi ſententia cedit religioni de

Figure 3.1 Cicero, *Epistolae ad familiares* (Rome: Conrad Sweynheym & Arnold Pannartz, 1467), first printed leaf, John Rylands 3455.

about this and I'm endeared to the unnamed French binder who left this small Easter egg in his work; you would only see it if you actually *read* the book, something one cannot necessarily assume.

Not where the Duc de la Vallière was concerned anyway, for this is yet another of Reviczky's acquisitions at that sale (lot 2311, 931 *livres tournois*).[13] This volume, however, gives us a longer vista into its past than the two previous Ciceros. Even La Vallière had his role models and one of those was Louis-Jean Gaignat (1697–1768), secretary to Louis XV, and another remarkable French collector, not just of books but of paintings as well. His beautiful early fifteenth-century manuscript of the great medieval allegorical poem the *Roman de la Rose*, graced with no less than 101 miniatures, is now in the Getty Museum and his imaginary view of the harbour near the Roman Capitol by Claude Lorrain is one of my favourite Lorrains in the National Gallery.[14] When Gaignat died, Guillaume-François de Bure, cousin to the man who prepared the La Vallière catalogue, presented the royal secretary's collection, not just as another auction catalogue but as a supplement to de Bure's own bibliographical dictionary; it was that impressive.

La Vallière bought heavily at the Gaignat sale in 1769. The 1467 Cicero cost him 430 *livres tournois*, less than half of what Reviczky paid for it, and its 1465 Subiaco sibling was probably also a Gaignat purchase as two copies were sold there, one for 116 and another for 103 *livres tournois*.[15]

Having reached Italy with Sweynheym and Pannartz in 1464, printing came to Paris with the trio of Ulrich Gering, Michael Friburger, and Martin Crantz in 1469. They had been invited by the rector of the Sorbonne and set up their press in that august institution. One of their first substantial productions was the *Epitome* of Livy written by the second-century AD Roman historian Lucius Annaeus Florus, a favourite of the Humanists due to its rhetorical flourishes and its convenient summary of early Roman history. Unlike the elegantly-shaped folios we have been handling so far, Gering's Florus is quite a small quarto, bound in French red morocco of the eighteenth century.[16] It is, to be brutally honest, a little disappointing inside. The type is ragged and uneven by comparison with that of Sweynheym and Pannartz, with more complex letterforms struggling to achieve a satisfying balance and evenness of line. The paper is a little grey and dirtied (it probably was not great stock to begin with) and the simple red and blue rubrication has left the guide letters visible. Still, the quality of the printing itself is good, with a nice even depth and colour of ink across the page. Overall, it would be an unremarkable piece of printing were it not for its place as one of the first works printed in France. Reviczky had bought it in 1786 at the sale of Michel-Louis Le Camus de Limare (1722–1794), another great collector of the *ancien régime*, for 801 *livres tournois*. La Camus must, in turn, have bought it not long before the sale of his collection as it does not appear in his 1779 privately printed catalogue.

By this point we and Spencer may have come to a few conclusions about the market for very early printed books at the end of the eighteenth century. First, these were already *very* expensive. Second, these beautifully bound, carefully preserved volumes were circulating, often at fairly high speed, through a comparatively small number of aristocratic libraries. In the case of the Gering Florus, it had known four owners in the space of a decade, from someone unknown to Le Camus de Limare to Reviczky to Spencer, apparently rising in price at every transfer. Did Spencer stop for a moment, maybe, and wonder whether there were ways to step outside this congested marketplace? It would have been a good question to ask.

* * *

So far we have been tracing the spread of printing through the Latin classics, but now we and Spencer might turn to their Greek counterparts. Although revived with Humanism and given an added head start—as well as a touch of urgency—by the presence of Greek refugees from the fall of Constantinople in western Europe after 1453, Greek was far less widely known than Latin in the fifteenth century and printing in Greek accordingly came later. Unsurprisingly, the first book printed in Greek was a grammar, by the Byzantine scholar Manouel Chrysoloras, and was printed in Venice about 1471, but more literary texts would soon follow.[17]

Do you know that great work of Homer, *The Battle of the Frogs and Mice (Batrachomyomachia* in the Greek)? Probably not. Although reasonably well known in Spencer's day, this heavy-handed parody of the *Iliad* is no longer thought to be by Homer and has receded into the comforting confines of academic monographs. A few hundred years ago, however, its stock was much higher and it has the surprising honour of being the first classical text printed in Greek. Its printer was the "experimental" and frankly mediocre Tommaso Ferrando of Brescia in Lombardy, one of whose more recent chroniclers felt the need to defend from the charge of "being merely a madman".[18]

One can understand why if we join Spencer in examining a thin, elegant quarto bound in midnight blue morocco, a pleasing rectangle of goatskin which gives us cause to reflect on the role of bookbinders and bindings in the marketplace we have been exploring.[19] Modern bibliographers and collectors more often than not value bindings that are contemporary or near-contemporary with the book itself; when buying an incunable, they will quite likely want it to be in a fifteenth-century binding if at all possible. This was not the case in our period. Reviczky, Spencer, and their peers would regularly have books in—to their eyes—tatty old bindings rebound in sumptuous full morocco by the fashionable London binders of the day. These binders were largely, though not universally, German immigrants and had established themselves as the leading members of their trade in London by the latter part of the eighteenth century.

Chief amongst them when Spencer came of age as a collector was the binder of the present volume, Christian Samuel Kalthoeber (1753–1819), who had been a favourite of Reviczky's as well.[20] A native of Berlin and former apprentice to the great Anglo-German binder, Johann Baumgarten, he had been active since the early 1780s and Spencer began sending books to him for rebinding as early as September 1789, hot on the heels of his first exposure to bibliomania.[21] Soon, however, he began to spread his custom more widely and in April 1792 we find the first receipt from Henry Walther (*fl. c.*1775–1815), another student of Baumgarten's and "a substantial, good, honest binder" according to the faint praise of Dibdin.[22] Personally, I'm very fond of Walther because of his minutely detailed invoices, in which he identifies the comparative richness of the binding, the materials used, and any conservation practised (e.g. "taking out the stains of the whole Second Vol[ume] and filling up a number of Worm holes").[23]

From 1797 onwards, however, Spencer—and many of his contemporaries—relied more than anyone on that indefatigable and brilliant practitioner of the "bibliopegistic art" (as Dibdin would have put it), Charles Hering (*c.*1763–1815).[24] Born in Göttingen, he rapidly established himself in the London binding scene in the mid 1790s and remained the leading figure in the profession for the rest of his life.[25] It was only after the deaths in quick succession of these three men that their younger contemporary Charles Lewis (1786–1836)—really Karl Ludwig and the son of a Hanoverian political refugee—came to achieve his dominant role in the high-end bookbinding trade.[26] We shall meet bindings by all of these men in due course, but we can do far worse than begin with the beautifully bound *Batrachomyomachia*.

Its distinguished outward appearance gives way as soon as we open it. This is a tremendously ugly book. The Greek type is miserably cut, the inking is uneven, the spacing is clunky, the Latin metrical translations which are present on the verso of each page are awkwardly spaced out leaving large and irregular gaps. Dibdin is spot on in describing it as "very barbarous".[27] In this copy, guide letters have been left for an illuminator but no illumination has occurred. What has occurred, however, is an incompetent attempt at washing which has only slightly faded the annotations but significantly stained the paper.

But this farrago has one very important thing going for it: it is *absolutely unique*. It first swims into our view in the Pinelli library and at the sale of that collection, when Reviczky first showed Spencer his Aldine Pindar, the Austrian count purchased it in a lot with the 1486 Venetian edition of the same text for a pricey but not exorbitant £27 16*s.* 6*d.*[28] Not unreasonable for the first book printed in Greek, even if it was ugly.

From such unprepossessing beginnings, Greek printing rapidly caught up with its Latin counterpart. Seeing the *Batrachomyomachia* must surely have caused Spencer to hunt out, if its sizeable bulk was not already visible in the same box, a slightly later printing of the genuine poems of Homer: the glorious 1488 Florentine *Works* of the blind bard, edited by Demetrios Chalkokondyles, a native of Athens who spent most of his life as a scholarly celebrity in the city of the Medici. After the near-weightlessness of the last little volume, Spencer might have done a double take on lifting the 1488 *Works*; this is a huge book, especially by fifteenth-century standards, both tall and physically large, which dwarfs the more common slim, neat folios of the incunable period. Our copy is bound in an almost violently red straight-grained morocco, very different in colour from the subtler wine reds of earlier French bindings, and its boards are decorated with classical swags, fleurons, and lyres.[29] The thick spine is intricately tooled with designs resembling open sunflowers in a spectacular style which is nonetheless not *quite* the right tone to set for Homer.

This is the work of Roger Payne (1738–1797), a genius and probably the best English-born bookbinder of the age, but an erratic drunk whose impoverished and tragic life contrasted strikingly with the rich, fantastical beauty of his bindings.[30] A famous engraving by Sylvester Harding shows Payne, bearded, ragged, and unkempt, bent over a book in the binder's press in a bare room whose cracked-plaster walls and small window describe what seems to be unrelieved poverty.[31] From such unprepossessing circumstances, he developed what may fairly be described as a new style of binding, one distinctively English which, in various iterations, would appear on many books in Spencer's library over the coming decades. What makes Payne so exceptional as a binder, I think, is not simply his choice and combination of tools, though that is outstanding, but a certain lifelike sinuosity to his tooling—how even to describe it?—which gives his work a moving three-dimensionality that is quite lacking in works of the binders of the mid- to late nineteenth century. Payne's work is that of an artist; his flowers are kissed by a gentle breeze.

But let us turn from binding to text. Skipping past the dedicatory epistle to Piero de' Medici, the spectacularly unsuccessful son of Lorenzo the Magnificent who lost Florence to the fanatical rule of Girolamo Savonarola, we come to the opening lines of the *Iliad* (see Figure 3.2).

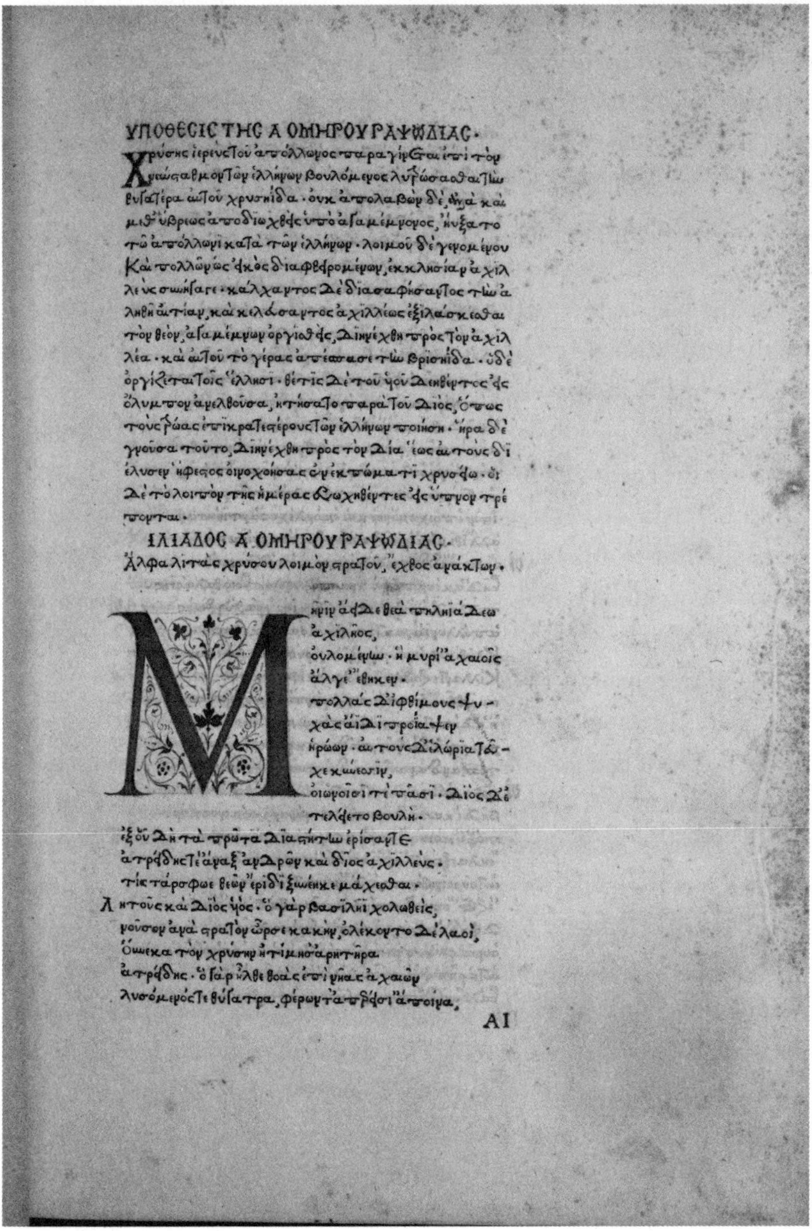

ΥΠΟΘΕΣΙΣ ΤΗΣ Α ΟΜΗΡΟΥ ΡΑΨΩΔΙΑΣ.

ΙΛΙΑΔΟΣ Α ΟΜΗΡΟΥ ΡΑΨΩΔΙΑΣ.

Ἄλφα λιτὰς Χρύσου λοιμὸν στρατοῦ, ἔχθος ἀνάκτων.

Μῆνιν ἄειδε θεὰ Πηληϊάδεω Ἀχιλῆος,
οὐλομένην· ἣ μυρί' Ἀχαιοῖς ἄλγε' ἔθηκεν·
πολλὰς δ' ἰφθίμους ψυχὰς Ἄϊδι προΐαψεν
ἡρώων· αὐτοὺς δὲ ἑλώρια τεῦχε κύνεσσιν,
οἰωνοῖσί τε πᾶσι· Διὸς δ' ἐτελείετο βουλή·
ἐξ οὗ δὴ τὰ πρῶτα διαστήτην ἐρίσαντε
Ἀτρεΐδης τε ἄναξ ἀνδρῶν καὶ δῖος Ἀχιλλεύς.
τίς τάρ σφωε θεῶν ἔριδι ξυνέηκε μάχεσθαι·
Λητοῦς καὶ Διὸς υἱός· ὁ γὰρ βασιλῆϊ χολωθεὶς,
νοῦσον ἀνὰ στρατὸν ὦρσε κακὴν, ὀλέκοντο δὲ λαοί,
οὕνεκα τὸν Χρύσην ἠτίμησ' ἀρητῆρα
Ἀτρεΐδης· ὁ γὰρ ἦλθε θοὰς ἐπὶ νῆας Ἀχαιῶν
λυσόμενός τε θύγατρα, φέρων τ' ἀπερείσι' ἄποινα,

AI

Figure 3.2 Homer, *Opera* (Florence: s.n., 1488), opening leaf of the *Iliad*, John Rylands 3246.

The Greek type is still not quite so beautifully cut as its Latin sibling, but its rugged, distinctive lines are far from the barbarity of Ferrando's attempt and its titling is gorgeous, looking more like Church Slavonic than the Greek founts which may be familiar to modern readers. This copy also has a pleasant gold-illuminated *mu* as its initial, whose interstices are filled with delicate vine leaves. Subsequent initials are not rubricated, which is a bit of a shame.[32]

Further on, the first page of the *Odyssey* tells a tragic story. It has evidently been washed to remove several marginalia just faintly visible as shadows in the margin, but in the process—alas!—it has also washed away what once must have been a beautiful illuminated *alpha* to match the *mu* at the beginning of the *Iliad*, now seen only as a ghostly outline. Under UV light—a common way of trying to read erasures is by lighting the page from behind with a plastic sheet which emits gentle ultraviolet light—the scrubbing away of the marginalium becomes very clear but the ghostly *alpha* vanishes completely—it can, paradoxically, only be seen in normal light.

What do I mean when I say a book has been "washed"? The story is a sad one, at least from the perspective of a modern scholar. Early books, especially Latin and Greek classics like the ones I've been describing, would often be annotated by their fifteenth- or sixteenth-century readers. Occasionally, these annotations would come to be valued if they'd been written by a famous scholar, but mostly they remained anonymous. We now consider them precious records of how a previous age interacted with texts, but as far as Spencer and his contemporaries were concerned they were unsightly blots marring the purity of the printed page. Hence, washing. A book would be unbound and its loose sheets floated in an acidic bath designed, not always successfully, to remove the annotations without affecting either the oil-based printing inks or the paper or vellum itself. Varieties of bleach or "acqua forte" were the most common solution used and, as has been repeatedly observed by more recent commentators, the brilliant whiteness which it could achieve in the short term has, two centuries later, too often led to stained and discoloured pages.[33]

The 1488 Homer was a landmark, but Greek printing truly came of age in the hands of Aldo Manuzio. Before the Pindar we met in Chapter 1 had come dozens of Greek works, quite often the *editiones principes*, and at the forefront of these, both chronologically and in terms of sheer size and achievement, were the *Complete Works* of Aristotle in six volumes (there had been earlier editions of medieval Latin translations, but this was the first in the original Greek).[34] Here the slightly rugged, blocky characters of the Homer have been smoothed out into a flowing stream of script, the capitals are like Athenian inscriptions, the ample margins balance the close-set wall of text. We can easily imagine Spencer turning from the Homer to the Aristotle, "large and magnificent, having many rough edges at the bottom of the leaves, and... beautifully bound in red morocco".[35]

When I was preparing for the research trip which would see me working with the books described in this chapter, the Aristotle was towards the top of my list. I looked in the online catalogue and there it was, as expected, but with a small note appended: "UML copy at 3107: Sold at Sotheby's, 14th April 1988". It had fallen victim to one of the great scholarly scandals of twentieth-century Britain.

In April 1988 the University of Manchester, which owns the John Rylands Library, decided to raise some quick cash by selling approximately one hundred "duplicates" from its collections. Of course, every early printed book is unique and the concept of "duplicates", especially when the collections they came from were Spencer's and that of the later nineteenth-century collector Richard Copley Christie, is absurd, as many pointed out at the time. Nonetheless, the Vice-Chancellor Sir Mark Richmond and the University Librarian Michael Pegg persisted, in a campaign which one contemporary observer described as "stupidity and duplicity go[ing] hand in hand".[36] Despite private entreaty and public outcry some of the best books in the Rylands, including sixty-seven from Spencer's collection, were quietly, almost secretively, despatched to Sotheby's for rapid sale. In this glittering array, the Aristotle could be described as, comparatively, "the least satisfactory of the great books"; it was sold for £110,000 to the London bookdealers Quaritch on 14 April and its current whereabouts are unknown.[37]

So, while Spencer had the pleasure of unpacking his Aristotle, I did not. As with every institution which parts with its patrimony for a mess of the proverbial pottage, the Rylands has had decades to rue what was accomplished in a matter of weeks and I do not wish to cast any further blame here, certainly not on the blameless (and, I might add, really quite wonderful) staff of the library today. Nonetheless, the "Rape of the Rylands", as it was somewhat melodramatically called at the time, was one of a growing number of sales by public institutions in the later twentieth century and the book historian Nicolas Barker was not wrong when he prophesised that "a disastrous precedent will be set for other historic libraries".[38] The precedent has been acted upon regularly and with vigour since, seeing many books which, one might have supposed, would have peacefully rested on library shelves for centuries being pitched into auction rooms for the sake of short-term gain. This modern-day failure at an institutional duty of care offers some intriguing parallels with the book world into which Spencer was about to plunge.

* * *

The printing press reached Spain in 1471–72, the Low Countries in 1473, England in 1476, Scandinavia in 1482, and even the Balkans by about 1491. In 1500, only forty-five years after the completion of the Gutenberg Bible, there were, according to one estimate, a thousand presses operating across Europe and something in the nature of eight million printed books in circulation.[39] The trickle had become a flood and the early days of printing, populated by isolated presses like that of Sweynheym and Pannartz in Subiaco, had been succeeded by a world in which print was normalised, was, indeed, the norm.

And, yet, precisely because of that sea-change, it was the earliest productions of the press, the first book printed *here*, the first edition of a classical text, the earliest use of this or that now-universal technique, that fascinated the collectors of the eighteenth century, as it still does their spiritual descendants.[40] By buying the Reviczky library, Spencer had bought into this fascination, this obsession with origins which defined the ways in which old books were valued. We can imagine him, by now exhausted, surrounded by open boxes, piles of folios stacked on the floor, quartos teetering on tables, Reviczky's catalogue, already well-thumbed, open in front of him, and candles burning low as he languorously reaches for just one more volume, one more wonderful revelation of ownership. Ownership, Benjamin wrote in the essay which opened this chapter, "is the most intimate relationship one can have to objects. Not that they come alive in him; it is he [the owner] who lives in them."[41] Spencer, alone in the deserted library, his household asleep around him, was alive in them in a way that could never be forgotten. It was this unpacking, unrecorded save implicitly in the echoes it left through the remainder of his life, which inaugurated *bibliomania*.

FOUR

The art of collecting

On 26 August 1789 the revolutionary National Constituent Assembly, sitting in Paris, adopted the "Declaration of the Rights of Man and of the Citizen", a deeply humane document which outlined, amongst other points, that "No man can be accused, arrested nor detained but in the cases determined by the law" (article VII), "No one may be disquieted for his opinions, even religious ones" (article X), and "Property being an inviolable and sacred right, no one can be deprived of private usage, if it is not when the public necessity, legally noted, evidently requires it, and under the condition of a just and prior indemnity" (article XVII).[1] On 2 November the same assembly voted that all property of the Roman Catholic church in France "be placed at the disposal of the nation".[2]

This was the beginning of the end, both for the high ideals of the revolution and for the millennium and a half of monastic life in France and, in the fulness of time, much of Europe. But while the nationalisation of church property was being discussed in Paris, Spencer and Reviczky were concerned with a much more pressing matter: the imminent sale of the unparalleled library of early printing formed by Pietro Antonio Bolongaro Crevenna (*d.* 1792), a wealthy Italian tobacco merchant living in Amsterdam who by 1789 owned over a thousand incunabula.[3] Crevenna's library was well known, for he had produced that crowning glory for book collectors, a lavishly-printed private catalogue, in 1775 and on-lookers were in no doubt that its dispersal would be an event of international importance.[4] The sale catalogues, issued by the booksellers Changuion and den Hengst in Amsterdam, proudly advertised that they could be obtained from "the principal booksellers of the towns of Holland" as well as shops as far-flung as Edinburgh (Charles Elliot in Parliament Close), Florence (Signor Molini), Leipzig (Weidmann's Heirs and Herr Fritsch), and even Moscow (the German emigré Christian Rüdiger).[5]

A copy reached Reviczky in September 1789. Having sold his library, the count remained invested in its development and almost immediately, supported by what seems to have been an instant and mutual liking, set himself up as Spencer's guide to the world of collecting. "I have noted some articles among the Classics which might suit you", he wrote, naming a number, including the second volume of the elusive 1471 Sweynheym and Pannartz Ovid as well as the De Spira Tacitus. But, overall, "this Library of Crevenna, whose Catalogue makes quite a stir, is not comparable to yours, at least in the classics, of which more than half of the first editions are missing". He did note, however, that a fine copy of Fust and Schöffer's 1462 Bible on paper was present and added that Crevenna had, he knew, bought it for 3,000 *livres* from De Bure in Paris.[6]

Spencer added his own wants list and the two men discussed strategy, with Reviczky, rather too sanguinely, averring that the Crevenna books, if obtained, and one or two others, "could advance your Collection so much, that there would remain afterwards almost nothing to do, especially in completing all the first editions of Cicero, which is the most difficult part".[7]

* * *

In the preceding chapter I introduced the John Rylands Library in Manchester, where Spencer's books are now preserved. Before we proceed much further, I should do the same favour for his family archive, from which I have been quoting the epistolary dialogue between Spencer and Reviczky. The Spencers' papers were divided up in 1984, with the manorial and estate papers going to the Northamptonshire Record Office while the family and political papers were acquired by the British Library. They form just under three thousand distinct entries in the library's catalogue, amounting to some millions of individual documents.[8]

The British Library (universally called "the BL") is probably known to many of my readers. In case you've not been there, it's a large, violently ochre 1990s construction in the heart of London. You access it from a central square and if, like me, you arrive at opening time, you'll probably have to wait in a long queue of library habitués before finally getting through the doors. I like people-watching in this queue: shambling old men clutching newspapers, smart American academics, tapping their feet with impatience, Sloaney students chatting volubly with their peers—the world is on display.

Once you pass through the doors and the obligatory security check, you try to squeeze your bag and coat into one of the awkwardly small lockers and then, lightened and carrying your laptop in a branded plastic bag (the "cool" academics always use the library bag of another institution, e.g., if you go to the BL, you carry your laptop in a Cambridge University Library bag or vice versa—I've never quite understood why this is) you mount the stairs to the manuscripts reading room. Passing students lolling in the open-plan study spaces, you go through another layer of security, and you're at the issue desk. The BL librarians are stern folk (they probably have to be) and I always feel a little intimidated when I ask for the items I've called up. Sometimes hiccups occur but in the case of the letters it is quite straightforward.

Fortunately for us, the Spencers kept just about everything. In the story that is unfolding, I have drawn especially on Spencer's correspondence, which is still loose and kept in solid wooden boxes. When you consult it, the BL's eagle-eyed guardians make you sit at an easily visible table and warn you against the perils of putting loose papers back in the wrong order. It's not that bad, really, and the feel of crackling two-hundred-year-old letters under your hands is a lovely one, especially when those letters are covered with the neat, distinctly Central European italic that is Reviczky's signature hand; this is where the early days of Spencer's collecting are to be discovered.

* * *

In the event, Reviczky opined that Spencer's best purchases at the Crevenna sale were the odd volume of the Sweynheym and Pannartz Ovid and an undated, but *circa* 1470, edition of Cicero's *Philippics*, both of which he thought were "quite beautiful" when he saw them safely arrived at the bookseller Thomas Payne's shop in London in July 1790.[9] We might gently demure and take at least an equal interest in the "other [books] of lesser importance" which Reviczky casually dismissed in the same letter, for here we begin to see a subtle change in Spencer's collecting. The advertisement to the sale had pointed out that, amongst other rarities, Crevenna had a collection of "numerous and unique early and rare editions, highly esteemed, of the Holy Books in Hebrew, with and without commentaries, and of works in the same language concerning the theology of the Jews".[10] Spencer bought at least a few of these, including a slightly stained but still desirable copy of the rare 1488 edition of the *Sefer Mitzvot Gadol* (*The Great Book of Commandments*), a thirteenth-century work of Jewish legal commentary by Moses ben Jacob of Coucy printed by the pioneering Jewish printer Gershom Soncino, as well as (and rather less desirably for modern tastes) the anti-Semitic screed, *Historia de infantulo*, printed in Rome in 1475.[11] Comparatively small acquisitions though they were, they hint that Spencer was already looking beyond the well-trodden fields of classical literature towards wilder and less crowded expanses of bibliophily.

But Spencer's most significant acquisition from the dispersal of the Crevenna library was not a book, but a man: the Italian collector's sometime librarian Tommaso de Ocheda (1757–1831). Ocheda had been born in Tortona to a Spanish officer in the Savoyard service, evidently with some obscure pretensions to nobility, studied with the Jesuits, and made a half-hearted attempt at studying law. His real interests, though, were philosophical and scholarly and through the intercession of some Jesuit acquaintances the twenty-seven-year-old Ocheda was, in January 1785, taken on as Crevenna's librarian.[12]

His time in Amsterdam was short, however, and one can only suppose that his final task—drafting the sale catalogue of his sometime employer's library—must have felt akin to knotting the rope with which he was to be hanged. Salvation came in the form of an offer from Spencer via the politician and diplomat Frederick North, then not long down from Oxford and not yet the distinguished book collector he would later become.[13] Ocheda wrote in overwhelmed tones on 5 January 1790, that "the generosity with which Your Excellency has deigned to offer me... the position of his Librarian, has supremely flattered my self-respect, and imbued me with the most lively gratitude and thankfulness. However, in the midst of the satisfaction I feel at seeing myself favored by such an illustrious Maecenas, I fear with all reason that I am well inferior to the portrait that [North] must have painted of me."[14]

Alongside such, undoubtedly forced, humility, Ocheda had also pointed out a more proximate problem: "I am sorry that I do not know enough of the English Language both to write and to speak, as I have learnt it largely without a teacher but by mere inclination. But as in the future I will perhaps have to consider it as a second mother tongue, so I will study better to learn it."[15] He did not, but he nonetheless arrived in London the following month and was delighted with the library put in his keeping; he would remain an indispensable fixture of Spencer's household life for almost three decades.[16]

* * *

As Reviczky's friendship with Spencer blossomed, he came to occupy a unique position vis-à-vis the younger and wealthier man. He acted as Spencer's agent, sourcing books from his well-established network of collectors and booksellers across Europe, but was also the earl's advisor, suggesting potential purchases, discussing conditions and prices, warning or encouraging: in effect, teaching him how to collect at the highest possible level. He also began to introduce Spencer directly to his network, gradually drawing him into the elite book world as it existed at the end of the eighteenth century.

The first acquaintance to whom he introduced the earl was one of the greatest collectors of this era and a near-contemporary of Spencer (only four years his senior): Angelo Maria Pannocchieschi, marchese d'Elci (1754–1824). D'Elci, the scion of a Florentine noble family, had entered the Knights of Malta in 1780 but never took religious vows and seems to have lived a life of modest wealth in Florence, decamping to Vienna during the Napoleonic occupation, and returning thereafter.[17] He first swam into Spencer's ken in August 1790 when Reviczky reported that the Florentine nobleman was willing to consider an exchange: the third volume of the Sweynheym and Pannartz Ovid, of which Spencer had purchased the second at the Crevenna sale, in exchange for the Tacitus printed by Wendelin of Speyer (better known by his Latinised name, Vindelinus de Spira), one of the earliest printers in Venice. "I know this part is missing from the volume purchased from Crevenna", wrote d'Elci, who had evidently been keeping an eye on his new competition. As added bait, he also mentioned that he knew where a copy of the *Metamorphoses* from the same edition could be found.[18]

This was to be the beginning of a correspondence by turns fruitful and maddening. Any hope of a swift exchange was dashed when d'Elci found his own De Spira Tacitus in October.[19] Instead, he suggested, a 1472 Plautus might be acceptable, no doubt aware that one was in the library of Cardinal Étienne-Charles de Loménie de Brienne, which was about to be sold.[20] Well before that library was sent to the auction block, however, the resourceful Reviczky had dug up a copy in James Robson's shop in London for the not inconsiderable sum of £36, "on the condition, however, that after about five weeks I can withdraw from [the sale], if I do not manage to make the exchange".[21] Even so, further negotiations were required and several more books mounted up as barter on both sides before d'Elci finally dispatched his share of the bargain in early February.[22]

Reviczky was exultant. Enumerating the books sold to d'Elci by Spencer—the Plautus, a four-volume set of the *Works* of Cicero, and the 1477 Asconius Pedianus—he triumphantly wrote, "listen now, My Lord, to what is due to you for this rubbish, and judge if I have succeeded in my negotiation. Here's what's in the crate that comes to you from Milan." The list that followed was certainly impressive. D'Elci had sent not only the *Fasti* but also the *Metamorphoses* from the Sweynheym and Pannartz Ovid as well as three other incunables and a rather nice 1505 Terence on vellum; not bad at all, the two concluded.[23]

D'Elci was one valuable—albeit exasperating—contact, but he was a collector first and foremost and the intricate transactions which mushroomed up between him and Spencer ultimately revolved around the swapping (or sourcing) of duplicates to improve their respective libraries. It took longer for Reviczky to let Spencer into his acquaintance amongst the trade. In 1790 he coyly mentioned "my correspondent in Italy", a mysterious figure who had an almost supernatural ability to provide choice incunables, usually with some hint of urgency behind them. That December, Reviczky's correspondent made a tempting offer, a "*superbe exemplaire*" of the De Spira Tacitus—Spencer already had a copy but not a very good one—for £25.[24] Reviczky had ordered it by the end of the month, but post was slow and it in March he could still write to Spencer that he had been at Edward's shop where he saw "the Tacitus of Spira, quite beautiful in margins, but it is very washed and a little dirty; it is a misfortune that one cannot compare the one which comes from Vienna" (alert readers will note that the Italian correspondent has changed residences).[25] Finally, on 14 April, the long-awaited package arrived. "Yesterday", Reviczky wrote, "I received the three packages that I have been so long waiting for… You were right not to hurry in replacing your De Spira Tacitus, because a finer copy than the one which arrived for you has not yet appeared in any sale since I began my collection. It is the copy of Prince Eugene, beautifully bound in red morocco and with his arms."[26]

The name of Prince Eugene of Savoy (1663–1736) was a talisman for Spencer's age in a way it no longer is for ours. Eugene, the younger son of a Franco-Italian count and Cardinal Mazarin's niece, entered the Imperial service at a young age and became one of the most celebrated commanders in Europe, fighting with spectacular success against the French and the Ottomans and doing much to preserve the integrity of the slowly ailing Holy Roman Empire. As a result of this he became absurdly rich. Some of this he laid out on the Belvedere Palace in Vienna and his other residences, more went on literary patronage, on a stupendous art collection, and on a truly enormous library. He never married and when his estate was inherited by his niece, she, like many an ungrateful heir of a bibliophilic relative, immediately sold the lot. The Emperor himself purchased his late cousin's library in 1737 and the *Bibliotheca Eugeniana* is now at the core of the Austrian National Library (as well as being recognised by UNESCO in its "Memory of the World" programme).[27]

It is a truly stunning collection and its books are instantly recognisable by their rich, wine-red morocco bindings, the arms of Prince Eugene stamped in gold on the boards and alternating arms and initials tooled on the spines. Inevitably, with such a large collection, books occasionally wandered or were disposed of as duplicates and the Tacitus is evidently one of these. It is a small folio of middling thickness and, like all of the prince's books, is an almost perfect example of sumptuous yet restrained early eighteenth-century binding.

I knew this and I had read Reviczky's accolade in the letters, but nothing could have quite prepared me for what lay inside (see Figure 4.1).[28] De Spira's neat Roman lines are enmeshed in a breath-taking profusion of illumination: clusters of peaches are surrounded by red and blue flowers and intricately-inked foliage; along the outside of the leaf are delicately drawn medallion portraits of the leading figures in Tacitus's history: Agrippina, Claudius, Messalina, and at the base is a fine medallion portrait of Tacitus himself, glowing like an intaglio, and surrounded by a laurel wreath. It is simply stunning and is the work of an anonymous Venetian illuminator known to modern scholars as the "Pico Master" who was active at the end of the fifteenth century.[29]

It is a slight surprise after this remarkable opening to find that the illuminator has not followed through and subsequent initials have been left unrubricated. De Spira's printing is good, but he has a tendency to over-ink and become blotchy; sometimes his type looks slightly off its feet, producing an unbalanced impression. Still, it is a wonderful book. It is also one of the first we have come across which has traces of its history before the eighteenth century still visible. Beneath the colophon (the small paragraph at the end of a work generally giving the name of the printer, often their city, and usually the date) is a faint (probably washed) inscription. I could just read it with the help of an ultraviolet light sheet: "this book belongs to the monastery [of Santa Maria della]

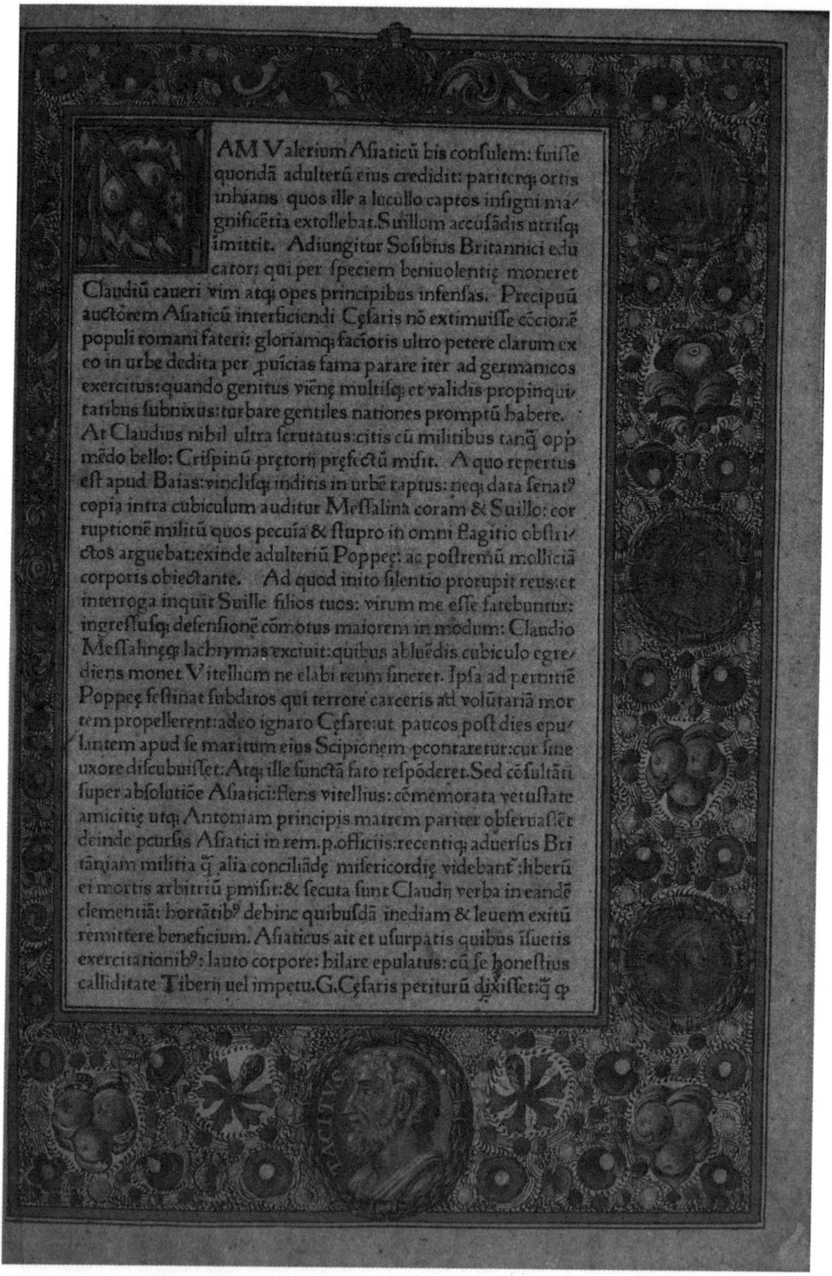

AM Valerium Asiaticũ bis consulem: fuisse
quondã adulterũ eius credidit: paritérq; ortis
inhians quos ille a lucullo captos insigni ma-
gnificẽtia extollebat. Suillum accusãdis utrisq;
imittit. Adiungitur Sosibius Britannici edu
cator: qui per speciem beniuolentię moneret
Claudiũ caueri vim atq; opes principibus infensas. Precipuũ
auctorem Asiaticũ interficiendi Cęsaris nõ extimuisse cõcionẽ
populi romani fateri: gloriamq; facioris ultro petere clarum ex
eo in urbe dedita per ꝓuicias fama parare iter ad germanicos
exercitus: quando genitus viẽnę multisq; et validis propinqui-
tatibus subnixus: turbare gentiles nationes promptũ habere.
At Claudius nihil ultra scrutatus: citis cũ militibus tanq̃ opp
mẽdo bello: Crispinũ prętorij pręfectũ misit. A quo repertus
est apud Baias: vinclisq; inditis in urbẽ raptus: neq; data senat⁹
copia intra cubiculum auditur Messalina coram & Suillo: cor
ruptionẽ militũ quos pecũia & stupro in omni flagitio obstri-
ctos arguebat: exinde adulteriũ Poppeę: ac postremũ molliciã
corporis obiectante. Ad quod inito silentio prorupit reus: et
interroga inquit Suille filios tuos: virum me esse fatebuntur:
ingressusq; defensionẽ cõmotus maiorem in modum: Claudio
Messalinęq; lachrymas exciuit: quibus abluẽdis cubiculo egre-
diens monet Vitellium ne elabi reum sineret. Ipsa ad pernitiẽ
Poppeę festinat subditos qui terrore carceris ad volũtariã mor
tem propellerent: adeo ignaro Cęsare: ut paucos post dies epu-
lantem apud se maritum eius Scipionem ꝑcontaretur: cur sine
uxore discubuisset: Atq; ille functã fato respõderet. Sed cõsultãti
super absolutiõe Asiatici: flens vitellius: cõmemorata vetustate
amicitię utq; Antoniam principis matrem pariter obseruasset
deinde ꝑcursis Asiatici in rem. p. officiis: recentiq; aduersus Bri
tãniam militia q̃ alia conciliãdę misericordię videbant: liberũ
ei mortis arbitriũ ꝑmisit: & secuta sunt Claudij verba in eandẽ
clementiã: hortãtib⁹ dehinc quibusdã inediam & leuem exitũ
remittere beneficium. Asiaticus ait et usurpatis quibus ĩsuetis
exercitationib⁹: lauto corpore: hilare epulatus: cũ se honestius
calliditate Tiberij uel impetu. G. Cęsaris peniturũ dixisset: q̃ ꝙ

Figure 4.1 Tacitus, *[Selected Works]* (Venice: Vindelinus de Spira, *c.*1471–72), Prince Eugene of Savoy's copy, first printed leaf, John Rylands 3463.

Carità in Venice and was given by Don Raffaele di Piacenza when he was prior of that monastery in the year 1475".

What happened to Tacitus between 1475 and his acquisition by Prince Eugene no later than 1736? We can only speculate. There do not seem to have been any great upheavals or bankruptcies in the monastery's history which could obviously account for the book's loss or sale, but we know far too little to say with any certainty. What we can say is that it is one of the many books already circulating in Europe before 1789 which had wandered from a religious to a secular home. It would soon be joined by millions more.

* * *

After two happy years of regular contact in London, Reviczky returned to Vienna in the summer of 1791. We do not know why, though the increasing shakiness of his handwriting suggests he may already have been in failing health and wished to spend his last years in a city familiar from his youth. His letters to Spencer slowed slightly, but were still full of information about the trade, books for sale, items he had seen in the Imperial Library, and the latest negotiations with d'Elci and other collectors. In what he may have known were the final months of his life, he became more open to Spencer about his sources. The mysterious Italian-Viennese correspondent had become "my abbé commissioner" in July and was charged with instructions to seek out books for Spencer on his next Italian journey.[30] By September, Reviczky was even prepared to name him: the Abbé Della Lena. And Della Lena had a prize well worth acquiring.

Soon after arriving in Vienna, Reviczky wrote to Spencer that "I saw here the copy of the *Offices* of Cicero on vellum 1466. It must be admitted that it is a very beautiful book from the Library of Prince Eugene, and I dare say more beautiful than the one of 1465 that you have, despite two or three pages with marginal notes, and a small hole in the last pages,"[31] It had been offered to the count for £70, but he had already bargained the as-yet-unnamed seller down to £35 and hoped for a still better deal.

By September, Reviczky revealed his source: it was none other than Della Lena. And, he added, "this abbé has once again played a trick on me for which I will not forgive him. After offering me his superb 1466 *De officiis* of Cicero on vellum for £35, he has left for Italy, and now that you authorize me to take it for this price, it is nowhere to be found in his house and probably he took it with him to see if he can get a better price; I know d'Elci is looking for him."[32] Reviczky's irritation with his favourite bookseller was evident, but it seems to have been unjust. He was arranging for the shipment of the Cicero by the end of October and Della Lena did not return from Italy until a month later, suggesting that the missing book must have turned up somehow.[33] It was in Spencer's hands by January and Reviczky reported his "extreme satisfaction" at Spencer's pleasure, adding with a note of self-congratulation that it "is indeed a very fine book".[34]

It really is. Its binding is like that of its Eugenian sibling purchased the year before and its opening leaf, to my surprise, was also illuminated by the Pico Master (see Figure 4.2).[35] This time it is Cicero staring sternly out at us from the mock-intaglio and the foliage is not quite so luxuriant (though it does boast a couple of hungry birds, nibbling at small golden fruits). The illumination suits the deep semi-Gothic of the type, perhaps rather better than it did De Spira's Roman. This is also something (almost) which we have seen before, for it is another product of Fust and Schöffer's workshop, an edition of Cicero's *De officiis* printed the year after the 1465 volume which we saw Spencer examining in the previous chapter. It is, once again, a classical text from the very cradle of printing.

Like the Tacitus, this volume also has surviving early provenance. On the final leaf are what look like two ownership inscriptions: "Ragnier" written in secretary hand in dark ink and "Cappel" written in italic in a lighter ink which has been slightly smudged (perhaps its author was left-handed?). It is just possible that the earlier of the two is Jehanne Ragnier, an otherwise unknown woman who also owned an early fifteenth-century manuscript copy of Christine de Pisan's *Livre du corps de policie*, now in the Bibliothèque de l'Arsenal; certainly the name sounds French.[36] With "Cappel" we are on sturdier, albeit still uncertain, ground. The Cappel

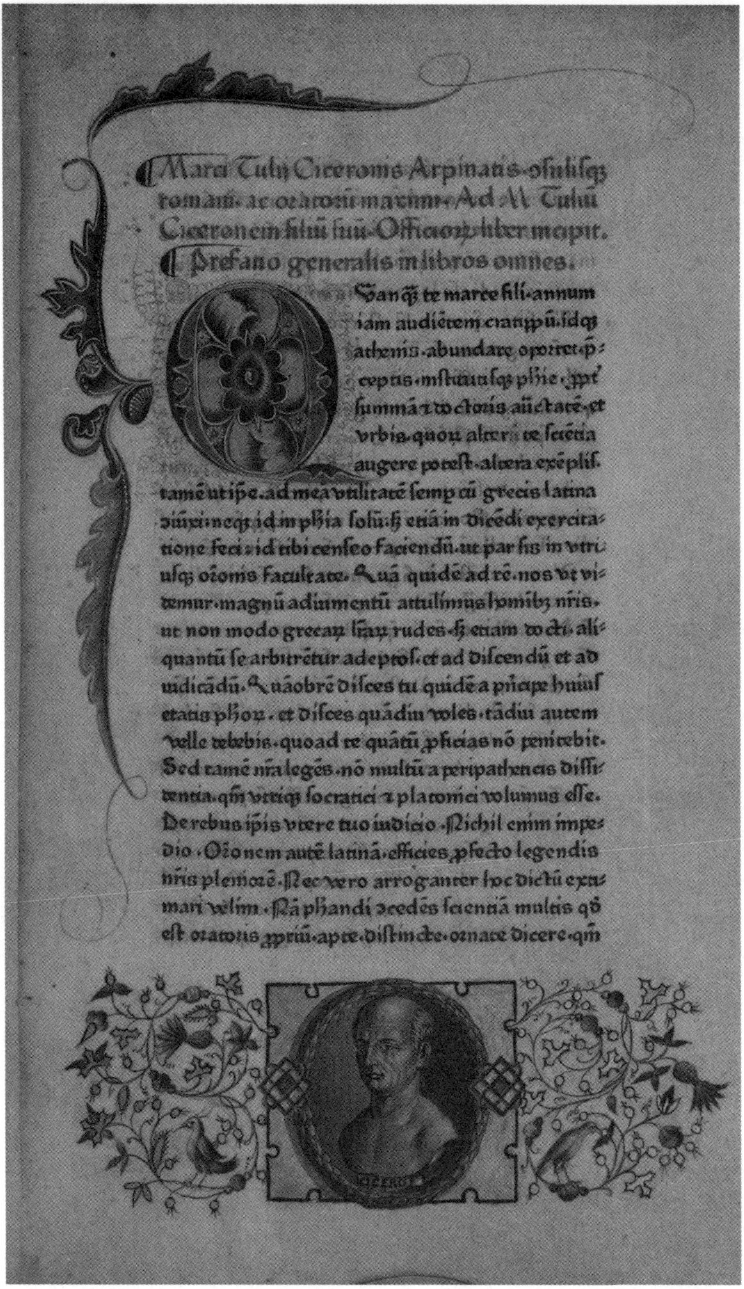
Marci Tulij Ciceronis Arpinatis. consulisque
romani. ac oratoris maximi. Ad M. Tuliu
Ciceronem filiu suu. Officiorum liber incipit.
Prefatio generalis in libros omnes.
Quamquam te marce fili. annum
iam audientem cratippu. idque
athenis. abundare oportet. p̄-
ceptis. institutisque phie. ppter
summa et doctoris auctoritate. et
urbis. quorum alter te scientia
augere potest. altera exemplis.
tamen ut ipse ad mea utilitatem semper cum grecis latina
coniunxi. neque id in phia solum. sed etiam in dicendi exercita-
tione feci: id tibi censeo faciendum. ut par sis in utri-
usque orationis facultate. Qua quidem ad rem. nos ut vi-
demur. magnum adiumentum attulimus hominibus nris.
ut non modo grecarum lrarum rudes. sed etiam docti. ali-
quantum se arbitrentur adeptos. et ad discendum et ad
iudicandum. Quamobrem disces tu quidem a principe huius
etatis phorum. et disces quamdiu voles. tamdiu autem
velle debebis. quoad te quantum pficias non penitebit.
Sed tamen nra legens. non multum a peripateticis dissi-
dentia. quoniam utrique socratici et platonici volumus esse.
De rebus ipsis utere tuo iudicio. Nichil enim impe-
dio. Orationem autem latinam. efficies pfecto legendis
nris pleniorem. Nec vero arroganter hoc dictum exti-
mari velim. Nam phandi concedens scientiam multis quod
est oratoris pprium. apte. distincte. ornate dicere. quoniam

Figure 4.2 Cicero, *De officiis* (Mainz: Johann Fust and Peter Schöffer, 1466), Prince Eugene of Savoy's copy, first printed leaf, John Rylands 7547.

family were a French dynasty of lawyers, scholars, and clergymen, descended from Guillaume Cappel, a late fifteenth-century rector of the University of Paris. Any one of them could be a possible owner, though the philologist and professor of Hebrew Jacques Cappel (1570–1624) is a particularly tempting choice.[37] Regardless, the book clearly had a French origin and may well still have been there when it was purchased by Prince Eugene.

* * *

It was around this time that the long-anticipated sale of the Loménie de Brienne collection finally came to pass. Étienne-Charles de Loménie de Brienne, Archbishop of Sens (1727–1794), had been another of the major collectors of Reviczky's generation, and had attempted some degree of accommodation with the new regime in France. Increasingly embattled, the sale of his collection was probably more a necessity than a choice as the wolves of the Republic began to close in (he would commit suicide in prison three years later).[38] His librarian, the sometime minim friar François-Xavier Laire, compiled a lavish two-volume sale catalogue of the archbishop's impressive collection of 1,332 incunables. Organised by date, it set new standards for detailed bibliographical description.[39]

It also, predictably, attracted Spencer's and Reviczky's attention. Reviczky wrote on 18 January 1792 cautioning Spencer that the tempting volumes of Cebes and Chrysoloras to be found there were probably already in his collection, but pointing out the 1497 Greek-Latin vocabulary and the 1490 Chrysoloras as potential acquisitions.[40] The sale itself took place on 12 March, but Reviczky had not yet heard the results when he wrote to Spencer five days later, gloomily predicting that "if the Bibliothèque de Paris [i.e. the new French National Library] has carte blanche, they will steal many of the lots from you" because they could pay in the new, dubiously valuable French *assignats*. He hoped, nonetheless, that Spencer would manage to get the Terence printed in 1470 or earlier by the first printer in Strasburg, Johann Mentelin, which Reviczky had previously missed, "Abbé Lena not having told me so that I could recognize the edition, and since then he gave it to the Imperial Library".[41]

This is one of the first hints that a new player was in the bibliographical field: the young Republic's national library, deep in the pocket, with an army at its (not entirely reliable) command, and ready to write to its foot soldiers that "nothing must be spared in assuring for the Republic the possession" of the earliest printed books.[42]

In the end, Spencer did manage to acquire the Mentelin Terence, in a faintly gaudy green morocco binding.[43] He also bought a book which Reviczky does not mention, but which was far more important: Fust and Schöffer's 1459 Psalter, one of the landmarks in the history of printing, but preceded—crucially, given Spencer's interest in chronological priority—by a 1457 sibling.[44] Here, again, reading Reviczky's letters gives only a partial, if a rich and revealing, sense of Spencer's collecting tastes which were rapidly expanding to include not just the Latin and Greek classics but almost every printed work which came off the press in the fifteenth century.

* * *

Reviczky made light of his bibliophilia, but he was an enthusiast nonetheless and one of the pleasures of reading his letters to Spencer is watching the ebb and flow of his enthusiasm for specific volumes. In the winter of 1792–93, with the 1466 Cicero and the mixed successes of the Loménie de Brienne sale some months in the past, a new focus for his attention presented itself. On 24 November Reviczky wrote to Spencer with barely concealed excitement, "my Abbé has returned from Italy and, though this time he did not bring me any of the articles I requested, he makes me hope for a very precious book…the first edition of Lucretius".[45] Conventional wisdom, he added, was that the first edition of the first-century BCE Epicurean philosopher Lucretius's poem, *On the Nature of Things*, had been printed in Verona in 1486, but Della Lena asserted that the book he had discovered had been printed thirteen years before in Brescia by Tommaso Ferrando. It was imperative, Reviczky wrote, that "an amateur of your merit, My Lord" should "ensure possession of it, and I ask in advance to be authorised to deal with the abbé, who thinks…he could obtain it for thirty or forty guineas".[46]

Reviczky was quivering with excitement and, not having had a sufficiently prompt reply, wrote again to Spencer in December, "I do not even know if you have received my letter in which I gave you an account of a first edition of Lucretius... which I have been led to hope for, and about which I have asked you for your instructions in advance".[47] Spencer responded with a mixture of enthusiasm and caution. Was it definitely dated or was the date only conjectural? Did it have signatures (the guides for binders at the bottom of each gathering of leaves which were only introduced in the middle of the 1470s)? What else was known? A slightly crest-fallen Reviczky replied that "the year 1473 is only conjectural and the edition has no date; besides, I still do not know if it has signatures". If it did not, it would certainly pass for the first edition, but if it did it would simply be an edition "most dubious and of little consequence".[48]

Distant from Della Lena's hunting grounds in Italy and slowed down by the leisurely speed of post between Vienna and London, Reviczky and Spencer were too late. On 16 March 1793 the count wrote with chagrin that "what I predicted unfortunately happened. The Chevalier d'Elci having betook himself to the very place, that is to say to Brescia, before we could conclude anything from here by negotiation, seized the book, at an exorbitant price, so they tell me, of about 200 ducats, or £100, and yet there is no date, and the subscription bears only: *Brixiae Thoma Ferrando auctore*; but the edition is without signatures, and it is known that this Thomas Ferrandus printed, or had work printed, in Brescia from the year 1473."[49] The still-lingering doubts as to the exact date of the work and the exorbitant sum paid did little to allay Reviczky's exasperation at having been pipped to the post by d'Elci. "The chevalier therefore triumphs, claiming to have a unique copy, and which, having no signatures, must be rightly counted as the first edition of Lucretius." It was only faint satisfaction to note that the recently deceased Count Otto Thott (1703–1785) in Copenhagen and possibly also the Imperial Library seem to have had copies as well.[50]

This was to be Reviczky's last bibliographical sally. Later that summer, on 25 July, he wrote deprecatingly to Spencer from Vienna that "I have been here for six months fighting against a languorous disease which takes a rather bad turn and which makes me incapable of the slightest occupation", but glossed this apology over with news of friends and books.[51] Two weeks later he died of tuberculosis, on 10 August 1793, aged only fifty-seven.[52] As has been repeatedly emphasised by later commentators, Spencer had made a good gamble buying Reviczky's library for an annuity rather than a lump sum. Less often mentioned, however, is the loss he must surely have felt for a man who, over the four years of their acquaintance, had become a valued mentor and friend. Reviczky had taught Spencer how to collect, what to value, how to acquire it, and who to know. He had passed some of his most valuable contacts, fellow collectors like d'Elci and booksellers like Della Lena, on to the younger man and had helped him purchase some of his most spectacular acquisitions to date.

Reviczky's death marked a period in Spencer's collecting. He was of age now and a collector of deservedly international fame. But both Europe and book collecting were changing. The month after Reviczky's death, the French Convention—the same which had passed the "Declaration of the Rights of Man and the Citizen" four years before—declared that "terror is the order of the day" and on 17 September the Law of Suspects was passed, allowing the mass arrest and execution of individuals suspected of disaffection to the new regime. The Reign of Terror had begun.

FIVE

Gutenberg's Bible

Let us pause for a moment at Reviczky's death, pause and then move in retrograde back to the autumn of 1790 when Spencer paid a rather expensive bill. We are fortunate to have the original, safely preserved within the Althorp papers, and I reproduce it in full below:

The R[igh]t Hon[oura]ble Earl Spencer	
Rec[eive]d of Tho[ma]s Payne 1790	
Mazarine Bible 2v.	
Psalter 1459 vellum	} £340
Biblia—Germanici	
Binding the above	£10
Exchange of the Catholicon	£20
	£370
Rec[eive]d in full October 29. 1790	
Tho[mas] Payne Jun[io]r.[1]	

Though Thomas Payne has briefly appeared before, now he is in the limelight. The elder Thomas Payne (1716/18–1799) had been selling books since the 1730s and in 1790 retired to his country house at Finchley, leaving his now flourishing business in the hands of his son of the same name.[2] Thomas Payne, junior (1752–1831) inherited what might not at first have seemed a terribly promising establishment: "an elbow-shed, rather than shop, and lighted by a skylight . . . at the gate of the lower Mews, opening into Castle Street, Leicester Fields" and opposite his family's "dwelling-house, the ground-floor windows of which, as seen from the street, were fairly barricaded with books".[3] It was, however, a centre for cultural and political gossip and the resort of some of the most talented and powerful people in London, Spencer among them.[4]

It is not surprising to see Spencer making large purchases from such a dealer, but £370 was a very substantial sum indeed and we may begin by wondering of what, exactly, did this transaction consist? There were three books, in four volumes, which were bought outright and subsequently bound, while another was "exchanged", probably by trading up for a better copy and paying the difference in price. This last was the first printed edition of the *Catholicon*, a widely-known Latin encyclopaedia, then assumed to have been printed in 1460 though modern scholars suggest several distinct dates for its printing across the 1460s and into the 1470s.[5] It is a common book and Spencer appears to have owned at least five copies at various stages in his life.[6] The 1459 Mainz Psalter, another landmark of early printing, was also subsequently sold when Spencer bought the Loménie de Brienne copy two years later, though in this case we can trace the item bought from Payne through subsequent owners to its present home in the British Library.[7]

Spencer *did*, however, keep the other two books he bought that day. The German Bible was the first printed edition of the Bible in that language, without date, place, or printer's name, though modern scholarship attributes it to Heinrich Eggestein of Strasburg and dates it to no later than 1470. It is a massive, heavy tome, bound in fairly plain brown pigskin, no doubt the binding paid for alongside its purchase.[8] On opening it, one is confronted with a manuscript table of contents of the books of the Bible, written in a neat *bastarda* of the fifteenth century and halfway down the page the eye meets a flowing eighteenth-century ownership inscription which has been heavily scored out. The opening leaf is surprisingly beautiful, with a delicately illuminated vine winding its way across the bottom of the page and neat illumination balancing the small type of the printed text. What fascinates me more, though, is the rather crude annotation in red ink at the bottom of the text of the

Apocalypse of John, "Johann Fust, doctor of laws, made this, anno 1472". It is, of course, false, and I cannot decide whether it is an ingenuous but inaccurate attempt at identifying the Bible's printer or a more calculated ruse to raise the book's value. Certainly by Spencer's day no such attribution was believed.[9]

But we have not given so much attention to a single receipt for any of *these* books, pleasing though they are. Instead, it is the item which heads the list that occupies us: "Mazarine Bible 2v.". What is a Mazarine Bible and why does it deserve particular notice? To answer this question, we must turn to the career of Guillaume-François De Bure le Jeune (1732–1782), one of an eminent Parisian dynasty of booksellers, printers, and bibliographers. In 1763 he published the first volume of his monumental *Bibliographie instructive: ou traité de la connoissance des livres rares et singuliers*, an early and extremely influential work of bibliography which focused especially on the first era of printing.[10] In it he described an old two-volume Latin Bible he had come across, "quite by chance", in the Bibliothèque Mazarin, the library of the Collège des Quatre Nations in Paris. This book, which had previously been owned by the famous Cardinal Mazarin, was, he asserted, none other than the semi-mythical first Bible, printed sometime between 1450 and 1455, known from various literary sources.[11] It was, in other words, the book we now call the Gutenberg Bible. This was the first time a scholar had connected the famous first Bible with a physical book and the name "Mazarine Bible" stuck, at least for another century or so, before it was displaced by the name of its printer.

Thus, amongst the other items purchased from Payne in 1790, Spencer had bought a Gutenberg Bible. This is not especially surprising. It was—and is—not a rare book. By 1790, at least fourteen other copies were known and many more would subsequently come to light (current censuses count forty-nine partial or complete copies as well as numerous fragments). Nonetheless, it was still an extremely valuable item and a jewel in the crown for a collector like Spencer. It may also hold the dubious title of being the first Gutenberg Bible to have sold for a price equal to its modern estimation in the tumultuous period of the French Revolution. To be sure, copies had sold for large sums in the heyday of the 1760s (Louis-Jean Gaignat's Gutenberg, a very nice vellum copy, went for 2,100 *livres* in his sale in 1769), but this boom had not lasted.[12] In May 1789 a copy had sold at Leigh and Sotheby's, the ancestor of the present auction house of that name, for a bargain £6 6*s.*[13] As late as January 1792, the book agent Jean-Baptiste Maugérard sold his copy to the Bibliothèque Nationale for a mere 240 *livres* (about £10).[14] Only a few months later, however, in March 1792, Guillaume De Bure l'aîné, cousin of the bibliographer, auctioned two Gutenberg Bibles which had been owned by Loménie de Brienne, at a reserve of 2,500 *livres* (about £100) each.[15] While they did not make their reserves—by how much we do not know—the direction of travel is clear. It would seem to be Spencer's purchase, the first really substantial sum paid for a Gutenberg Bible since the Gaignat sale thirty years before, which reignited collectors' obsession with this first of all printed books.

But what *did* Spencer pay for his Gutenberg? The receipt suggests a package deal: £340 for the Gutenberg, the 1459 Psalter, and the German Bible. Bundling like this is still a common practice in the trade. Usually the buyer, by virtue of buying more, gets each book for a bit less than might have been the case were they bought individually, but such discounts are often impressionistic and rarely granular. We may suspect something similar here, but we should equally be aware that both Spencer and Payne will have had prices in their minds for all three individual books. What would they have been? We must remember that 1790 lay at the beginning of a curve which would see book prices skyrocketing over the subsequent two decades. In 1798 Spencer was offered a vellum 1459 Psalter for 300 louis d'or (about £180 at contemporary exchange rates) and in 1797 the same correspondent reported the sale of a Gutenberg Bible the previous summer for the same sum.[16] By contrast, we can compare this with the prices of the Gaignat sale in 1769: the Gutenberg there made 2,100 *livres* and the 1459 Psalter (also vellum) only 326 *livres*, or about £157 and £25 respectively.[17] Numbers for the German Bible are less easy to come by, but we may presume that it was the least expensive of the three. Regardless of how one divides the £340 paid to Payne, then, it is hard to imagine that Spencer could have paid less than about £150–200 for his Gutenberg Bible—a stiff price indeed.

What he got for his money, though, is undeniably spectacular.[18] It was not until I'd made a few visits to the Rylands, working on less iconic books in Spencer's collection, that I looked at the Gutenberg itself (there were, predictably, security issues and it took the library a little while to decide who had to be in the room with me). If you haven't handled a Gutenberg Bible before—and I was in that category at the time—you'd be surprised at just how big one is. We're used to thinking of Bibles as thick but rather small volumes, printed on onionskin paper and left in hotel rooms by well-meaning dissenters, but these are *enormous*: two doorstop volumes, closer to elephant folio than anything else. They have been rebound for Spencer in dark-blue straight-grained morocco over exceptionally thick and heavy boards with a foliate border of three repeating tools and his arms blind-stamped in the centre of the boards. It's almost as though he didn't quite have the courage to put his arms in gilt on this, of all books. Though it is now in a box, it must once have been shelved and examined regularly, probably by gawkers, for the bottom board edges are heavily worn. There are wide inner dentelles but no doublures (board interiors fully covered in leather and likewise usually highly tooled in gilt), again more modest than I might have expected, and the endpapers are a plain purple painted paper which is now showing signs of spotting on the free leaf. There are many more richly bound Spencer volumes (maybe a testament as much to when he bought it as anything else). The pages following the endpapers contain two attempted collations, the first by Spencer or one of his librarians, the second dated 8 November 1873, pointing out that the first one is wrong. A detailed printed bibliographical discussion of another Gutenberg Bible from an 1836 sale catalogue has been pasted onto the recto.

After all this, I was still in the nineteenth century; the pages I'd been looking at were all added around the original textblock during rebinding and I could see my hands trembling as I moved closer to Gutenberg's printing itself (see Figure 5.1). It is mesmerising. And perfect. The characters are so crisp and well distributed on the page, the chunky late textura quadrata so solid, the illuminated initial on the opening leaf appropriately profuse in gold but somehow quite overshadowed by the

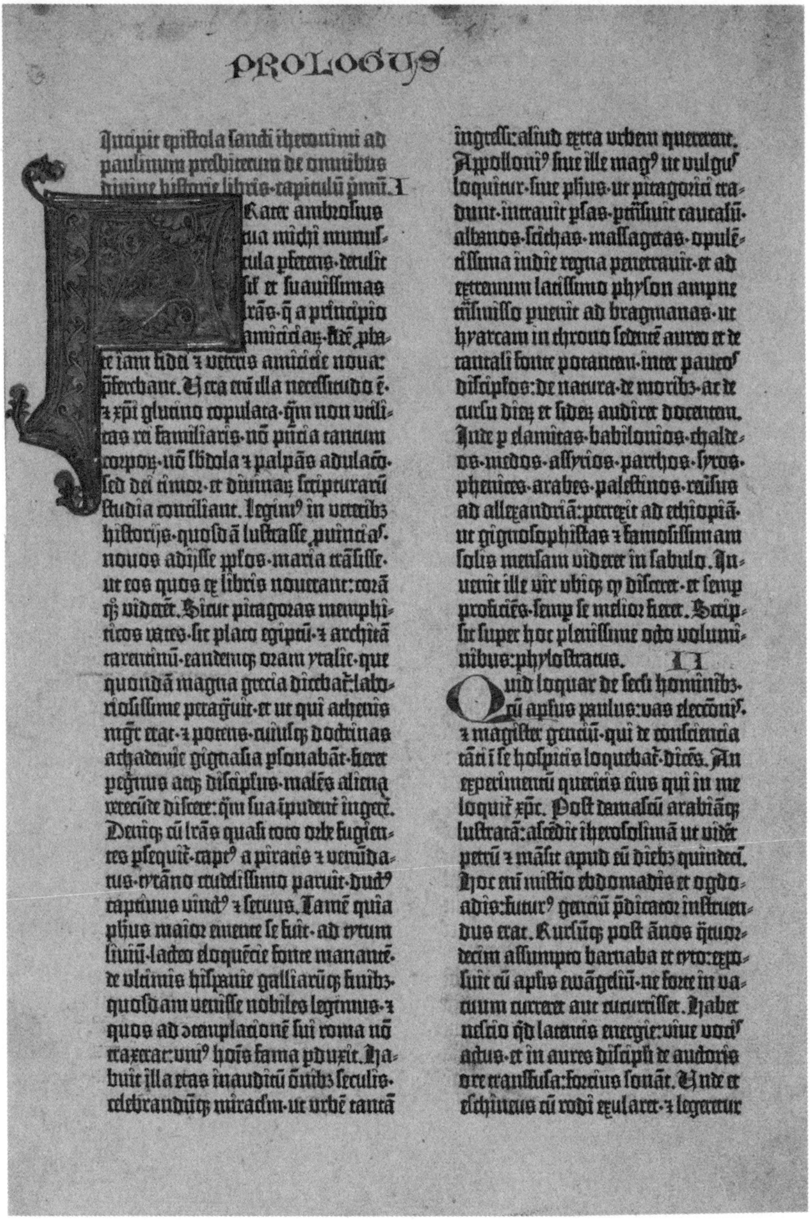
PROLOGUS

Figure 5.1 *Biblia Latina* (Mainz: Johannes Gutenberg, 1455), Vol. I, first printed leaf, John Rylands 3069.

sheer reality of the first printed book. The now almost entirely erased ownership inscription at the top of the first folio seems so perishable and frail by comparison with the print below as if—and I know I wax romantic—the written word simply cannot stand up beside print. The recto of the first folio shows a bit of grime and extra wear, amounting almost to a kind of shininess at the edges, which makes me think it must have been conjugate to the front board at some early stage in its life. Within, on the verso, it is so fresh that the ink still glistens and shines.

We might expect to find the first page beginning with Genesis, but this is the Vulgate Bible, not the modern English editions to which we're used, and instead it begins with the letter of Saint Jerome to the Presbyter Paulinus, abbreviated as the "prologus" in the red and blue running titles. When we reach Genesis we find another noticeable difference from a modern Bible for it begins, "Incipit liber bresith que[m] vos genesim diximus" ("here begins the Book of Bresith which we call Genesis"), "Bresith" being Bereshit, the name of the first *parashah* (essentially a section) in the Hebrew Bible.

The paper is stiff, white, and fresh with an audible crackle as you turn the pages (I felt slightly self-conscious). Note also that this is before two-colour printing. The red explicit/incipit statements are all neatly(ish) handwritten and so vary somewhat in terms of contractions and lay out from those in other copies.

Volume one concludes with the Psalms. As I moved into volume two I noticed it is a bit more scuffed and faded and I chatted with John Gandy, the Incunabula Cataloguer at the Rylands, who was sitting opposite me (here as elsewhere fulfilling the regulation that the library must keep an eye on anyone using its most precious books) speculating that it was out on display for many years, more or less permanently, in the earlier days of the Rylands. Maybe linked to this is the fact that the library couldn't resist putting a frankly enormous bookplate onto the front pastedown of this volume—it's larger than many octavos. It's engraved by C. W. Sherborn, a fine bookplate engraver of the late nineteenth century, and is a nice piece of bookplate art, but it hardly sits right in this context.

Figure 5.2 A rubrication accident. *Biblia Latina* (Mainz: Johannes Gutenberg, 1455), Vol. II, fol. 267r, John Rylands 3069.

Every hand-rubricated book is unique in its own way, but there is one thing that makes this Gutenberg Bible especially so and that is folio 267r: Galatians 3 and 4 (see Figure 5.2). Described by Eric White, the historian of the Gutenberg Bible, as a "rubrication disaster", the unfortunate rubricator has accidentally tipped some of the red *minium* used to illuminate initial letters onto the page. Left alone, this might have just resulted in a not-unattractive splatter pattern, a sort of 1455 Jackson Pollock, but—perhaps panicked at his accident—the poor scribe attempted to wipe the liquid off, instead spreading it only further until it covered almost the entire page.[19] A later reader, evidently amused at the accident, has written "usque ad sanguinem" (literally, "unto blood", but more colloquially, "to the death!") in the margin; it does look rather like a splash of blood across the words of the New Testament.

* * *

I want now to consider more closely the erased ownership inscription on the first folio of volume one. It is impossible to read under normal light. In 2013, however, the Rylands subjected the mysterious scribble to multi-spectral imaging, revealing the faint ghosts of letters which were tentatively read as "Conventus Colmariensis Ord: D: Augustini", i.e. "The Colmar Convent of the Order of St. Augustine". This reading was supported, as White observed in 2017, by the existence of other early books belonging to the Augustinians friars of Colmar with the same inscription formula.[20]

I returned to this inscription in July 2024. Further manipulation of the digitally-enhanced image left me in no doubt that the proposed reading was correct: volume one had come from Colmar. What worried me, though, and what no one seemed to have noticed, was that volume two had an erased inscription on its first folio as well and that, though quite unreadable, it was definitely *different* from that in volume one. The rubrication and illumination is consistent across the two volumes, so this couldn't be a made-up set, but did this represent, I wondered, another mark of provenance which would complicate our understanding of the Bible's past ownership?

The inscription in volume two was much more heavily erased than its sibling, making identification of any characters with the naked eye an impossible task, but with the aid of further multi-spectral imaging, together with digital manipulation, comparison with different forms of eighteenth-century script, and pen trials with a similar pen to determine the plausibility or implausibility of certain reconstructed strokes, I was able to read the inscription in its entirety: "Fr[atrum] Ere[mitarum] Con[ven]tus D[iui] Augustini Colmariensium", "[The book] of the Eremite Brothers of St. Augustine of Colmar". It didn't take long to find another Colmar book, a 1508 edition of the works of Thomas Aquinas, with exactly the same inscription formula.[21]

On the one hand, confirming that both volumes had Colmar ownership inscriptions was less exciting than discovering previously unknown provenance. On the other, it gave me an additional degree of certainty that this was where we should look for Spencer's Bible. These were eighteenth-century inscriptions and there was every reason to suppose that both volumes had been in possession of the Augustinians, one of the mendicant religious orders, until not long before Spencer acquired them. What had happened?

* * *

The Couvent des Augustins in the town of Colmar, on the present north-eastern border of France, was, in retrospect, doomed from the moment when on 2 November 1789 the National Constituent Assembly issued its decree beginning with the simple but explosive statement: "all ecclesiastical property is at the disposal of the nation".[22] This far-reaching act would transform the bibliographical landscape of France in a few short years. Revolutionary officials reached Colmar on 11 May 1790, inventorying the goods of the monks, including a library of 1,900 volumes, with an eye to their confiscation by the state. The Augustinians were far from being a priority however, and it was not until 3 May 1791 that the convent was marked for closure, provoking a brief revolt by the people of the town, where on 22 May a "mob forced the gates of the church", which was temporarily re-opened for worship two days later.[23]

The convent was finally closed and the remaining monks ejected between 10 and 16 June 1791.[24] It is a simple, brutal, and common story in revolutionary France.

But what of the Bible? We do not know when Payne had sold it to Spencer, but it must have been some weeks or months before 29 October 1790 when Spencer paid his bill. This was, in other words, in the twilight period between the inventorying of the monastery's goods in May 1790 and its closure in June 1791. We do not know and, barring the discovery of new archival evidence probably can never know, precisely what happened, but we can guess by analogy with similar situations across Europe: the writing was on the wall, the monks knew their hours were numbered and they would soon have to shift for themselves as best they could. A book agent, who we do not know, appeared offering ready money for their oldest volumes. Faced with an existential threat and needing to prepare for the future, they said "yes". From the agent, it reached Payne and from Payne, Spencer, all in the course of a few tumultuous months in 1790. Had they been slower or more reluctant, we might now be consulting these volumes in the Bibliothèque Nationale.

But Spencer's Gutenberg Bible was only a drop in an ocean of pillaged books. The initial decree of 2 November 1789, confiscating church property, was expanded on by another of 30 March 1792 which confiscated the property of all emigrés and others of doubtful allegiance. These latter properties, a further decree of 27 July 1792 declared, were to be sold for the benefit of the state.[25] From these three governmental acts arose a bureaucratic regime of book confiscation that has not yet been equalled for sheer size. Enormous "book depots" (*dépôts littéraires*) were established in towns and cities across France where the books confiscated as a result of these decrees were sifted through by bureaucrats of the new revolutionary state.[26] By 30 September 1791, just under two years after the initial decree of confiscation had been promulgated, 107 districts across France reported that they had confiscated a total of 1,463,069 volumes, with a further unspecified number of districts not yet reporting.[27]

This was only the beginning. The scale of these activities would not begin to be equalled until the Nazis attempted a similar programme of confiscation and looting during World War II.[28] To give only the example of Paris, Hubert-Pascal Ameilhon, future director of the Bibliothèque de l'Arsenal and, we are told, "a man of action, of rare activity and with a marvellous sense of order", had charge of the city's confiscated books, which were collected into three depots, all themselves located in confiscated religious properties. These books came from 170 distinct religious institutions in the département of Paris and by 1791 numbered 990,738 volumes, of which only about half seem to have been apportioned between various public libraries.[29]

The traditional estimate is that 300,000 volumes from these depots were retained by the Bibliothèque Nationale itself, many more were given to newly-created regional libraries, with an unknown further number being sold or discarded and, while it is clear that the librarians organising this immense operation prioritised much the same things as collectors—incunables, books printed on vellum, large paper copies, beautiful bindings, and so forth—much slipped between the cracks, officially or not, enriching the book market well beyond France in consequence.[30]

Meanwhile, the depots continued to grow. In March 1795 the, we may imagine exhausted, Ameilhon saw the arrival of new carts full of books plundered from the monasteries and convents of Belgium to add to the first crop of French religious libraries and the subsequent addition of books seized from emigrés and enemies of the state.[31] The initial three Parisian depots had now expanded to no fewer than eight and even that was barely enough to absorb the incoming tide.[32] The depots in the provinces had expanded proportionally as well, so much so that no precise count could be made, though one revolutionary official, Henri Grégoire, estimated that by December 1795 the provincial depots—exclusive of those in the département of Paris—contained about six million volumes.[33] A report of autumn 1796 estimated that the Parisian depots then contained the contents of around 1,100 ecclesiastical or lay libraries totalling something in the nature of 1.8 million volumes.[34] With such staggering numbers, it is unsurprising that a substantial staff was required to even begin to maintain order. In summer 1795 the depot on the rue Saint-Marc—and we must bear in mind that this was only one of eight scattered across Paris—had nineteen full-time employees.[35]

Within the depots, the greatest task after the first and most basic one of maintaining some sort of order was to triage the incoming books and direct them accordingly. It took years for this process to be standardised and it was only on 1 January 1798 that a four-part sifting system was put in place. First, all books printed prior to 1550 and all written in exotic languages would be set aside for closer examination. What remained would be divided into three classes. The first, containing "good editions" of Bibles, Church Fathers, councils, and the first twelve copies of "the most esteemed authors" would be kept for the state. The second, containing scholastic and moral theologians and copies beyond the twelfth of items in the first category, would be sold or exchanged. The third, containing "useless and worthless books" and "bad editions of good books" would be sold at auction by weight or delivered to the needs of the artillery (presumably to aid in the packing of cannon balls).[36] Further, increasingly complex systems were devised, but all foundered when faced with the sheer enormity of the task.

Nineteenth- and twentieth-century French scholars have emphasised the books which went from the depots into public institutions and there can be no doubt that the modern libraries of France have been built, so far as their older collections are concerned, from the quarries of the depots. But it is also undeniable that a very large proportion of the books confiscated were ultimately sold, flooding the book market with vast quantities of older texts (remember that anything post-1550 could be fair game for sale or even destruction). If this had been the full extent of the French Revolution's impact on the book trade, it would have been immense. But it was not. Indeed, the books which passed through the depots were probably not even the most significant casualties of the revolution and its aftermath. Side by side with this internal confiscation, the advancing French armies, working in concert with the librarians of the Bibliothèque Nationale, were systematically acquiring manuscripts, incunabula, and other treasures for the French state, plundering them with impressive precision from the towns and cities through which they marched.[37]

In the end, however, the largest and most important transfer of books was probably neither through internal confiscation nor external looting. It was, instead, the many sales, thefts, and other more or less honest transfers of property that occurred because of the times themselves, of which Spencer's acquisition of the Bible we have been discussing was only one. Monks who read the signs of the times were suddenly willing to sell treasured possessions for ready cash; unscrupulous caretakers of secularised institutions could be tempted to part with a few unconsidered trifles for the right amount; and booksellers, always alert to a good deal, were everywhere, making sure that anything left by the army and the state would find its way into auctions in London, Paris, Vienna, or elsewhere. Never before or since in European history have so many books changed hands so quickly as they did in the years between 1789 and 1815. Spencer, like so many of his wealthy contemporaries, benefited, both directly and indirectly, from the chaos of these decades. Indeed, his library could not have been assembled without it. Until now we have seen Spencer the younger collector, buying his books in the established *ancien régime* channels which had helped collectors to assemble their libraries for generations. Now, we shall see a new side of collecting: one which was reliant on the horrors of war and the brutalities of a new regime for its crop of treasures.

SIX

The wreck of Italy

The Bagni di Lucca are thermal springs nestled in the Tuscan hills, a destination for tourists and pilgrims since the Middle Ages. By the end of the eighteenth century, they were a regular stop for English travellers on the Grand Tour and one of those sites of wealthy idleness which for Britons would come to define southern Europe. A Milanese noblewoman, in conversation with Dr. Johnson's friend Hester Piozzi, was succinct in her estimate of the Bagni, "if you would find out the place where common sense stagnates, and every topic of conversation dwindles and perishes away by too frequent or too unskilful touching and handling, you must go to Lucca".[1]

In the late summer of 1793 two of those whose common sense was stagnating and whose conversation was dwindling were Spencer's mother, the dowager countess, and his sister, the society hostess Georgiana, Duchess of Devonshire.[2] Georgiana, an altogether more scintillating and mercurial personage than her brother, had finished up a decades-long career at the centre of London society in 1791 by conceiving an illegitimate child, the daughter of her lover Charles Grey. The Duke, her husband, offered her the choice of divorce or exile, she chose the latter, and the summer of Count Reviczky's death found her wandering Europe with her mother, her sister Harriet, and Harriet's husband, the Earl of Bessborough (these last two were also in the midst of divorce and adultery, which was something of the order of the day for the Spencer children).[3]

While at Lucca the dowager countess and one of her daughters—I like to imagine it was Georgiana, who shared some of her brother's collecting enthusiasm—were waited upon by a middle-aged priest, none other than the Abbé Eusebio Maria Della Lena, Reviczky's source for so many fine books out of Italy. "[W]e spoke", Della Lena recalled in a fulsomely deferential letter to Spencer which he sent on the strength of this chance meeting, "of the superb Collection that you have enriched and embellished by your exquisite taste, and by your generosity."[4]

Della Lena went on to eulogise Reviczky. "I heard of his death here, which made me desolate. I was greatly attached to his merits out of both duty and gratitude and his memory will always remain with me." Having made his respects to the dead, he got down to business: "Her Excellency Madame your Mother will have told you that I found the Tibullus, Catullus, and Propertius of 1475, and Statius's *Silvae*. The copy [of this latter volume] is very beautiful, and it has only a small defect, that the first leaf before the text is framed. The price: ten pounds."[5]

* * *

Eusebio Maria Della Lena had been born in 1747 to an old Lucchese noble family. Their palazzo was a rambling, half-medieval building in archetypal Tuscan style which clung to a steeply-ascending hillside, partly wooded, partly given over to small fields, above the town (Della Lena had a bucolic view of his ancestral home engraved in 1802 and dedicated to the Polish Princess Lubomirska).[6] He was one of three talented brothers: the eldest, Giacomo, was Spanish vice-consul at Venice and a dealer who heavily criticised the spoliation of art from Venice by foreign collectors (while eagerly assisting in that spoliation); the second, Innocenzo, was a doctor, a long-time resident in London, and a critic of the Italian theatre.[7] Eusebio, the youngest, was destined for the church and while still a young man had been prefect at Empress Maria Theresia's elite school, the Theresianum, in Vienna.[8] From there he seems to have drifted slowly into antiquarian and book-collecting circles, perhaps with the aid of his dealer brother. He lived between Venice and Vienna, was a close friend of Casanova, an intimate of many of the literary men of both cities, and himself dabbled in poetry.[9] The future Sardinian Prime Minister, Massimo d'Azeglio, whose family holidayed at Lucca in the early decades of the nineteenth century, recalled Della Lena in old age as "a curious original, immensely tall, wearing a floral overcoat" who once made the journey from Lucca to Paris and back alone save for a horse and buggy.[10]

The first definite evidence we have of Della Lena as a bookseller comes from 1782 when he offered a list of books for sale to Daniel Cornides, book agent for the Hungarian nobleman and literary patron Count Gedeon Ráday. Ráday bought an incunable Virgil from him, some indication that he was already dealing in high end volumes.[11] It seems likely that Reviczky may have come to know the abbé in this Hungarian bibliophilic milieu and they seem to have worked together, not without occasional friction, for some time by the point at which Della Lena swam into Spencer's ken.

When he began corresponding directly with Spencer, Della Lena was at the peak of his game and gave the impression of having access to an almost inexhaustible supply of the best books from Italian collections. His letters are often simply long lists of books for sale with attached prices and frequent admonitory notes ("I had two other collectors who wanted it at all costs") reminding Spencer that his was not the only place at the table.[12] These lists arrived on Spencer's desk in profusion throughout 1794, with one example, dated 12 February, standing in for all:

1. Martial's *Epigrams*, folio, Venice, 1475. £5
2. Juvenal and Persius's *Satires*, folio, Milan by Zurotus, 1474. £6
3. Livy's *History*, folio, Milan, 1480. £6
4. Cicero's *On Offices, Paradoxes, On Friendship*, and *On Old Age*, folio, Milan, 1474. £6
5. An ancient commentary on Homer's *Iliad*, folio, Rome, [Printed] in the House of Angelo Colocci, 1517, Greek, very rare. £3
6. A commentary on the seven tragedies of Sophocles, quarto, Greek, Rome, [Printed] in the Medicean Gymnasium, 1515, very rare. £2[13]

Et cetera, et cetera. This was heady stuff.

Spencer's time was not entirely his own, however. Much of 1794 was spent on a diplomatic mission and his return home saw the Prime Minister, William Pitt the Younger, appoint him to the post of First Lord of the Admiralty just before Christmas. He knew nothing about the navy—nothing about boats, for that matter—but he proved himself a good administrator and a shrewd judge of character, two talents that were particularly needed in what would become near-constant wartime. Nonetheless, letters from Della Lena continued to pour in and Spencer continued to buy, at times receiving books through the medium of Della Lena's London-based brother Innocenzo.[14]

Meanwhile, the War of the First Coalition was going badly for the Allies. The French Republic had placed a young Sardinian officer, one Napoleon Buonaparte, in charge of their Italian army on 2 March 1796 and within months much of northern Italy was under French control. The Cisalpine Republic, a French puppet state, was established in the summer of 1797 and a similar "Roman Republic" was proclaimed in February 1798. Italy became the scene of incessant plunder. The French took everything worth taking, at least everything they could find, spurred on by the orders of the government itself, which was determined to acquire as many cultural items of any value as they could lay its hands on.[15] Art was the primary target, but books were included as well and these spoliations were rapidly augmented by the French suppression of monasteries in the occupied regions of Italy, their libraries thrown to the winds, or into the pockets of astute bystanders.

The French government was by no means the only victor. James Edwards, the bookseller who had dispersed the Pinelli library and with whom Spencer had long done business, was known to his contemporaries for "following the rear of the French armies, [where] he might on easy terms obtain his choice of what he most wanted".[16] His most spectacular acquisition, though it never reached Spencer, was the 1469 Sweynheym and Pannartz Livy, printed on vellum and illuminated for its first owner Pope Alexander VI, which had long resided in the Benedictine Library at Milan, but which was sold in the chaos of the Napoleonic occupation to Abbé Matteo Luigi Canonici (1727–1807) and thence to Edwards.

It seems to have been a favourite of the bookseller and remained in his possession until his death.[17]

Abbé Canonici's role as middleman illustrates the ambiguous position agents like him and Della Lena occupied during the sack of Italy. Like Della Lena, Canonici was both an Italian and a cleric with the self-appointed goal of building a library which he might eventually bequeath to a restored Jesuit order (he himself had been a Jesuit before their suppression by the papacy in 1773). High motives, but this did not stop him happily benefiting from the spoliation of other religious houses. In the end, the Jesuits were restored seven years too late for Canonici, who had died in 1807, and his manuscripts were purchased by the Bodleian Library in Oxford and by another English collector, Walter Sneyd.[18]

Nor were Italian laymen slow to benefit. The most famous example is that of Giambattista Sommariva (1762–1826), a lawyer who had immediately thrown in his lot with Napoleon and was rewarded with the secretary-generalship of the flimsy Cisalpine Republic. He filled his palace on Lake Como with looted artwork, ancient and modern, and—somewhat miraculously—survived the upheavals of the century to die in his bed in Milan in 1826.[19] But there were others. Amongst bibliophiles we may note the enterprising Luigi Serra, duca di Cassano (1747–1825), who, while prudently maintaining an arm's distance between himself and the occupying forces, had no great love for the former Bourbon monarchs of his Neapolitan kingdom and happily enriched his collection with spoils from the suppressed monasteries of southern Italy and Sicily. We will meet him and his books again in the fullness of time.

But what of Della Lena? Like so many of Spencer's associates he was scrupulously vague about the sources of his acquisitions, though he emphasised the challenges involved, dwelling on his "difficult and dangerous voyage by land and sea in Istria" while engaged in "typographical researches"—i.e. book buying—in a letter of 4 September 1797 and lamenting the "very difficult circumstances" in Italy in the following year.[20] At one point he mentioned discretely that Count Balbi of Genoa wished to sell his art collection—for the modest sum of £13 or £14,000—due to "*les malheurs de sa Patrie*", but one would hardly guess that the abbé was skirting round armies on the march and picking through still-smoking ruins.[21] This, combined with the almost universal and likely deliberate erasure of any marks of provenance in the books Spencer sourced through Della Lena leaves us largely in the land of conjecture when imagining where and how these books were found. The book themselves, however, are eloquent in their own ways.

Della Lena's familial interest in art had already provoked a discussion with Spencer concerning the famous 1481 Florentine edition of Dante, a very early example of copperplate engraving (in the end, Spencer owned a series of copies of the Dante, replacing inferior with superior copies throughout his life).[22] In early February 1797, however, Della Lena reported a new acquisition which put the Dante quite in the shade. "I take the liberty of submitting to Your Excellency", he wrote, "the description and the history of the painful acquisition that I made of the *Monte Santo di Dio* 1477 which inaugurates the first period of the art of engraving on copper and on silver, an art without contradiction invented in Florence."[23] Copperplate engraving had been developed independently both in Germany and Italy about the middle of the fifteenth century and the book in question, the Franciscan Antonio Bettini's devotional treatise *Il monte santo di Dio*, is generally considered to have been the first, or at least one of the first, printed books to incorporate the new art form, with three spectacular engravings, traditionally supposed to have been by Baccio Baldini after designs by Botticelli.[24]

The book was not in itself tremendously rare—twenty-six more or less complete copies are known today—but, as Della Lena was quick to point out, most known copies were imperfect: "the two copies in Florence and the one in Venice have copied figures; Loménie bought his for £30 which was missing the first print; the copy of the Duc de la Vallière only has the print of Hell and it was sold at a higher price". The book was heavily used by its monastic readers, he noted, "and that is why copies were consumed". Even the copy he had eventually secured "was twice at the mercy of being lost and passed freely through the rapacious hands of the looters of Italy. The barque which was to carry it from Venice to Portogruaro in twenty-four hours was tossed by the bad weather in the Lagoon for eighteen days and was almost shipwrecked. To make this acquisition has cost me not only a great deal of money, but pains, journeys, much patience, and three years of time."[25] Little wonder, after such difficulties, that Della Lena, who had originally written a price of £45 at the bottom of this sales pitch, subsequently altered it to £50.

Spencer was hooked. In April Della Lena reported that he had given the *Monte santo di Dio* to a Signor Olivieri, a language teacher, who would present it in person to Spencer in London and purred that such "an article [is] well worthy of your superb collection". Half the purchase price, he noted, "you will be kind enough to pass on to my brother as he is still in London".[26]

Whatever the *Monte Santo* was originally bound in (I fantasise a rather tatty vellum but could be entirely wrong), Spencer had it rebound in olive crushed morocco decorated with vaguely oriental arabesque tooling on the boards.[27] There is no binder's ticket, but we know from Dibdin's description that it is the work of Roger Payne.[28] Inside, it is unrubricated and the printing, from the workshop of Nicolaus Laurentii, a German working in Florence, is not the best: blodgy, uneven, frankly rather poor. There is also an orange tint to the edges of the pages which I suspect is left over from a washing process that was just a touch too heavy on the bleach.

But we're not here for the letterpress. We're here for the plates. All three engravings are present. First is the ladder to heaven. Its would-be scaler, a monk (unsurprisingly, given the audience Della Lena described) is climbing the rungs of humility, prudence, temperance, and so forth against the background of a craggy mountain with Christ on the cross partway up its height. Above is the sphere of heaven with Christ in glory surrounded by angels. A man in secular clothing stands to one side, his hand blocking out the seraphic vision and a rope around his ankle marked "cecita", blindness, which is being yanked upon by an enthusiastic-looking devil. A scroll to one side contains the opening of Psalm 121, "I will lift up mine eyes unto the hills, from whence cometh my help. My help cometh from the Lord."

Figure 6.1 Antonio Bettini, *Il monte santo di Dio* (Florence: Nicolaus Laurentii, 1477), plate two (Christ in glory), John Rylands 9389.

The first plate is purely medieval in its conceit and execution. The second, Renaissance (see Figure 6.1). Christ in glory is surrounded by an oval frame, like an upturned eye, which is being supported by angels. Jesus himself has departed from conventional archetypes and closely resembles depictions of Socrates: snub-nosed, a touch chubby, bearded, and closer to middle age than youth. The angels look like they're feeling the weight and the one at the very bottom, on whose head the entire celestial assemblage is resting, has a decidedly put-upon expression.

Finally, we come to the third plate. The first two are full page, but this has been slotted into the bottom half of the last letterpress leaf. A capital "AMEN" gives way to a faintly embarrassed Satan, sitting up to his midriff in a sort of stone bath, munching on three sinners and holding another two in reserve while devils do various ambiguous but clearly unpleasant things to other sinners in small sinkholes around the edge of the plate. The influence of Dante is unmistakable and, indeed, Della Lena was at pains to point out that this plate was copied from Nardo di Cione's Dantesque vision of hell painted for the Cappella Strozzi di Mantova in Florence's Santa Maria Novella around the middle of the fourteenth century. I do not see that striking a resemblance myself, but I take his point.

The engravings are fascinating from a technical point of view as well. Viewers used to more modern copperplate might be disappointed. Their colour is grey, almost cloudy, and the engraving itself is not the subtlest. In many ways they seem rather like woodcuts done on copper, though there is still a precision of detail unobtainable in wood which hints at what is to come.

* * *

Later in the same year, writing from Trieste on 4 September 1797, Della Lena reported an even more explosive discovery. Bibliophiles do not always get second chances and the sting of losing the Ferrando Lucretius to d'Elci in 1793 must have been considerable, but now Spencer was once again presented with a copy of this fabulously rare book. "The French", Della Lena wrote, "who stripped Italy of all the rarest editions" had missed it, its companion, lost four years before, was the rarest and most precious book in d'Elci's collection, and, quite honestly, he could sell this one in a flash to the Imperial Library in Vienna, "but [because] Your Excellency's library is even closer to my heart", he was prepared to let Spencer have it for the bargain price of £100. It was a matter of haste, though, and Spencer must act quickly.[29]

It is not clear to me how far Spencer read Della Lena's practised salesman's patter with a cynical eye. Surely it must have been fairly obvious?

Showmanship or not, though, it was still the Ferrando Lucretius and the terse note appended by Spencer to the letter, "that I would take the book at the price asked", says it all. The circumstances resulted in a slow and circuitous delivery, but it reached Spencer in the end and so reached me a little over two hundred years later.

I should really have been used to *editiones principes* by the time I came to the Lucretius, but there's something particularly exciting about this one. The Roman philosopher has been a darling of twenty-first-century scholars who, rightly or wrongly, see his atomistic Epicureanism and his emphasis on the role of chance rather than the divine in shaping the universe as fundamentally modern. Without buying into the contemporary cult of Lucretius, most fulsomely expressed in Stephen Greenblatt's *Swerve*, I had still been brought up, in a way, on his *De rerum natura*, both in its classical and early modern iterations, and felt a tinge of giddy anticipation opening the smallish folio, bound in straight-grained blue morocco (probably by Hering).[30]

It has sky blue moire silk endpapers, now faintly discoloured from historic damp, but then one is straight into the characteristically ugly, unstable types of our acquaintance (not, I think, friend) Tomasso Ferrando (see Figure 6.2). He really is a miserable printer. There are several layers of early annotation in different hands, but, puzzlingly, some pages, especially those towards the end, are more thoroughly washed than others. The different layers of annotation, or, rather, the different inks in which they are written, have fared variously as well. One confident early hand is beautifully legible with its summaries and cross-references, but—alas!—what was once a bold inscription across the top of the opening leaf, seemingly in eighteenth-century italic, has been thoroughly scrubbed out so that even seen under ultraviolet light it is only a ghost. What I would give to be able to read it, for it is surely a provenance very close in time to Della Lena's acquisition. I turned and twisted both the book and my neck, half-turned the page to hold it closer to the light, slid the UV light sheet which the library staff had kindly lent me underneath the leaf, but all to no avail; the washing had done its job.

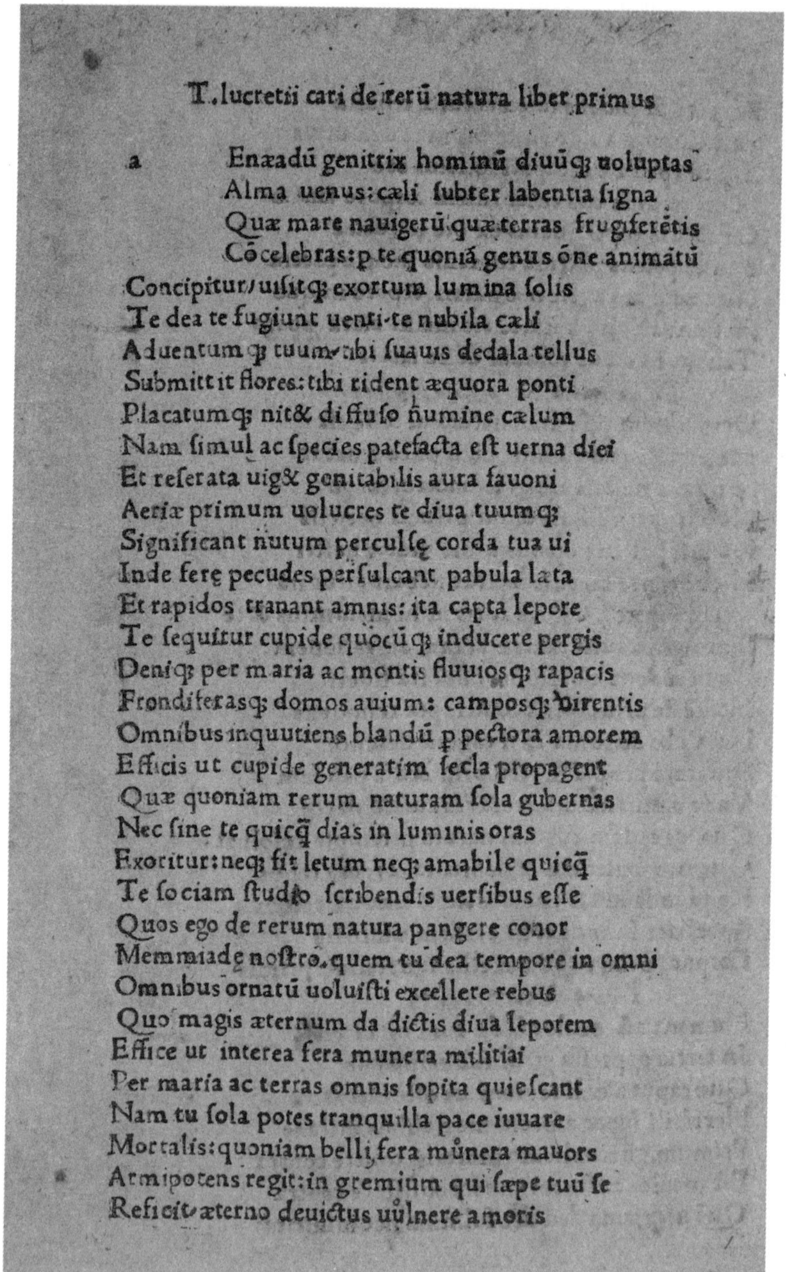

T. lucretii cari de rerũ natura liber primus

a Enæadũ genitrix hominũ diuũq; uoluptas
Alma uenus: cæli subter labentia signa
Quæ mare nauigerũ: quæ terras frugiferẽtis
Cõcelebras: p te quoniã genus õne animãtũ
Concipitur: uisitq; exortum lumina solis
Te dea te fugiunt uenti: te nubila cæli
Aduentumq; tuum: tibi suauis dedala tellus
Submittit flores: tibi rident æquora ponti
Placatumq; nit& diffuso numine cælum
Nam simul ac species patefacta est uerna diei
Et reserata uig& genitabilis aura fauoni
Aeriæ primum uolucres te diua tuumq;
Significant nutum perculsę corda tua ui
Inde ferę pecudes persulcant pabula læta
Et rapidos tranant amnis: ita capta lepore
Te sequitur cupide quocũq; inducere pergis
Deniq; per maria ac montis fluuiosq; rapacis
Frondiferasq; domos auium: camposq; uirentis
Omnibus incuutiens blandũ p pectora amorem
Efficis ut cupide generatim secla propagent
Quæ quoniam rerum naturam sola gubernas
Nec sine te quicq̃ dias in luminis oras
Exoritur: neq; fit letum neq; amabile quicq̃
Te sociam studio scribendis uersibus esse
Quos ego de rerum natura pangere conor
Memmiadę nostro: quem tu dea tempore in omni
Omnibus ornatũ uoluisti excellere rebus
Quo magis æternum da dictis diua leporem
Effice ut interea fera munera militiai
Per maria ac terras omnis sopita quiescant
Nam tu sola potes tranquilla pace iuuare
Mortalis: quoniam belli fera mũnera mauors
Armipotens regit: in gremium qui sæpe tuũ se
Reficit: æterno deuictus uulnere amoris

Figure 6.2 Lucretius, *De rerum natura* (Brescia: Tommaso Ferrando, *c.*1473–74), first printed leaf, John Rylands 8677.

The acquisition of the Lucretius was a major coup and quite possibly one of the most significant additions Spencer had yet made to Reviczky's classical collection. Today only four copies of this edition are known. Spencer's and d'Elci's are there, of course, and another is in the astounding Roudnice Library at Nelahozeves Castle near Prague, the private collection (still, after many vicissitudes) of the Princes Lobkowicz. A fourth is in the library of the Musée Condé in the Château de Chantilly and it was this last, once owned by the Italian bibliographer Gaetano Melzi and later by the eccentric English expatriate Frank Hall Standish, which came to occupy my attention.[31]

Standish died childless in Cadiz in 1840. He had hoped, quite unrealistically, that he might succeed to a baronetcy held by a distant relative and, nursing a lasting grudge against the English government for failing to deliver said baronetcy to him, he bequeathed his entire vast collection of books and art to the French state. The art was sold in 1852–53, but the books eventually went to the Duc d'Aumale, son of Louis Philippe, and so, with the Château de Chantilly, to the Institut de France and the present collection.[32] At some point, probably after the death of Standish, a bibliographer (blessed be their unknown name) added a note to this copy. It was, they observed the "editio princeps [and] rarest among rarities". There were only three copies—the Lobkowicz copy was not yet known—d'Elci's, the present volume, and "that of Lord Spencer which came from the Abbé Boni".

This hit me like a thunderbolt. Abbé Mauro Boni (1746–1817) is not an unknown name by any means. A Genoese, he became a Jesuit and displayed an early interest in antiquities, spending time in Ragusa (modern-day Dubrovnik) studying the collection of the Counts Durazzo. When his order was abolished, he, like his contemporary Canonici, had to shift as best he could. After time spent teaching in Cremona and Bergamo, he landed on his feet as tutor in the household of Giacomo Giustiniani, scion of an old patrician family in Venice.[33] It is here that he likely met Della Lena. It is also here that he conceived of his most ambitious scheme.

Abbé Boni came to know a skilful Venetian goldsmith by the name of Meneghetti. Together they took advantage of the antiquarian tendencies of Boni's employer Giustiniani, together with those of the artist Giandomenico Tiepolo and the art collector Teodoro Correr, by producing a cornucopia of forged antiquities. Coins, manuscripts, lead sheets with engraved characters, perhaps even more elaborate work in precious metals, all were fed into the collections of the dupes, all the more willingly as these precious Venetian antiquities consistently mentioned worthy Giustinianis, Tiepolos, and Corrers of the Serenissima's glory days. The spectacular scale of the fraud was only revealed much later, though suspicions had been voiced before, in a review published in the *Archivo Storico Italiano* for 1866.[34]

Thus far Abbé Boni. But how did he come to acquire the Lucretius, assuming, of course, that the annotator of the Musée Condé copy knew what they were talking about? To understand this, we must return to the theatre of war. On 18 April, five months before Della Lena reported his acquisition of the Lucretius, the Peace of Leoben had been signed between the Holy Roman Empire and the French Republic. This contained both public and secret articles of agreement, one of the latter of which was that the empire should acquire the Republic of Venice once it had been conquered. France declared war on the Republic on 1 May and two weeks later the ancient city had fallen. It formally became Imperial territory under the Treaty of Campo Formio, signed on 17 October.

In other words, Della Lena had acquired the Lucretius from Boni in the midst of Venice's downfall and we may suspect that Boni's acquisition of it had occurred in the same tumultuous period. Unless the erased ownership inscription can finally be read, we may never know Boni's exact source, but the library of a Venetian monastery or noble family is perhaps the most likely guess. Spencer, a world away in London, was benefiting from the increasing state of chaos into which the continent had been plunged.

* * *

These were not the last of Della Lena's discoveries in the wake of Venice's erasure from the map of Europe. A "superb" 1471 Schöffer Thomas Aquinas (£35) in September 1798, an even more tempting 1470 *editio princeps* of Petrarch's poems with miniatures (£65) in February 1799, more works printed by Ferrando, who was fast becoming an obsession of Spencer, or at least of Della Lena, and Gershom Soncino's 1490 edition of the rabbi and philosopher Maimonides's *Mishneh Torah* (a mere £5) all followed in 1798 and 1799.[35]

In 1797, however, the First Lord of the Admiralty had other matters on his plate. The mutinies at Spithead (16 April–15 May) and the Nore (12 May–5 June) were the two largest revolts against the tyrannous discipline of the British navy in its history and both happened, unfortunately for him, on Spencer's watch. He managed things about as well as could be managed, negotiating with the mutineers himself and doing his best to genuinely address some of their concerns, but it must have been a thoroughly trying time, not least as he underwent the rather ignominious necessity of requesting aid from the Russian fleet under Admiral Makarov against his own men.[36] The extent to which he exercised undue force in bringing the mutinies to a close is debatable. Writing to Admiral Duncan on 14 June and reporting the end of the Nore mutiny, he sternly observed that "we shall lose no time in taking the necessary steps for bringing [Parker, one of the ringleaders] and the other delegates to justice; and I hope some examples will be made in every ship concerned, by which means alone we can flatter ourselves to restore anything like order or discipline again", but later family tradition was insistent that he was "so grieved at being obliged to sentence Richard Parker to death" that he offered his widow a pension.[37] The truth is likely to fall somewhere in between the two extremes; Spencer was no better or worse than his contemporaries, but his role as villain or mediator is dependent more on the political and social opinions of modern historians than on the equivocal historical evidence available.

The harder question, at least for our purposes, is: how does the Spencer of the mutinies relate to the Spencer of the library? Our sense, at least so far, of Spencer's personality, of the man himself, remains slightly fuzzy. This is confirmed rather than elucidated by the portrait, now in the National Portrait Gallery, painted within a year or two of this time by John Singleton Copley (see Figure 1.1). The earl's hair is discreetly powdered, his coat a quiet brown with a minimal amount of lace falling from his cravat. He wears the Garter but no other decoration, and his face, which on first glance seems severe, is, on closer examination, faintly strained as if he found the whole affair of sitting for a portrait rather embarrassing. Spencer could be autocratic and deprecatory in the same sentence, but one is left, most of all, with the impression of a deeply private, retiring man, one with a talent for organisation and investigation which served him in good stead as both bureaucrat and collector, but who had little relish for the grand theatre of war and politics into which his position and the times had catapulted him.

SEVEN

A monk for all seasons

It is the end of October 1802 and we are in the library of the Imperial Abbey of Prüm in the newly formed "departments of the Rhine", Imperial lands occupied by French forces. The abbey is depopulated. It has been secularised and its Benedictine inhabitants ejected after just over a millennium of continuous devotion. We can imagine the room, perhaps already ransacked, books and papers scattered across the floor, and moving across them with purpose, a middle-aged man with an iron glint in his eye. He works methodically through the books on the shelves, selecting some, discarding most. His assistant walks by his side with a growing armful of volumes. This is the man most hated by later German bibliographers: the "Bloodhound", Jean-Baptiste Maugérard, "government commissaire for researches into the sciences and the arts in the four departments of the Rhine". He is one of the greatest book thieves in the history of the modern world.[1]

In the glimpse we have just had, Maugérard was confiscating books for the French national collection in Paris, with letters instructing him to do so from the highest sources in his pocket, but this was only one episode in a long and tangled life. We should not be surprised to find that, dutiful Commissaire Maugérard though he may have appeared in 1802, he had begun life as a young Benedictine monk in the ancient abbey of Saint-Arnould in Metz, at the north-eastern corner of *ancien régime* France. There, as librarian of the abbey, he had begun a profitable career in buying and selling books as early as the 1760s. Subsequently he went from strength to strength, serving as librarian to Cardinal Montmorency, sourcing rare items for the Duc de la Vallière's collection, selling, under an assumed name, books out of Metz to Loménie de Brienne, dispensing with his holy orders in 1790 after the suppression of his monastery, and only fleeing French territory in time to escape the Terror. He would spend a decade in exile in Germany before changing circumstances brought his return as a Napoleonic commissaire and professional book looter.[2]

He enters our story during this period of exile. Italy was not the only part of Europe where Spencer had contacts. The latter part of the 1790s saw him growing beyond Reviczky's network and co-opting new book agents into his enterprise. Like della Lena, they tended to be learned churchmen making the best of tumultuous times, and so we are not surprised to see that on 12 January 1797 Maugérard wrote to Spencer from his temporary home in Erfurt, introducing himself and adding that as "the current situation has changed my state, I trust to be of service for whatever is needful".[3] He laid his credentials on the table by following this with a lengthy discussion of early German printing, citing especially the important *Historie von Joseph, Daniel, Judith und Esther* a 1462 Bamberg imprint by Albrecht Pfister which, he mistakenly claimed, proved that Pfister had printed the Gutenberg Bible.

Spencer bit, guardedly, and Maugérard followed up with a long but unpriced list of early printing later in the month, framing it as his "collection" but making it clear that everything was for sale. Amongst these were none other than the *Historie* he had referenced as crucial for understanding the early evolution of printing in his previous letter.[4] Like any good dealer, in subsequent letters he gradually increased the pressure, reminding Spencer of the rapidity with which he must act if he was not to be beaten to the punch by his rivals. Only "last summer", Maugérard noted,

> an English lord, accompanied by an equally English bookseller, searched all the ancient libraries of Franconia and Bavaria, and took from them at any price what they agreed to sell; then went to Italy for the same purpose. I'm sure they paid three hundred louis d'or for the Guttenberg Bible 2 vol. in fol. well preserved; and as much for the Psalter of 1457 … I did not learn that they went to Swabia, but because the search for these sorts of old books is being done with more ardour than ever, I would like your Excellency to give me his orders as soon as possible.[5]

By May, the original coy list of his "collection" had become a catalogue, totalling sixty-nine articles which he offered for a total of 25,960 louis. This was too much for Spencer, but he recognised the potential value of Maugérard as a contact and noted on this letter that: "I would be glad to hear from him of old Editions of the Classicks with Condition & the price & if the Psalter of [14]57 could be found in good Condition & perfect I would like it even at a high price."[6] This was the great Mainz Psalter printed by Gutenberg's sometime partner Johann Fust and his son-in-law Peter Schöffer. Spencer already had the edition of 1459, but he badly wanted the first, 1457, printing.

Meanwhile, Spencer had cherry-picked some of the best items out of Maugérard's initial list, offering him 3,500 *livres* in June for seven books, including the *editiones principes* of Florus, Virgil's *Bucolica*, Lucan, Cicero *De Senectute*, and Vegetius—fine additions to his collection of classics.[7] What is particularly interesting about the draft letter in which he accepts these volumes is Spencer's explanation of his own collecting at this stage. "As for the explanation you requested", he wrote,

> I can only generally point out that I have few editions after 1470 unless they are undoubtedly *editiones principes*. I am also not looking for the first editions of authors who are not in the original language, such as for example Josephus, Dionysius of Halicarnassus &c, nor the first Editions of the Holy Fathers, or the decretales of the Popes. For old Bibles, I already have some of the rarest ones, and I will happily acquire a few others, provided they are in very good condition and that the age of the edition is well guaranteed.[8]

Spencer in 1797, then, had a set of collecting priorities that were still strikingly similar to his mentor Reviczky: *editiones principes* of the classics, very early printing, and a selection of the best early Bibles; patristics, papal documents, and later incunabula were not yet of interest. This would change dramatically over the ensuing decades, though we can already see the reality of his purchases belying any rigorous application of his rules in the later 1790s.

Meanwhile, Maugérard gladly accepted the 3,500 *livres*, but he replied with embarrassment that one item, Seneca's *Opera* without date or place, was actually in Bamberg and the other, Bemler's 1466 Latin Bible, in Ratisbon; it would take time to collect them.[9] While these may have been books which Maugérard had deposited elsewhere due to lack of space or instability of residence, it is equally likely that he had not yet bought them, offering them to Spencer speculatively in the hopes that their purchase might be worth his while. This was not uncommon practice in the chaotic book market of the 1790s.

As with most of Spencer's correspondence with his agents we have only the incoming letters, but he kept unusually full drafts of his responses on many of Maugérard's, which gives us some sense of the volume of books—and money—flowing between Erfurt and Spencer House in these years. A good example is Spencer's response of 9 March 1798 to Maugérard's letter of 20 February. The sometime monk had sent a multi-page letter filled with possible sales, mostly unpriced, including the tempting proposition of a *Life of Saint Ludvina*, allegedly printed in 1456 by Gutenberg, as well as a *Speculum humanae salvationis* with engravings "certainly" printed in Augsburg at the Monastery of St. Ulrich and cited in Carl Heinrich von Heinecken's pioneering 1771 bibliography of engraving.[10] Spencer's draft response reads:

> That I will pay him 500 livres for the service & German Bible.
>
> Refusing the Seneca by Ulric Zel also the 2 works of Bernardus Silvestris, & the Bible by Therhoernen, & the S: Augustine de Arte Predicandi.
>
> Asking the Price of the Histoire de Griseldis.
>
> Declining to buy the other Copy of Bemler's Bible.
>
> Desire he will not send me any Prints without date.
>
> Ask for a more exact description of the Book by Guttenberg [*sic*] in 1456 as I suspect some deceit in it, but if genuine will give a good Price for it.
>
> Offering 80 or 100 livres for Summa Oratorum.
>
> I will answer him at another opportunity about the Speculum Humanae Salutis printed at Augsburg not having Heineken by me at present.[11]

This was only one of several substantial moments of acquisition from his Erfurt agent in 1797 and 1798. Maugérard was offering good books and Spencer was buying them with pleasure. Early editions of Josephus,

Poggio, Ovid, Seneca, Augustine, and more made their way across the Channel. These are the books which align with Spencer's professed collecting practices. What is more revealing however, is the list of books Spencer did *not* purchase. With surprising tone-deafness, Maugérard persisted in offering Spencer manuscripts throughout the period of their correspondence, waxing lyrical, for example, on a manuscript of Ovid in "large characters of gold" or an early manuscript life of S. Oswald.[12] Spencer was adamant in refusing them; he did not collect manuscripts.

Even more revealing was Maugérard's offer of the *Life of Saint Ludvina* [*sic*], dated "1456" and, he was certain, printed by Gutenberg.[13] Unsurprisingly, Spencer doubted the authenticity of this otherwise extraordinary unknown work and requested more details. Maugérard dutifully wrote back on 9 March 1798 that he had examined the "Gutenberg" more carefully and saw that the date had been added in manuscript (perhaps having forgotten he had already done so, he gave substantially the same information in another letter a month later).[14] Would he have been so meticulous if Spencer had responded instantly, offering—what?—£50 or even £100 for this rarity of early printing? I am very doubtful. Maugérard's letters are an unsavoury mixture of self-evident expertise with wide-eyed naiveté, all the while slowly turning up the pressure and emphasising the need to make quick decisions. They are the work of a profoundly amoral and manipulative man.

* * *

We have seen that one of the items on Maugérard's initial sale list was the *Historie von Joseph, Daniel, Judith und Esther*, whose reception he had already prepared with a discourse on its importance and which he described as follows:

> 65 folios in folio with 64 woodcut figures. [Printed at] Bamberg by Albrecht Pfister, 1462. This is the first German printed book with a certain date; and also the first to have woodcut figures with a date.[15]

This is all true. The *Vier Historien* is one of the earliest and most important vernacular works to be produced, not just by the German press, but by any press in Europe.[16] It is also one of the rarest, with only two copies presently known to survive, a likely side-effect of its popular character (all the other copies were probably read to pieces). Its printer, Albrecht Pfister, worked in Bamberg, an ancient cathedral city in the east of Franconia, and was certainly in business by the early 1460s, only a few years after the printing of the Gutenberg Bible. We know entirely too little about him, but he has long been recognised as a pivotal figure in the development of printing, expanding it beyond simply the reproduction of manuscripts to something altogether new and strange.[17]

By the time interest in early printing had revived in Germany, the *Historie* was completely lost to view and it was only in 1792 that a copy was rediscovered in Augsburg by Matthias Jakob Adam Steiner, the minister of the church of St. Ulrich in that city. He published a learned article on his discovery which produced a sensation; the hunt was up.[18] Probably spurred on by Steiner's article, the Carmelite prior and librarian of the order's library in Bamberg, Bonifacius a S. Elisaeo (born Michael Seuffert), reported an even more remarkable discovery amongst the books of the Carmelites at Würzburg.[19] In the library of the convent of St. Barbara there he discovered another copy of the *Historie*, this time bound together with two other early works by Pfister, the *Biblia pauperum* and *Belial*. It was an altogether astounding find.[20]

This was in 1792. What happened next is unclear. Father Bonifacius seems to have been a conscientious and bookish man, aware of the importance of early printing and unlikely to easily allow works like the *Historie* to stray out of Carmelite hands, but he was in Bamberg and the situation in Würzburg is less clear. What is clear, however, is that by January 1797 the Würzburg copy of the *Historie* and its two accompanying texts were in the hands of Maugérard; this is what he was so eager to sell to Spencer.[21] And this was not even the first copy of the *Historie* Maugérard had obtained. In a December 1795 letter to Joseph Van Praet (1754–1837), the omnivorous and relentless librarian heading up the Bibliothèque Nationale, he reported that he had obtained a copy lacking a number of leaves and it is not beyond the bounds of possibility that this earlier *Historie*, which is now lost, may have been gutted to perfect one or both of the other two surviving copies.[22] Van Praet did not purchase this volume, but the French had only to wait; in 1799 the Augsburg copy was looted by the advancing French armies and sent to the Bibliothèque Nationale where it still resides.[23]

One might imagine that Spencer would have jumped at the chance of owning a treasure as choice as the Würzburg volume and he was certainly intrigued, but he did not immediately make an offer and Maugérard repeated in a letter of 24 June that "there are a few items which I would be very happy to see included in your Excellency's rich collection", mostly notably the *Vier Historien* as it helped establish datings and contexts for Pfister's types.[24] Spencer made an offer of 1,000 *livres* (about £40) but Maugérard demurred. "It seems", he wrote, that Spencer did "not understanding the binding of this volume". The *Vier Historien* was bound with two other pieces of Pfister's printing and the whole volume would cost not less than 1,800 *livres*. Of course, if Spencer wished only for the *Vier Historien*, something could be arranged. He followed this parry with a long panegyric sucking up to Spencer and praising his collection.[25]

Spencer evidently felt the extra price was worth it and the additional works from Pfister's press no bad thing, for a list of books ordered dated 25 August includes the entire volume marked at 1,800 *livres*.[26] Modern scholars would have dearly liked it to stay as it must have been when it was shipped to Spencer, but the tastes of the 1790s demanded otherwise. The three items have since been separated.

Instead of whatever primitive binding it might originally have possessed, Spencer's copy of the *Historie* is now bound (by the inimitable Hering) in rather excessively red morocco with intricate gold tooling imitating metal bosses at each of the book's four corners (see Figure 7.1).[27] It is a small folio and the first thing you notice when you open the volume is that it must have been found in terrible condition. When you open the Paris copy you are presented with a creamy white page, as crisp and fresh as if it had just come off the press (in reality, it has probably been washed), but the Spencer copy is not only dirty, it has evidently been damaged at the edges and the surviving portions of each sheet subsequently inlaid in more modern paper frames.

Figure 7.1 Binding by Charles Hering to *Historie von Joseph, Daniel, Judith und Esther (Vier Historien)* (Bamberg: Albrecht Pfister, 1462), John Rylands 9375.

This does not, however, affect the crisp, deep inking of the text, which is up to Pfister's usual standards. And it certainly does not affect the colouring of the woodcuts. These are bold and fresh with rich greens and fiery reds: flat, strong blocks of colour like a 1950s comic book. While modern scholars have spilt much ink on the role of works like this in the creation of a market for "popular print", i.e. works read by somebody other than scholars, clerics, and aristocrats, this is hardly "popular" in any meaningful sense. It may not be in Latin, but it has still been made for a literate audience with the spare cash to buy a very beautiful book. The Paris copy has eighteenth-century annotations by the head of the Augsburg goldsmiths' guild, Johann Jeremias Lutz, and we can imagine a similar wealthy bourgeois audience would have read it when it first appeared. The only evidence we have for earlier ownership in the Spencer copy is a thrice-repeated death knell on the final leaf: "4 February. Doctor Marius was buried". The name is too common to permit secure identification, but the hand looks seventeenth century.

There are other intriguing peculiarities here. On folio 12r a woodcut has been placed in the press upside down and is not illuminated, but has a large cross through it. A pencil note at the beginning of the volume comments that the same print had been fixed and placed the right way up by the time the Paris copy was printed. Elsewhere, we see another woodcut repeated on folios 10r and 13v and someone has added, in an eighteenth-century hand, a manuscript colophon giving the printed German in Latin on the recto of the final printed page. This is a book which began life in one world and ended it in a very different one.

For us moderns, though, it is the woodcuts themselves which inevitably grab our attention. They are delightful. Daniel topples an idol with a suave two-finger gesture while Nebuchadnezzar looks on nonplussed, pointing at the prophet as if to say, "and who exactly is this clown?" (see Figure 7.2). On the facing page, Daniel sits in the lions' den, praying calmly, albeit rather cramped, as the lions, like oversized house cats, snuggle in around him. An angel looks on, as does Nebuchadnezzar, now grown, in the surreal geometry of late medieval art, to such a size that he can gaze over the ramparts of his city, one hand casually resting on a

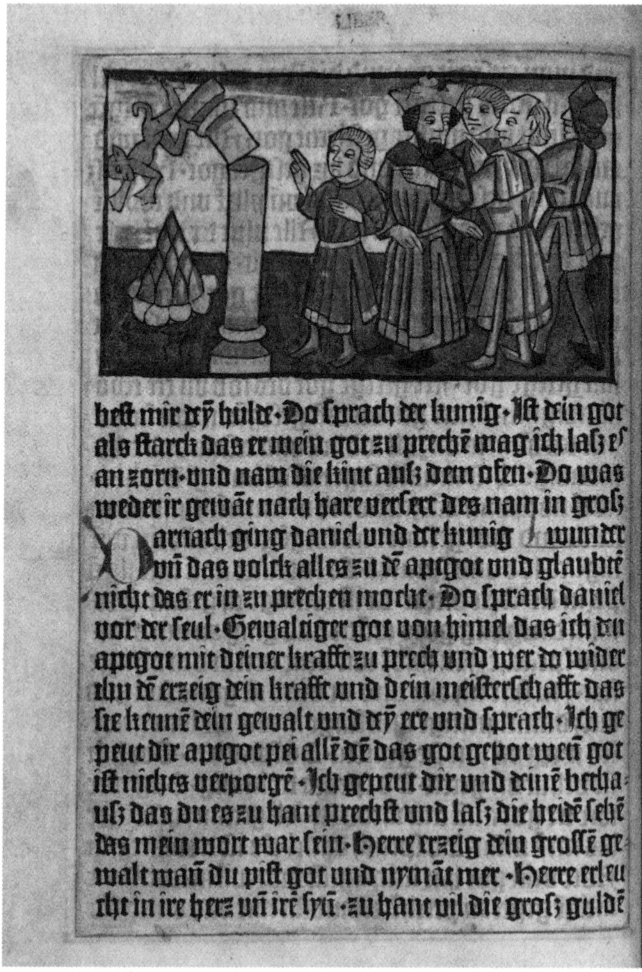

Figure 7.2 *Historie von Joseph, Daniel, Judith und Esther (Vier Historien)* (Bamberg: Albrecht Pfister, 1462), detail from fol. 18v, John Rylands 9375.

battlement. We are too apt to see the ridiculous in images which would have inspired sincere devotion in a citizen of the fifteenth century.

* * *

Spencer only bought heavily from Maugérard for a very brief period, essentially the months between June 1797 and November 1798. If Maugérard was such a good supplier, why did their relationship not last? As his subsequent career attests, Maugérard retained his skills as a book agent for many decades after his employment by Spencer. The answer must be read between the lines, but we can see it clearly enough. One factor was undoubtedly Spencer's recognition that Maugérard's conduct was not above suspicion and that one could not entirely rely on the descriptions he provided of the items sold. Even if it was not a case of outright fraud, like the "1456 Gutenberg", confusions arose leading, for example, to Spencer exasperatingly writing that he had received the wrong Bibles and, as such, had "made over [these] to Mr Edwards to dispose of in the most advantageous manner he can".[28]

Dubious descriptions and unwanted offers were part and parcel of the book trade. The larger issue, though, was Maugérard's ability to acquire what Spencer wanted and the demands he placed on his patron in return. As early as September 1797 Maugérard was making plans to decamp from Erfurt to Brunswick if the war came any closer and he maintained, at least to Spencer, a generally pessimistic assessment of the situation, writing on 27 January 1798 that:

> A general terror hangs over all of Germany; all the monasteries, fearing their secularization or suppression, put aside what has not been looted; and we can't have anything in terms of books, they are hidden here and there.[29]

Paradoxically, however, he wrote in April that "there is a facility at this moment to buy in the monasteries because they fear their suppression", but that there was nothing left to be had in Erfurt and that a journey (anticipating the journeys he would make as French commissaire in a few years' time) was required. All very well and good, but "to be able to do so it would be necessary that some prince of Germany honour me with some character". He went on,

> For example, if your Excellency would deign to grant me in the Electorate of Hanover some title, whether of Councillor, or Archivist, or Librarian or Secretary, then I would not be detained anywhere and I could go everywhere.[30]

And this was the sticking point. Maugérard wanted Spencer to use his political influence in Britain to secure him a sinecure in Hanover, still a British continental dependency, in exchange for the promise of further acquisitions. It was in the same letter that he offered the manuscript Ovid in "large characters of gold", evidently as an example of the sorts of things he might be able to send if Spencer secured him a post.

No reply from Spencer survives, but it is clear that he either passed over Maugérard's suggestion in silence or responded with a resounding "no". The effort and political capital involved in securing Maugérard an appointment, even if it could be achieved, was entirely disproportionate to the reward promised, not least because, as we shall see, Spencer was already developing another contact who provided far better results and made far fewer demands. This particular misstep by Maugérard, in April of 1798, marks the souring of the two men's relationship. Spencer refused the former's new offers in June and in his draft response to a letter of 7 July coldly shut down a new line of enquiry by writing that "I have [already] procured a Copy of the Psalter of 1457".[31] The Mainz Psalter had recurred several times in their correspondence and it was a snub to Maugérard that someone else had succeeded where he had failed. The only new proposal from Spencer was that he would pay £30 if Maugérard could obtain the legendarily early woodblock print of St. Christopher from the Charterhouse of Buxheim, but that was much easier said than done and would not be achieved by Maugérard.[32]

Maugérard's letters in the winter of 1798–99 turned from offering new items to working out the often complex logistics of paying for and shipping Spencer's purchases from the previous year. In April 1799 he made another bid for patronage, touting Petrus Niger's early antisemitic polemic, *Contra perfidos Judaeos de conditionibus veri Messiae* (Esslingen, 1475), and then offering a Bible and Psalter in 1800 which Spencer refused "as the character was not fifteenth century".[33] Maugérard's final letter to Spencer, written on 2 August 1800, well after the ship had sailed, gave a reckoning of their accounts and a last desperate offer of a French wine called Stein Wein, "bon et estimé", Spencer's for only 4–5 *livres* a bottle. Spencer politely "declined his offer of Wine & thanked him for it" and that was the end of Maugérard, at least as far as the earl was concerned.[34] The former monk would return to France in 1802 and take up his new post as commissaire on 27 July (four years later he would buy a house and vineyard in Metz where he lived out the remainder of his life in happy retirement).[35]

It is tempting to imagine what might have happened had Maugérard proved a more trustworthy and less importunate agent. Spencer's library and the movement of books in Napoleonic Europe might have looked very different. But it was not to be. Though Maugérard could at best only have guessed at this, he had been decisively replaced by another agent, altogether more tractable and more useful to Spencer, both as a source of books and, crucially, as a source of political information. In short: a man who could be both book agent and spy. To locate this intriguing personage, we must go back to 1794 and Spencer's last visit to the continent for almost a quarter century.

EIGHT

The talented Father Horn

The summer of 1794 had found the British government increasingly worried, not only by the activity of the French but by the inactivity of its allies. Particularly egregious was the Austrian position, "infinitely too languid and little for the object", which saw that creaking remnant of the Holy Roman Empire looking on while revolutionary France was winning victories on all fronts.[1] In an attempt to rouse the Austrians to action, Britain had sent one of its own cabinet ministers, accompanied by the foreign secretary's brother, to Vienna at the end of July. The cabinet minister: Spencer; the foreign secretary's brother: his good friend and fellow bibliophile Thomas Grenville (1755–1846).[2]

The mission was not notably successful, at least not where British foreign policy was concerned. After two months of slow and frustrating negotiations, offers, and counter-offers, Spencer and Grenville left Vienna at the beginning of October having gained little more than a cordial dislike for the Austrian foreign secretary who, according to Grenville, behaved "more like a haberdasher of small wares than the Minister of a great Empire".[3] In other spheres, however, the summer of 1794 would change Spencer's life and, through its consequences, the lives of many others.

For a diplomatic mission was never only about diplomacy. Spencer made the most of his time on the continent, a rare opportunity as war continued to spread, and his time in Vienna had been spent haunting bookshops as well as ministerial antechambers. From the ennobled bookseller and printer Johann Thomas von Trattner's shop he bought an expensive pile of reference works on early printing, adding some additional items (including several choice incunables) from the more modest range offered by Trattner's enemy, the unsuccessful poet-cum-bookseller Aloys Blumauer.[4] His purchases were, if not excessive, certainly extensive as he did everything he could to take advantage of the opportunities presented by the Viennese book market. A characteristic example is his bill for purchases—about a hundred items, including many multi-volume sets—from Pierre Besson, a Warsaw bookseller seeking refuge in Vienna from the unsettled times, for which he paid a total of 1,230 florins on 29 September.[5] Nor did he hurry unduly on his way home. Stopping in Frankfurt, he and Grenville found the time to buy a staggering amount of German wine, Spencer's half of the bill alone coming to £244 for, amongst other things, 717 litres of hock.[6]

But travel, then as now, had its inconveniences. Before reaching Frankfurt, the two men had been delayed near Nuremberg when their carriage broke down. Perhaps the springs were ruined by muddy autumn roads, perhaps a shaft snapped, perhaps a wheel was shattered, we do not know. When they reached Nuremberg itself, Spencer wrote a letter (which unfortunately does not survive) describing the incident to a new correspondent and it is to this correspondent, this new star on the horizon of our narrative, that we must now turn.[7]

* * *

He is "such a wild young fellow, that it is a real shame that he should have the monkish habit", wrote Betsey Wynne in her diary after spending several days in the company of Father Maurus Horn later that year.[8] The Anglo-Italian sixteen-year-old Wynne was worldly wise for her years and knew what she was talking about. But who was Father Horn? The thirty-one year-old Benedictine monk had begun life as plain Alexander Horn[9] and had been born into an impoverished family, part of Scotland's embattled Catholic minority, in the North Sea port of Montrose, in 1762.[10] Catholics were still refused access to public education in Enlightenment Scotland and the tender age of ten found him and five other Scottish boys conducted from their homes to one of the few places they could receive a Catholic education: the seminary at the Scottish

Monastery in Regensburg.[11] There he studied under Father Benedict Arbuthnot, a talented mathematician who became abbot of the monastery in 1776, finishing his preparatory schooling with, as he rather smugly puts it in his autobiography, "unprecedented Applause".[12]

In retrospect, at least, Horn presented his entrance into the priesthood as a necessity rather than a vocation for one who "had no Fortune at Home, no Friends there capable of promoting my Interest, nor any Prospect of providing for myself abroad". He consoled himself, however, with the thought of the monastery's library and the "liberal Conduct of its Members", a lively society of intellectually-minded, somewhat quarrelsome, Scots abroad. In 1779 he was tonsured and joined his Benedictine brethren with the religious name of "Maurus".[13]

Monk or no, the centre of Horn's life was not God but history. He "rummaged, compared, and weighed" ancient and medieval historians, wrote "a long historico-geographical Dissertation on the famous Question about the Homage done by the Scottish Kings to those of England", and planned and partly executed a revision of the vast but entirely untrustworthy history of Scottish monasticism begun by his predecessor at Regensburg, Marianus Brockie, a half century before.[14]

This arrogant, clever young man, still only in his twenties, offered a tempting opportunity for older and more cynical intellects. The Perpetual Imperial Diet, a dysfunctional but long-running meeting of the leading politicians in the Holy Roman Empire, convened at Regensburg and it was not long before the young monk attracted the attention of some of the diplomats present (no doubt he over-acted his part as usual, thrusting his erudition in their faces and leaving them to make their own judgements). Amongst these was Johann Eustach Graf von Görtz, sometime tutor to the princes of Saxe-Weimar-Eisenach, friend of Goethe, Diderot, and Frederick the Great, and eventually a career Prussian diplomat.[15] Görtz took Horn under his wing "and laid before me an Account of all his Negotiations in Bavaria, Russia, and Holland, with all the Papers relating thereto, in order to correct, as he said, and to regulate my Ideas". "Probably", the mature Horn later recognised, the count "intended me as one of his political Emissaries"; in other words, he had tapped Horn on the shoulder to be a spy.[16]

This singling out did not immediately result in daring cloak and dagger deeds, but the rather more prosaic task of translating an anti-Russian propaganda pamphlet into English. Meanwhile, however, in 1789, Horn was in Munich visiting another of his diplomatic acquaintances, Graf von Lehrbach, and met the British diplomat and spymaster, Thomas Walpole. Horn seems to have had no qualms about shifting his allegiance from Görtz to Walpole (indeed, he may not have viewed the two roles as mutually exclusive) and promptly began feeding him information on the inner workings of the Imperial Diet.[17]

This was the situation in 1794 when Horn first came to the attention of Spencer. Judging from the former's first letter, they must have met during Spencer and Grenville's outbound journey to Vienna in the late summer of that year. The young monk had no doubt been brought to the earl's attention in his role as a British agent, but their talk seems to have quickly strayed from politics to books. Horn's early fascination with history and the study of manuscripts—"diplomatic", as it was called then, echoing back to its origins in the practical need to study and verify public documents—had blossomed into an obsession with early books, helped along by his appointment as librarian to his monastery.

We can both imagine and partially reconstruct the conversation which took place between Spencer and Horn in the library of the Scottish monastery of St. James in Regensburg during the summer of 1794. Before we can do so, however, a bit of history. In the time of Abbot Bernard Baillie, in the earlier part of the eighteenth century, a new library had been constructed in the monastery, "a beautifully arched hall, decorated with stucco work... about fifty feet long and twenty-five wide". Soon it "became too small, so that three other rooms were added, which were then filled with works of lesser value; because in the great library they try to keep a selection of beautiful works until the plan of building a new room in which the entire stock of books can be held is realised".[18]

When the bibliographer Georg Wilhelm Zapf visited the monastery in 1782 he commented of the library that "although it is not numerous, it does have some large, splendid works consisting of many volumes", with a particular strength in British history. "There is", he added dismissively, "little or nothing to be found in the way of old books; the entire library consists largely of new works and is large enough for such a small society."[19] Damned with faint praise, this was the state of the collection when Horn was coming to maturity.

By the time the younger and more enthusiastic Friedrich Karl Gottlob Hirsching, later known as an almost implausibly prolific author of biographical dictionaries and similar reference works, visited the monastery in 1788, the library had been transformed. The "main focus" Hirsching agreed, describing a collection which he estimated to contain about 14 or 15,000 volumes, was still on the collection of historical works, "which is constantly increasing and takes up well over half of the large library", but there were also numerous new volumes, especially in English, which "deserve the attention of every traveling scholar". As for early printing, "this collection owes its existence to a mere accident, but such a lucky chance that few libraries could equal it so quickly. About six or seven years ago, barely two pieces of ancient printing were there. Presumably, when new editions were acquired the old books were sold or even ——", here Hirsching breaks off with two long and telling dashes, unable even to write the sordid fate which might have met St. James's books. But he soon recovers his composure and, mentioning Zapf's unimpressed visit of a few years before, compares it with the present date. Horn, "a very talented, active, and extremely good man...and my beloved friend" had "had the greatest inclination for learning and books from his youth...and even though he was not a librarian at the time but still at his studies" began to collect early printing for the library, exchanging, trading, and doing everything he could to expand the collection such that by 1788, the year of Hirsching's visit, St. James could boast one hundred and forty incunables and as many volumes again from the first fifteen years of the sixteenth century.[20]

There is something quite touching about Hirsching's effervescent account of the library's renaissance. He and Horn were of an age, both only twenty-six when they met, and one can imagine them excitedly clambering up ladders and exclaiming over the astonishing collection which Horn had assembled in so short a time. The first meeting with Spencer must have had a very different character. A diplomat on his way to his posting would most probably have been received by Abbot Arbuthnot and the other worthies of the monastery, at least at first, and it seems likely that the inevitable and probably lengthy ceremonies and forms would have been followed before Spencer could begin to take an interest in the serried ranks of books beneath the elaborately stuccoed ceilings of the main library.

Horn, with his usual mixture of enthusiasm and self-assurance, must have asked Spencer what he would like to see. Perhaps the many folio volumes of national and local histories for which the library was so famous? No? Something older? That could easily be arranged. The monastery boasted of a number of early manuscripts. Consider this, a supposedly ninth-century manuscript of the Gospels, formerly owned by Anscharius, Archbishop of Bremen. Or this fine fourteenth-century Bible with its brilliant illuminations?[21] No? Ah, your Lordship, prefers printed books! Well... And then the conversation would have really begun.

Horn had some fine things to show Spencer on that front. The 1465 Fust and Schöffer *Decretals*, a 1466 St. John Chrysostom printed by Ulrich Zell, a rather nice 1475 Ptolemy from Vicenza, the 1477 works of St. Anthony on "the largest paper", a German Bible printed in Augsburg in 1490, and so forth.[22] It was perhaps predictable, though, that what we know, rather than suspect, they spoke of, were books they didn't have. One book they discussed was the first Bible printed in Italy, by Sweynheym and Pannartz in 1471. In his letter of 15 October 1794 Horn recalled this conversation and added that he knew of a religious house which possessed a copy, but though "they have given me leave to strip their Library of the Cicero of 1465 the Decretum Gratiani &c &c for a trifle", they "will not part with their Bible for no sum in the world, they even tell me they have a tradition that their Bible is more worth than their Monastery". Horn, never inclined to tolerate such beliefs, waspishly added that "had they said it was more worth than their Library they might have been pretty near truth for I should be sorry to give £5 for all that is contained in it".[23]

They had apparently also discussed a Tacitus without date or place of publication which Horn judged, based on its appearance, to date from before 1470; he would be happy to send it to Spencer along with the Psalter of 1457 which they had discussed (as we shall see, this proved less easy to obtain than Horn sanguinely supposed). In sum, he wrote, "the only pieces which I now have are the Cicero de Oratore of 1465 printed in Subiaco the Decretum Gratiani a Superb Copy by Schoffer 1472 Claudian's Editio princeps 1482 and the Tacitus and I do not think them over rated if I charged the whole at £70".[24]

But what was Horn doing here? Surely not selling books out of the Regensburg library? I do not think so, at least not in this instance. Describing the four volumes as "the only pieces which I now have" seems to suggest a side hustle in incunabula distinct from his work as librarian, though it also seems clear that bookselling and librarianship could overlap for Horn in ways which did not always sit well with his contemporaries. It was probably the Bohemian naturalist Kaspar Graf von Sternberg who authored an anonymous travel account of 1792 which described how at the Scots monastery, "the library is richly stocked with diplomatic and historical works, and also has a large collection of incunabula, which the tidying librarian, because they are nothing more than rarities, sells to England for large sums and in return buys useful works with which to enrich the library".[25] One could imagine that such early essays in book dealing provided useful funds for the expansion of what was clearly a cherished library (cherished by Horn, at any rate), though the ethics of these transactions, like so much of what Horn was to embark upon, were rather murky.

Spencer and Horn must also have discussed politics and from the date of their first correspondence until its final termination many years later the young monk was continuously passing on political news, gossip, and intelligence to the First Lord of the Admiralty. In that respect, he was doubly valuable: an excellent finder-out both of books and information with a single-minded determination to acquire only the best in both categories.

* * *

The relationship between Spencer and Horn grew only gradually in the latter half of the 1790s. Preoccupied with Maugérard, Spencer seems not to have taken Horn's initial offers very seriously. On 7 April 1796 the librarian wrote bombastically that "after long and laborious researches I have now the pleasure of laying before your Lordship a capital Collection of ancient Classic Editions and flatter myself it will meet with your Lordship's approbation"; Spencer declined them all.[26] A similar list followed on 15 July 1797, apparently with little more success, though to my own mind the "Plinius historia naturalis Jo de Spira Venice 1469 exceptionally broad margins, gilt and painted initials superb in every respect" sounds nicer than the rather plain copy of that magnificent book which Spencer eventually acquired.[27]

What set Horn apart from many of his contemporaries was not his tenacious determination to make a good sale, but rather his ability, as both intelligence agent and bookseller, to read the political room and strike at the right moment. Writing to Spencer on 13 October 1797 with French forces advancing on southern Germany he pleaded that "if your Lordship would but give me a List of those [classics] still wanting in your Collection I might perhaps in the present hour of General Apprehension be able to succeed in procuring them all".[28] Here, and not for the last time, Horn demonstrated both a keen sense of when political misfortunes could shake loose desired books and a sociopathic disregard for the calamities which such moments implied. What matter if Germany fell to Napoleon as long as the right incunabula could be obtained?

This came into sharp focus in what we may imagine to have been Horn's proving moment so far as Spencer was concerned. In 1794 he had already ingenuously claimed he could send his new correspondent a copy of the 1457 Mainz Psalter, printed by Gutenberg's collaborator Johann Fust and Fust's son-in-law Peter Schöffer and one of the earliest substantial printed books after the Gutenberg Bible, but this, as we have seen, did not materialise.[29] It was not until 13 October 1797 that he could write that "I shall now be at the heels of the Psalter 57", adding with characteristic unconcern, "perhaps war will do the rest".[30] Unbeknownst to Horn, however, Spencer was playing Maugérard separately for the

Psalter, perhaps deliberately seeing which of his agents could prove more resourceful. On 3 October he had asked Maugérard whether a copy could be found at Metz. Later that month the abbé replied in discouraging tones:

> The Pseautier of 1457 which Monseigneur heard of as being in Metz was the one I possessed; but it was stolen from me 13 years ago, despite the precautions I took to keep it safe; I never knew where it went, and only suspected another thief like a mason or a carpenter... If God wills it, I will do everything in the spring to get you the one of which [the Abbé Desaunays] spoke to me. I won't be able to succeed at any price in terms of money, but I have another way which I believe will succeed.[31]

"Another way", indeed. Fortunately for Horn, Maugérard did not succeed. Instead, a few months later, in February 1798, the younger monk wrote triumphantly to his patron:

> It scarcely began to appear that the great Monasteries in Suabia would be fixed upon as a kind of indemnification to those Princes who had lost their territories on the other side of the Rhine when I thought that now or never I should be able to procure the Psalter of 1457 for Your Lordship. I do not well recollect the price your Lordship authorised me to give yet I remember that Edwards afterwards desired me to offer 300 £ which were refused by the Monks as they said they would not take a sum under, I think, 10 or 12,000 florins.
>
> As I did not now doubt but that these Messieurs would in case of the dissolution of their Monastery be glad to divide a sum of 3000 florins between them rather than leave the Psalter behind I wrote to them a fortnight ago represented to them the danger they incurred and concluded with repeating my former offer of 300 £ which I said was hourly at their service in consequence of which I received the inclosed Letter by which they inform me that aware of their impending dissolution they are determined to put up their Psalter for sale but that I am to have the preference if I will pay down 4000 fl immediately.[32]

It was a triumph worth celebrating, but who were the monks with whom Horn had so masterfully dealt? They were the Premonstratensian fathers of the Imperial Abbey of Rot an der Rot (generally known in the English of the day as "Roth") in Upper Swabia. How long it had been in their possession we do not know; perhaps it had even been bought by the community when it was first printed. What little we do know about its life at Rot comes from a letter from Father Sigismund Hogl, the librarian there, to Horn, dated 23 February 1798. Hogl recounted that the Psalter had still been in use for liturgical purposes as recently as fifty years ago, but that now it was seen exclusively as an object of historic and antiquarian value.[33]

As with similar early books in monastic libraries, a change in valuation had occurred in the latter half of the eighteenth century. No longer was it a book for practical use, but one for aesthetic and scholarly appreciation. If Hogl's dating is accurate, its removal from use in the abbey church predates its "discovery" by secular sources. The first reference there is by the bibliographer Johann Georg Schelhorn in 1768 who, describing the surviving copies of the 1457 Psalter, wrote that,

> a few years ago I unexpectedly enjoyed the special pleasure of discovering the fifth [known copy of the psalter] in the choir of the Premonstratensian Reichs-Stift-Roth, which is next door to us, [and] which, in my opinion, serves as an adornment to the local library.[34]

Schelhorn's discovery was repeated by Carl Heinrich von Heinecken in his widely-read *Idée générale d'une collection complette d'estampes* (1771) which Horn referenced in his victorious letter to Spencer.[35] Scholars like Schelhorn and von Heinecken did great work and we owe them an enormous debt for their foundational labours in the history of early printing, but the copy-specific discussions of these Enlightenment bibliographers would, by the 1790s, become a check-list for men like Horn, Maugérard, and the oncoming armies of the French.

Once obtained, it was not entirely a straightforward matter to ensure the Psalter, or any other package, reached Spencer. Horn had to navigate English bills of exchange via the international banker and fellow Scot Sir Robert Herries, then pack the Psalter, "carefully wrapt up in waxcloth", and send it to another Scot, Mr. Fraser, at Hamburg by the chariot de poste. Fraser would then ensure this was embarked on a ship for England.[36] It would not reach Spencer until later in the year.

The Mainz Psalter was certainly not the only book Horn was acquiring for Spencer in this period, nor should we discount his value as a political correspondent and spy, but it marked a turning point in their relationship. From being one, relatively minor, agent in Spencer's stable, Horn gracefully vaulted into the role of his patron's chief book buyer, advisor, and correspondent on bibliographical matters, a position he would retain for the better part of a decade. The talented Father Horn had made good.

* * *

I could not easily contain my excitement when the Psalter was brought out to me in the air-conditioned hush of the Rylands reading room. It had been kept in a morocco box when Dibdin described it, but this had long since been discarded for a more practical archival box with a large printed label beginning "STOP!" in red letters on the outside.[37] Inside this box was another and inside that…the Psalter itself.[38] My first sight of the binding was a surprise, even though I had read descriptions. It is bound in a by now rather shabby midnight velvet, probably early nineteenth century, which has been strengthened with midnight blue morocco at the hinges. It's like nothing else I've seen in Spencer's library, though it is not unlike the similar velvet binding on its sibling in the Royal Collection.[39]

The endpapers are, quite frankly, in shockingly bad taste: dull gold cloth which sparkles in the light like something from an eighties disco. John Gandy, who was following Rylands protocol by sitting opposite to me and making sure I didn't do anything untoward, commented that it looked as if they were covered in clingfilm, which is about right. But I was not there for the endpapers, nor did I give them much mind. I was too taken with the textblock itself.

It is such a stunningly beautiful thing (see Figure 8.1). It's big—a large, heavy folio—and big in its types as well; something to be used in public devotion. The opening page hits you in the face with its heavy, beautiful blackletter as well as the fine, though surprisingly minimalist and abstract, rubrication. The vellum is heavy—more like a proper medieval

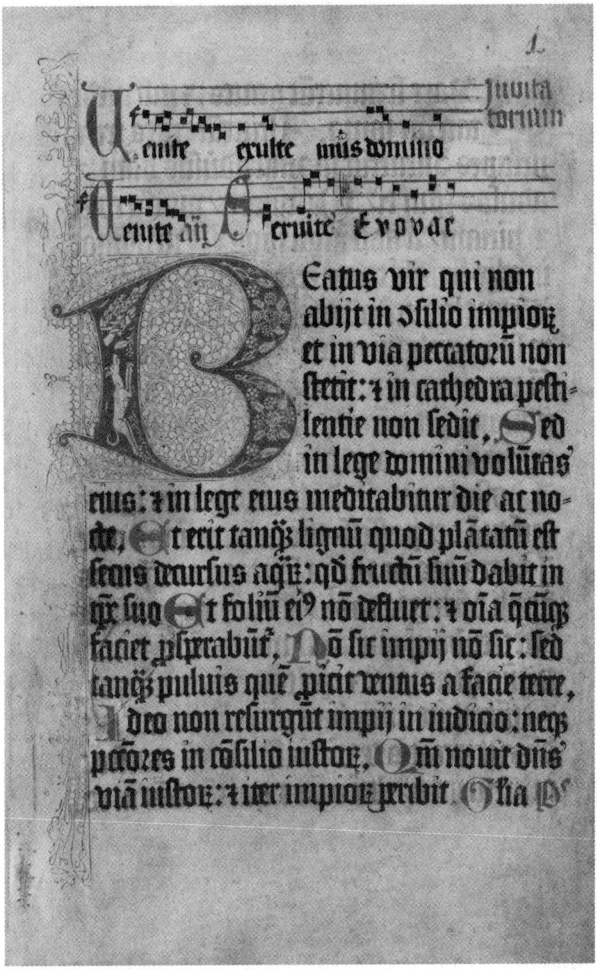

Figure 8.1 *Psalter* (Mainz: Johann Fust and Peter Schoeffer, 1467), first printed leaf, John Rylands 9784.

manuscript than, say, an Aldine on vellum—and a creamy yellow, deeper at the bottom of each leaf.

It is also a fascinating example of the meeting of print and manuscript. The music is entirely in manuscript but so are the lines of text immediately below the musical staves. It looks as if Fust & Schöffer wanted to be sure they had left enough space for the scribe and their caution was justified: the lines of text are a bit squeezed in and are smaller than their printed brethren. There are actually numerous scribal touchings up, including dashes representing word breaks across lines. It might be more appropriate to think of this as a mixture of print and manuscript than a purely printed text. Sometimes words and lines are corrected. On page 63, for example, a line of the *Gloria* has been missed out and added by what looks like a seventeenth-century hand. Presumably a monk at Rot became tired of having to come across the missing passage. It probably hadn't been fixed before simply because it was such an obvious part of the liturgy.

Without having you there, it's difficult to express how *beautiful* this printing is, especially compared to many of the incunables of a couple of decades later. In its richness and depth of colour, its precision and pleasing regularity, it's so much closer to a manuscript of the period than to later printing. Slowly leafing through its pages I reflected that I've held many Victorian books which were in the last stages of disintegration, practically dust. This is more than half a millennium old and feels as rich and fresh as if it had just come off the press. This is *good printing*.

I lingered for a long time over this volume and could linger as long here, but if we are to follow Spencer we must leave it for the time being. Time was marching on. Spencer's picked man, Horatio Nelson, had defeated the French fleet at the Battle of the Nile in August 1798 and the Second Coalition against France was brewing. It would lead not only to political and military disaster, but to a cultural upheaval, the wholesale secularisation of the south German monasteries, which could hardly have been imagined a decade before. Spencer, and Horn, were going to make the most of it.

NINE

"I have renewed the Attack"

On 9 November 1799, 18 Brumaire, Year VIII, in the French revolutionary calendar, Napoleon had returned to Paris and successfully engineered a coup which made him First Consul, almost absolute ruler of France (he would not be crowned emperor until 1804). As the fortunes of the French state entered a new phase, war continued and the situation on the continent looked more dire at every moment. Five days after the coup, Horn wrote to Spencer, with political news to be sure, but only after he had triumphantly announced that: "I have at length the pleasure of informing Your Lordship that I have succeeded in purchasing the following valuable articles

1 The Litteræ Indulgentiarum [i.e. a papal indulgence] on vellum 1455.

2 a beautifull Copy of Pliny 1469.

3 Ciceronis Orationes folio maximo, unknown Edition

4 Livy 1470 by Spira

5 and a superb Copy of Boethius 1473.

The first and third your Lordship shall have the refusal of but I am in too great a hurry to settle any thing by this poste and therefore beg leave to refer to the next."[1]

This was only the latest in a series of astonishing coups—in the bibliomaniacal rather than political world—which Horn had pulled off in the turbulent libraries of southern Germany. In this case, Horn's source had been the Benedictine monastery of St. Emmeram in his own home of

Regensburg, the burial site of a seventh-century wandering holy man named Emmeram or Heimramm. As usual, Horn supplied only the best.

The papal indulgence was the first of several of these early and ephemeral pieces of printing which Spencer would purchase.[2] Another was supplied by Horn in the following year, almost as soon as Spencer had received the first, this time from the private library of the Prinz von Hohenlohe-Öringen, who had, in turn, acquired it from the library of the German theologian and historian Johann Georg Schelhorn (1694–1773).[3] It was an altogether better specimen and, as Horn was quick to note, had "*the original seal hanging to it*"; he charged £20 more (£60 in total) accordingly.[4] Both of these outstanding examples of early printing are described at length in the *Bibliotheca Spenceriana*, but the St. Emmeram indulgence is no longer in the Spencer collection.[5] Why? The answer lies in another, particularly unsavoury, transaction which occurred almost three decades later. In 1829 another papal indulgence had been discovered in the library of the University of Louvain by its librarian Baron Frédéric de Reiffenberg, but within a year or two it had been stolen.[6] When it reappeared, it was in the hands of the dealer and collector Jacques-Joseph Techener (1802–1873), who sold it to the elderly Spencer. As it duplicated the St. Emmeram indulgence, Spencer traded up, buying the Louvain copy and disposing of the St. Emmeram one. If we were in any doubt as to the legality of the transaction, later in the 1830s the Belgian government formally demanded the Louvain copy back from the Spencer family and were refused; it remains in the library.[7]

Let us turn, however, from the indulgences and linger a little longer on the "beautifull Copy of Pliny", which was also amongst the books from St. Emmeram. It is the *editio princeps* of that writer's *Natural History*, printed at Venice in 1469 by Johann de Spira (of Speyer), brother of the Wendelin de Spira who printed Spencer's glorious Tacitus (see pp. 58–61). We have seen printing spread gradually from southern Germany to Italy, but aside from the Aldine Pindar with which we began our story and with Wendelin's own brief cameo Venice has remained unvisited.

Johann of Speyer was a Mainz goldsmith, like Gutenberg, and at the centre of the earliest printing there. By 1468, he and his brother Wendelin were in Venice and their *Epistolae* of Cicero, the first book printed in that city, was issued in 1469.[8] The Pliny soon followed. As a classical text it proved a failure, with Giannandrea Bussi's rather more elegant and scholarly edition of the *Natural History* appearing in Rome the following year and being widely read while the Venetian *editio princeps*—apparently printed in only a hundred copies—was quickly forgotten.[9] As a target for bibliomania it retained its mystique as the first printing of this foundational text of the Renaissance.

For Spencer, it was not the first copy of this edition he had possessed. Reviczky had owned a copy of this work, bound in violet morocco with gold inner dentelles (it sounds a bit gaudy to me) and he was trading up, probably because of the exceptionally wide margins in this copy.[10] It is another enormous book, the size of a large bible and as thick, in straight-grained blue morocco, richly gold- and blind-tooled by Hering, whose ticket is on the verso of the front flyleaf. On the recto of the first folio is the neat inscription "Monasterii S. Emmeram Ratisbonæ" conveniently written into a space left blank for a never-inserted illuminated initial.[11] And this is a puzzling thing about this volume—it is only partially rubricated and that quite plainly. Spencer was clearly buying it for its size and freshness as a printed book rather than for any manuscript fripperies. This is not to say that it lacks character. There is a tremendous ink blot in the table of contents—the scribe's red *minium* has splashed across the page, though not so badly as in Spencer's Gutenberg Bible—and there are minute ink sketches of manicules and tonsured heads in the margins, so many that they hardly seem very useful in pointing to specific passages. The annotator was nothing if not determined and continued throughout the entire text of this book so large that vellum tabs have been pasted onto the fore edges to guide the reader to different sections. The real reward, for a book historian at least, comes from a boldly-scribed manuscript note on the verso of the final leaf stating that one Ulrich Prossinger gave this book to the monastery of St. Emmeram in 1492. The Pliny, then, had resided in its monastic home for just over three hundred years.

But neither Horn nor Spencer were interested in provenance; what mattered to them was that this was a large, clean, and beautiful copy of a rare book, one of many which formed a steady stream from Horn in Regensburg to Spencer in London over these years. Horn exhibited a quite remarkable disregard for anything other than the chase in these letters, writing almost casually on 6 September 1800 that:

> We are now on the eve of hostilities which begin on the 10th at 6 in the afternoon and though both Mr Wickham and Mr Drake [the British agents there] insisted on my leaving this place yet I preferred to stay and hope to be the first to send good news.[12]

It is characteristic of Horn that this is an aside at the end of a long letter concerning his discovery of a new printed papal indulgence. With equal casualness Horn discusses French troop movements in a letter of 26 October, noting that "they are going to leave this town in three divisions on Monday the 29th"; he, a British spy, had been living in an occupied town for more than a month.[13]

A spy? Yes. From political intelligencer, Horn was taking on a more active role as British spy and agent in the eye of the Napoleonic storm. He was also passing this information directly on to Spencer as First Lord of the Admiralty and, later, Home Secretary, putting Spencer in the peculiar position of being handler for his book agent.[14] In between dodging the French and passing on the latest news, often from surprisingly high sources, Horn continued to send books Spencer's way, including one little short of the Gutenberg Bible in rarity and prestige: the so-called 36-Line Bible. This anonymous work, evidently printed in Bamberg and possibly by Albrecht Pfister, certainly no later than 1461, is another exceptionally early piece of German printing. Horn had reported in August 1798 that he had had the offer of one, but negotiations became protracted and we hear no more until 12 November 1800.[15] Then Horn wrote:

> I have the pleasure of informing Your Lordship that I have got a Copy of Pfisters Bible but unfortunately the minor Prophets are wanting and the first two leaves are mended in the upper part of the margin: au reste it is a beautifull Copy with the leaves in many places uncut and I do really believe there is not another Copy in Germany.[16]

Spencer must have wanted it badly to consider a substantially incomplete copy and evidently offered for it, but Horn wrote on 1 January that:

> I am sorry to be under the necessity for the first time since I had the happiness of becoming acquainted with your dear Person to refuse the Bible of Pfister for the sum you offered as including money Books &c which I gave for it, it cost me more. I had been bargaining for it these 3 years past and but for the present unhappy Circumstances and the Additional offer of David's Herculanum (which I was tired with tho' it cost me 200 florins) over and above what I had offered before I scarcely believe I would have ever got it. I therefore cannot value it under 50 £ however your Lordship shall not be disappointed so I shall send it in hopes of being able to complete it and your Lordship may keep it either for yourself or for me.[17]

Spencer eventually gave in. One wonders if he would have been surprised at what he saw when the Bible finally reached him. Horn emphasised the Bible's early provenance, quoting a parchment leaf at the beginning of the first volume which established that in 1468 George I, Prince-Bishop of Schaumburg, gave the Bible to the Benedictines of Kloster Aurach in Bavaria. This is fortunate, as the leaf has subsequently been lost.[18] What Horn did *not* mention was that the Bible had come from the Benedictine Schottenkloster in Würzburg, the sibling house to his own home monastery in Regensburg: it had been there since at least 1615.[19]

Again, Spencer most probably did not care, but we, at least, may be faintly surprised that Horn was so ready to alienate the property of another Scottish Benedictine house. There were only three of these, in Regensburg, Würzburg, and Erfurt, all medieval foundations which had been taken over under dubious premises from the Irish by exiled Catholic Scots shortly after the Reformation.[20] There were only ever a handful of monks in each monastery and by and large they seem to have had a strong degree of fellow feeling as exiles from their own homeland, but any Scottish solidarity Horn may have possessed was overwhelmed by his far more intense drive to acquire old books. For their part, the Scottish monks at Würzburg must have known that their days were numbered and they ought to prepare for the worst. They were right to do so—the seven-hundred-year-old monastery of St. James was closed with the rest in 1803, its books confiscated, its Scottish exiles left to fare as best they could.[21]

Acquiring an incomplete book is always a cross awaiting the unwary book collector and Spencer may have subsequently had reason to rue buying the Würzburg 36-Line Bible. Horn had casually suggested that he complete it with the copy sold in the Pinelli sale of the previous decade, but this was much easier said than done.[22] Meanwhile, Horn had begun bargaining for another copy as soon as he had sold the first to Spencer. This bears the inscription of Joachim Schmidt, a sixteenth-century Augustinian canon at Heidenfeld and it seems likely that it was still in Heidenfeld when Horn began his negotiations. With secularisation, Heidenfeld was looted by the new Bavarian state and the Bible passed into the university library in Würzburg; it was not until seven years later, in 1810, that Horn finally acquired this second copy for Spencer.[23] And it was not until 1814 that Spencer made a deal with Charles Jenkinson, the owner of the Pinelli copy, swapping leaves of their respective Bibles in a dizzying dance which eventually allowed Dibdin to proudly proclaim that Spencer was "in possession of a *perfect copy* of the BAMBERG BIBLE".[24]

Therefore, when we lay these two heavy folios on our desk at the Rylands, we must always bear in mind that we are working with hybrid beasts, heavily tampered with and far from representing what any part of them might have looked like in the fifteenth century.[25] They are bound by Hering in the midnight blue straight-grained morocco which Spencer favoured for Bibles and Biblical commentaries and, while the boards are unadorned save for his armorial supralibros, the inner dentelles are spectacularly wide and glorious, echoing in their shapes the tracery of a cathedral window. The opening leaf, which we will recall is from the Heidenfeld copy (it bears an almost entirely erased ownership inscription at the top of the page) has an elegant red, blue, and black rubricated initial, but it is the typeface which steals the show (see Figure 9.1). It's a particular spiky, sharply defined textura which sits, rich and black, on the page, and seems to shimmer slightly if you allow your eyes to unfocus and gaze lazily at the forest of vertical minims. But it's not Fust and

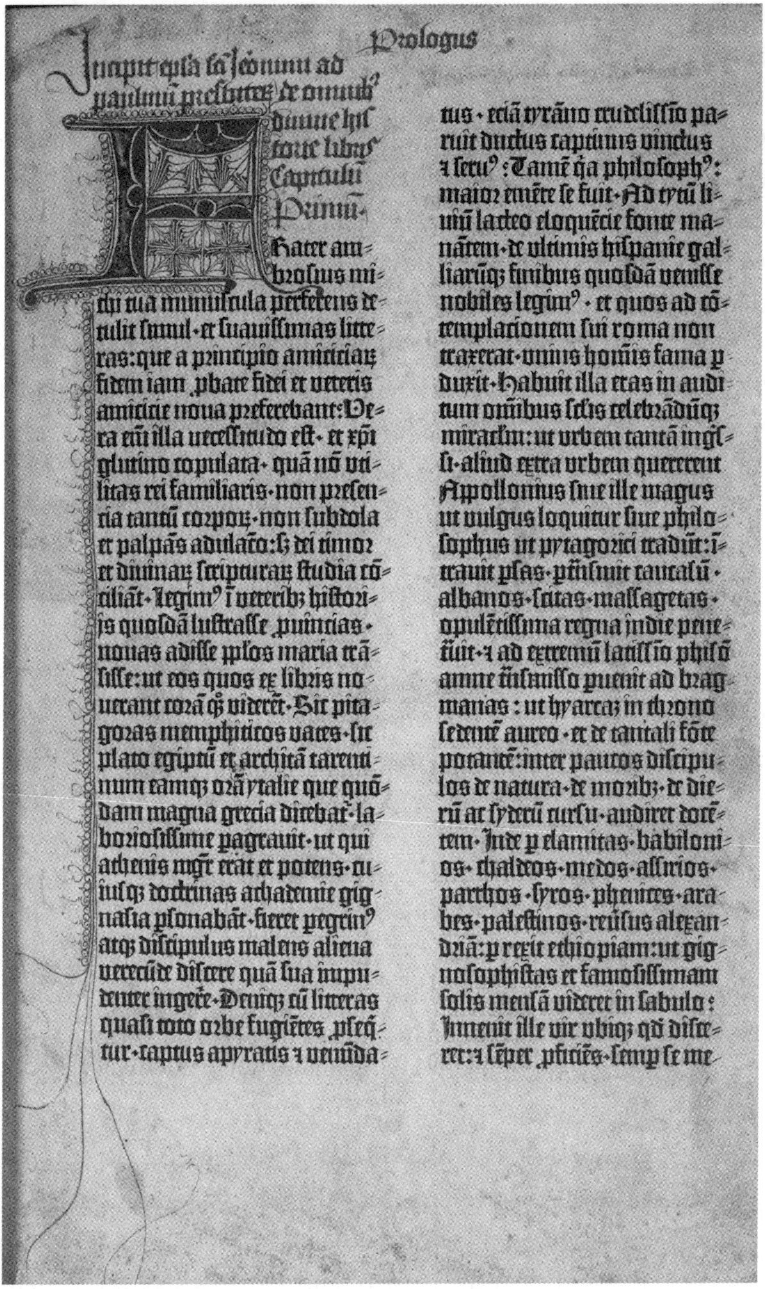

Figure 9.1 *Biblia Latina* (the 36-Line Bible) (Bamberg: s.n., not after 1461), Vol. I, first printed leaf, John Rylands 15365.

Schöffer. When I first saw these volumes, I had come straight from the Mainz Psalter and the difference was noticeable. This is good printing, the other, truly great.

Once you begin looking for it, it becomes obvious that this set has been made up from three copies for in each case the rubrication is distinctive. The Heidenfeld rubricator loves elaborate, sometimes enormous initials—the "I" of the "in principio" of Genesis takes up the entire outer margin of the page—but is sparing with his ink otherwise. The Würzburg illuminator, by contrast, has very simple large red initials, but is more enthusiastic about adding splashes of colour to printed characters within the text block, and the Pinelli rubricator likes larger, bolder red initials (he has done a very nice, feathery 'P' on the opening leaf of volume II) but adds only tiny dashes of red to the text block. Its composite nature means that most of the leaves are in excellent condition, but occasional hints of the truth shine through, as with the last leaves of the Würzburg fragment, which have been inlaid with modern paper on their outer edges, evidently an attempt to repair substantial damage. Still, there are only fourteen reasonably complete copies of the 36-Line Bible and most of those are somehow imperfect; Spencer had to make do.

* * *

One of the characteristics which made Horn such an excellent bloodhound was that, if Spencer really, *really* wanted a book, he would stop at almost nothing to obtain it. And a book that Spencer had really, *really* wanted, almost from the moment he began collecting, was the *Meditations* of the fifteenth-century Spanish cardinal Juan de Torquemada, the first edition of which had been printed at Rome by Ulrich Han (another German immigrant to Rome who set up his press around the same time as Sweynheym and Pannartz) in 1467.[26] At first, this seems like an odd choice of obsession given that Spencer had always been more interested in the ancient world than the modern and certainly had no particular fascination with modern Catholicism. But the *Meditations* was not just any book: it was the first illustrated book printed in Italy and was exceptionally rare (it was also the first dated book to be issued from Han's Roman press, but that was almost by the by). In Spencer's time only two copies were known. One was in the Imperial Library in Vienna, but there was no hope that would ever be sold, leaving only the copy in the Nuremberg Stadtbibliothek as a possibility.

Accordingly, on 9 July 1798 Horn wrote that he had "made overtures to Nuremberg for the Turrecremata" (this Latinised form of Torquemada's name was the standard in Spencer's time).[27] He was rebuffed, but remained undaunted and two years later wrote that while "I have again failed in my attempt upon the Turrecremata [of 14]67 and Boccacio at Nuremberg though I offered for both 80 Guineas however I do not yet entirely despair".[28] This Boccaccio was a rare 1472 Mantuan edition of the *Decamerone* (even today it is only known in four copies). Spencer bid Horn "renew his attempts" and in January 1801 Horn announced that he was travelling to Nuremberg in person, "though I have but little or no hopes of success".[29]

Horn arrived in Nuremberg "in a very low state of health" on 21 January 1801. Nuremberg was one of the Free Imperial Cities of the Holy Roman Empire, acting largely independently of the states around it, but had become increasingly cramped in its territories and powers by its larger neighbours over the previous decade and now had the additional worry of the French armies on its doorstep. "I found the whole place in confusion", Horn wrote,

> on account of the exorbitant demands of the French and the distress still heightened by the Prussians who are doing every thing to engage or oblige the Magistrates and Bourgeoisie to throw themselves a second time into the Arms of Prussia for protection.
>
> I flattered myself that in the Situation of Affairs something reasonable about the Library might be expected and accordingly introduced myself to the Librarian. But I soon discovered that with respect to the Turrecremata 1467 all kind of negociation was unavailing and to no purpose as the book is too well known!
>
> As to the Boccacio 1472 which is a beautifull copy in large folio he very openly and honourably declared that there could be no Idea of having it under 100 Louis.
>
> That if I could consent to give him that sum of which he would account 80 for the Library and 20 for his pains he would remove all difficulties by telling the Magistrates that it was among the books which the French had put in requisition but that hitherto he had found means to conceal it.

> If the demand had been more reasonable I should not have failed to close with it. however he has promised to lay it aside untill I have received further orders.[30]

Horn was so tantalisingly close and the librarian was so evidently corruptible, but the Torquemada remained just out of his reach. One can hear him grinding his teeth. But he did not despair. Enquiring discretely, he found at least one Nuremberg magistrate who "was not against selling it" and urgently asked for instructions from Spencer who responded almost as soon as Horn's letter reached him, authorising £50–60 for the Torquemada alone and £80 if the Boccaccio could also be secured.[31]

But all to no avail. Even then, Horn kept the desired book in his sights and five years later, on 13 February 1806, asked Spencer for a revised offer "as soon as possible". What had changed? "[A]s that Town [i.e. Nuremberg] seems now to be threatened by the French with a Change of Masters I might possibly succeed in getting them. I request Your Lordship to state your highest Price with Precision".[32] Horn was planning to use the threat of impending invasion and sack—or the chaos occasioned by it—to make his move. By 14 March, it was almost his,

> in Consideration of sixty Louis offered in my last Letter to the Librarian for the Meditationes I have brought this Business so far that in case of a change in the Independence of Nurnberg my Letter is to serve as a Proof that the Book was sold in the Beginning of the Month of May when the Magistrates had yet the Right of disposing of it, and the Book is in the mean Time to be removed out of the Library and deposited in the Hands of one of our mutual Friends in Order to be either delivered up to me for the 60 Louis or reclaimed in case of the Town's remaining independant.[33]

Nuremberg was awarded to Bavaria on 12 July, but this was largely a notional gift in the tumult of the times and the French continued to menace the former Imperial city. On 25 August Horn wrote with considerable irritation that a Nuremberg had been showered with (largely empty) honours deputation by their new Bavarian masters and "that now every one of the Magistrates, either afraid of committing himself, or looking up for similar Honors, is adverse to the Surrender of a Book which they imagine will be coveted by their new Sovereign". He added that "[i]n Return the Librarian gives me all possible Hopes that in Order to get rid of me they will make no Difficulty in giving up the Decamerone di Boccaccio 1472".[34]

In the end, Horn obtained neither book. On 11 March 1807 the French army marched into Nuremberg, occupying it, rather dubiously, in the name of Maximilian I of Bavaria, and later in the year executing one of the city's booksellers, Johann Philipp Palm, for selling anti-French pamphlets.[35] All hope of obtaining the Torquemada and the Boccaccio was extinguished, but surprisingly they were not appropriated by the French and sent to Paris; instead, both volumes remain safely on the shelves of the Stadtbibliothek, despite the best efforts of both Horn and the librarians of the Bibliothèque Nationale.[36] As we shall see, another, unknown, copy of the Torquemada would eventually be unearthed by the indefatigable Horn, but Spencer would have to wait a further decade for that minor miracle. He also eventually obtained a rather grubby and incomplete copy of the Boccaccio on whose flyleaf he wrote wistfully that "[p]erhaps the finest copy of this book in the world is in the public library at Nuremberg".[37]

* * *

Horn's Nuremberg adventure was one of his biggest failures, albeit a failure which could hardly have been anything but given the situation, and we only do him justice if we follow it with one of his greatest successes: a single triumphant haul which put him in possession of more than a dozen of the best books in Europe. This was the plunder of the library of the Carthusian monastery of the Blessed Virgin Mary at Buxheim in Swabia.[38]

The Charterhouse, as Carthusian foundations are called in English, at Buxheim had been established in 1402 and from an early date was both exceptionally wealthy and well supplied with early printing. To a considerable extent this was due to the donations of Hilprand Brandenburg (1442–1514), sometime rector of the University of Basel and a patrician of the small town of Biberach.[39] His gifts, according to the *liber benefactorum* of Buxheim, amounted to "450 books large and small".[40] This collection, almost all incunabula, remained at Buxheim, largely in their original fifteenth-century bindings, for the remainder of the monastery's existence and their importance was well known by the end of the eighteenth century. Martin Gerbert, Abbot of St. Blasien, could, for example, write in 1765 that the monastery library "abounds in books from the first epoch of the art of printing" and could spend several pages of his bibliographical travelogue, the *Iter Alemannicum*, describing at length the 1462 Bible and other treasures of the house.[41]

Such riches made Buxheim a prime target for book hunters like Horn. It also loomed large in Spencer's mind for a very particular reason. Amongst its rows of incunables it contained what might at first have seemed a rather modest item: a single manuscript, written in Bohemia in 1417, of the Matins of the Virgin and gifted to Buxheim in the first half of the fifteenth century by Anna von Gundelfingen (*c.*1400–42), a canoness in the nunnery of Buchau.[42] This manuscript was remarkable, however, not for itself, but for a woodcut pasted inside its cover: a large, hand-coloured woodblock print of St. Christopher dated 1423. It is (probably) the earliest known dated example of a woodblock print in Europe.[43] The importance of the St. Christopher woodcut for the history of printing was first noted by Buxheim's librarian, Franz Krismer, "a polymath and great lover of the arts and belles lettres", who showed it to the art historian Carl Heinrich von Heinecken on his visit to Buxheim.[44] Krismer subsequently published a study of early woodcuts in 1776, including the St. Christopher.[45]

It was probably from the works of either von Heinecken or Krismer himself that Spencer came to learn of the St. Christopher and its significance.[46] In a draft reply to Maugérard from autumn 1797, he had scribbled imperatively "get me the Print of St. Christopher at Buxheim", but Maugérard, if he attempted, did not succeed, and it was left to Horn to take up the challenge.[47] Horn, initially, met with no better success, later writing that:

> I recollect that being in 1802 at Buxheim where I intended to buy some old Editions and procured [*sic*] your St. Christopher those rich Carthusians were convinced that they alone would escape the general Fate of the Monasteries because they having nothing to do with the World, the World had nothing to do with them.[48]

But the "Principal Conclusion of the Extraordinary Imperial Delegation" changed all that. The "Principal Conclusion", usually referred to in English as the "Final Recess", is one of those documents of modern history which cast the most drastic and unhappy of decisions in the most boring prose. Dated 25 February 1803, it began with what seems an entirely positive goal, "to end the war which has broken out between His Imperial Majesty and the German Empire on the one hand and the French Republic on the other".[49] It continued, however, by laying out a comprehensive plan of "Entschaedigung", compensation, for the losses suffered by the Imperial states following on from the surrender of the left bank of the Rhine. How might this compensation be achieved? Through "Saekularisationen", which historians commonly and blandly translate as "secularisation", an entirely inadequate word to describe the forced closure and looting of hundreds if not thousands of monasteries across the Holy Roman Empire.[50] Horn was there. "In the present uncertain state of the Bavarian Monasteries I have renewed the Attack" he wrote triumphantly to Spencer on 5 March, only days after the Final Recess had been signed and sealed and Buxheim was one of his main targets.[51]

When Buxheim was secularised in 1803, its property, including its library, went to a minor and altogether unimpressive nobleman, Johann Friedrich Carl Maximilian Graf von Ostein (1736–1809), as compensation. Most of it was eventually inherited by Ostein's kinsmen, the Grafen Waldbott von Bassenheim, and was sold by that family in a high-profile auction in Münich in 1883, but not quite all.[52] Horn was hot on the trail and wrote to Spencer on 4 July 1803 that "[t]he Monks of Buxheim who before in hopes of not being suppressed refused all the offers I made them secreted their principal Articles and now I am invited to meet their collection at Ulm".[53]

The chance to acquire the Buxheim books was so tempting that Horn seems to have spent much of the summer of 1803 at Ulm, working on the unnamed refugees from Buxheim in the hope of securing their treasures for himself. By September, he announced the acquisition of the St. Christopher and other high-profile items, including a 1462 Bible and a Fust and Schöffer Cicero, but the full extent of his success only became apparent in a letter of 12 January 1804.[54] Horn here wrote with an odd coyness, given that Spencer knew quite well he had been negotiating for the Buxheim books, merely informing his patron that:

> Since my last I am become possessed of a Superb Collection which I should wish to get rid of in a lump perhaps they might suit any of Your Lordships friends and therefore I take the Liberty of giving You the following List…[55]

What followed was a list of fifteen items, plus the St. Christopher, the likes of which had probably never been offered as a single lot before and certainly never would be again. It contained a Gutenberg Bible, a 1459 *Rationale*, a 1460 Catholicon, a series of early and exceptional classical texts, and more. "I would give the whole including the St. Christopher", Horn wrote, "for 700 £."[56]

Unfortunately for Horn, Spencer, who already had copies of most of these, demurred, taking only the St. Christopher and leaving Horn out of pocket and unexpectedly at loose ends. The immediate consequence of this was that Horn found he could not pay the exiled Carthusians who kept back the St. Christopher as security until their account was finally settled.[57] When he did arrive with the money in hand, in the early autumn of 1804, he reported that "the Proprietors of the St. Christopher… showed a Determination to get rid of that part of the Bargain which concerned him and even offered to restore the Money" but "[a]fter a great Deal of wrangling" Horn prevailed and triumphantly brought away the woodcut and its enclosing volume.[58] To recoup his losses, Horn would later resort to publicly advertising his Buxheim books for sale in German and French periodicals, eventually unburdening himself of his ambitious purchase over the subsequent four years (the Gutenberg Bible, if you were wondering, was bought by another English collector, Mad Jack Fuller, and is now in the library of Eton College).[59]

In the end, Spencer paid £50 plus an additional £15 gift to a poor relation of Horn's for the St. Christopher, possibly his most expensive purchase by the page.[60] In return, he received a competent but crude woodcut leaf, hand-coloured in pale greens, blues, pinks, and yellows,

Figure 9.2 St. Christopher Woodcut (1423?), John Rylands 17249.2.

depicting a giant St. Christopher carrying the Christ child across a stream as a monk looks on and two minute peasants go about their labours (see Figure 9.2). The saint's brows are furrowed and he is leaning on a palm tree as a staff while the young Christ, unconcerned, holds the Imperial orb in one hand and blesses us with his other. It is a woodblock print which would undoubtedly have remained in the obscurity of learned journals and catalogues were it not for the electrifying date: "1423" (or, more precisely "millesimo cccc° xx° tertio"). Whether it is true or not, it has for two hundred years put the St. Christopher in the position of *the* first: "the most ancient specimen extant, with a date", as Dibdin would put it, "of the use of PRINTING INK".[61] It is item number one in his catalogue of Spencer's collection.

* * *

Spencer had profited from the tragedy unfolding in Europe ever since he had begun collecting, but nowhere did he benefit more directly from others' misfortunes than in the years just before and just after secularisation. A central thread in the social, political, and religious life of Europe for the past millennium, the monasteries, had been violently torn out of the fabric of the continent and Spencer, Horn, and their bibliophilic contemporaries greedily supped up the treasures left over. Even if, as has often been observed in their defence, each individual transaction was perfectly legal (money or new books given in exchange for old), the morality of these transactions, examples of which could easily be multiplied, to the dozens, even to the hundreds, amongst books in Spencer's collection alone, remains difficult to justify.

We have not yet seen the last of secularisation, nor of Father Horn, but for the moment we must return to yet another agent-cum-collector who has figured in these pages and, more importantly, to the question: how was Spencer going to pay for the books he had collected so rapidly and single-mindedly over the previous fifteen years?

TEN

The limits of a fortune

On 6 November 1845 the ailing sixty-six-year-old Charles Stuart, Baron Stuart de Rothesay, died at Highcliffe, the Gothic Revival palace he had built for himself on the Dorset coast.[1] A decade later, his widow and heirs dispersed the massive library which this inveterate collector and connoisseur had acquired over the previous half century.[2] I am holding one of those books now. It is a compact little volume, just under 14cms tall, *Histoire des evenemens tragiques d'Angleterre et des derniers troubles d'Ecosse* (Cologne, 1686). Stuart had it rebound at some point in or after 1812 by the great French binder René Simier (he had long served as British ambassador in Paris and his tastes were thoroughly French). Whatever its earlier binding may have been, it is now wrapped up in sumptuous black crushed morocco, so heavily tooled in the style of the First Empire that one can barely see anything but gold. It is a beautiful little gem of a book (I can fit it in the palm of my hand) and a favourite volume in my collection.

This little volume, one of thousands once at Highcliffe and now spread across the world, captures in miniature the bibliophilic, if not bibliomaniacal, ambition of its sometime owner when he was at the height of his diplomatic career, a key figure in European political circles, and a peer and landowner in his own right. But let us go back some years earlier, to Vienna in December 1802. The baron, then plain Charles Stuart, was a twenty-three-year-old secretary in the British legation there and he had just been given a package with strict orders to send it home by the first extraordinary courier.

The package had been delivered into his hands by none other than the Chevalier d'Elci, that sometime friend of Count Reviczky and thoroughly troublesome source of books for Spencer. In it was a copy of Henry VIII's *Assertio septem sacramentorum*, printed by Richard Pynson in 1521, a defence of Catholicism which has been somewhat overshadowed by Henry's later career (see Figure 10.1). But this was not just any copy. It was, as its sender wrote, "a magnificent copy printed on vellum, decorated with miniatures, and which can be said to be truly unique".[3] D'Elci did not exaggerate. Originally a gift from Henry VIII to Christian II of Denmark and subsequently in the library of Pope Pius VI, it is a book which almost glows with colour, its illuminations (possibly not contemporary, but undeniably beautiful) leaping off the page with undimmed vividness.[4] Its ultimate recipient, we will be unsurprised to learn, was Spencer. Did d'Elci show this volume to the young secretary Stuart, I wonder? And was that, perhaps, a turning point in his life, a single, crystallising moment in which he first understood the love of beautiful books? I imagine the gentle, round-faced young man with his shock of red hair (he was paternally a Scot) gazing with rapt admiration at d'Elci's prize while the older, more worldly-wise Florentine looked on with satisfaction.[5] This is, of course, all speculation.

* * *

What we do know is that d'Elci's decision to give the *Assertio* to Spencer and the correspondence which ensued from it were no accident. When Reviczky mediated between d'Elci and Spencer for the exchange of books in the early 1790s, the Italian was living in Milan, where he had gone to be with his long-time mistress Costanza Brusati. When the French invaded in 1796, however, the inveterate royalist and ultramontane d'Elci returned to Florence, but, faced with the ongoing French sack of the peninsula, by September 1800 he had fled onwards to Vienna, where he remained for the rest of his life.[6]

It was in his Viennese period that he finally dispensed with intermediaries and began, on 5 October 1802, to correspond directly with Spencer. He comes across as a precise, somewhat pernickety, occasionally

Figure 10.1 Henry VIII, *Assertio septem sacramentorum adversus Martin. Lutherum* (London: Richard Pynson, 1521), Christian II of Denmark's copy, title page, John Rylands 18952.

infuriating, but also in his own way charming figure, a cluster of traits which show themselves from the opening of his first letter. "It has been a long time since I wished to have the honour of writing to you", he wrote,

> as I well know the insights and advantages which I could draw from correspondence with a Person of such distinguished reputation and merit as your own. I have, so to speak, a right of inheritance, having been a close friend of the late Count Reviczky, who perhaps will have sometimes spoken to you about me and my books. Fortunately, an opportunity presents itself to me to write to you and send you a book, which will certainly be to your taste...[7]

The book was, of course, the *Assertio septem sacramentorum*. This was a princely gift. Or was it? A bill from the booksellers James Payne and John Mackinlay records, under the date 6 March 1803, the *purchase* of this volume by Spencer for the substantial sum of £52 10*s*.[8] If d'Elci gave the book to Spencer, how could he have purchased it from a bookseller?

The answer lies in a closer examination of just what d'Elci was doing. In his initial letter he proposed what sounds, on the surface, like a gentlemen's agreement between two collectors:

> tell me what I could do for your superb and famous Collection of old Editions; certainly I will neglect no opportunity to show you the eagerness I have to contribute to your satisfaction, but I dare to implore your help in favour of my Collection of *editiones principes* of the classical authors, which to tell the truth, is one of the most complete in existence, but which I would never dare compare with yours.[9]

By 2 December, he was asking Spencer for "precise knowledge of your Desiderata" as well as offering a list of items, perhaps for sale or trade, though "I am only indicating them to you, without being able to commit to anything."[10]

One of these was the *editio princeps* of the Roman poet Statius, which Spencer was keen to acquire. D'Elci was encouraging, but could promise nothing. First, he had to ensure it was not already promised to Payne and he was quick to add that the Imperial Library in Vienna was "making every effort to get it out of my hands".[11] This begins to sound suspiciously like the language employed by any other book agent, but we could still, if generously inclined, imagine it to simply be that of a collector determined to get the best price for a duplicate. On 1 February 1803, however, he wrote further that he had, unfortunately, sold the volume to Mr. Payne and "it is therefore my duty to inform you of it, because, although I must undoubtedly send it to Mr. Payne, he will keep it at your disposal".[12] Sure enough, the same bill from Payne and Mackinlay which itemised the *Assertio*'s sale also itemised, under 5 July 1803, Spencer's purchase of the Statius for £31 10*s*.[13]

In other words, d'Elci was playing a delicate game. He *was* a serious collector, that was perfectly true, but he was also acting as a book agent for James Payne (1765–1809), younger son of the elder Thomas Payne and yet another resourceful and ruthless member of this bookselling dynasty (it is no coincidence that Payne was in Vienna at the time of this correspondence), carefully sourcing and selling books to Spencer via Payne, presumably for an appropriate commission from the latter.[14] It is difficult, then, to be confident as to where a particular book is when d'Elci mentions it in his letters. Was it a duplicate in his collection? Was it an item he had or could source for sale? Was it even already in the hands of a bookseller like Payne and was d'Elci merely serving as an intermediary for the trade? At different times, all three possibilities seem to have been true.

This is not to say that d'Elci was not sending good quality items, regardless of his subterfuges. The Statius, if not quite so resplendent as the *Assertio*, is a rare book (only eight other copies are known) and a pleasing exemplar, with very generous margins and occasional early annotations, including corrections of textual errors (see Figure 10.2). Dibdin disliked the printing, sniffily writing that "the entire impression wears the aspect of a work executed in the rudest period of the art by an unskilful printer", but on examining it myself I couldn't help but think he had been a bit too harsh.[15] The printer had certainly struggled and the lines suggest a very loose and unevenly assembled forme, but it is not entirely unpleasing. Spencer had had it rebound by Hering in straight-grained blue morocco and any provenance that had previously been present must have been discarded along with whatever endpapers and

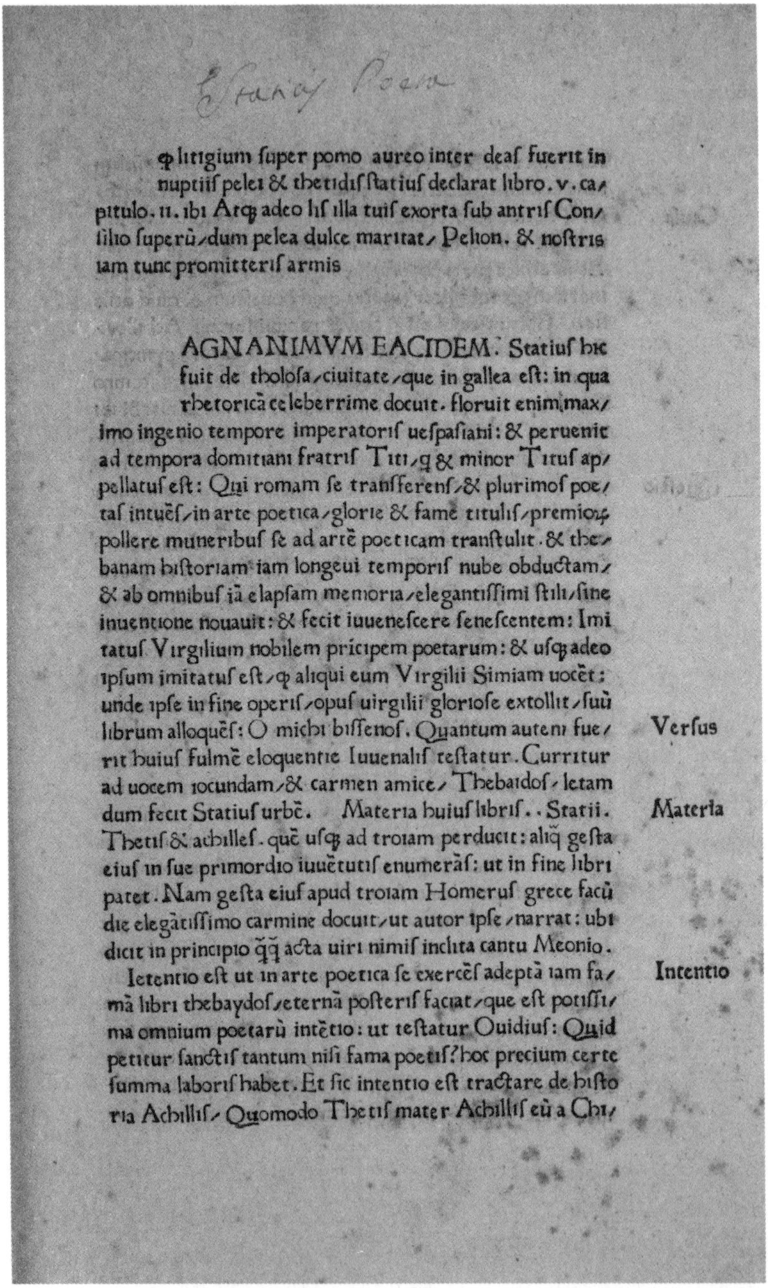
Statius Poeta

ꝙ litigium ſuper pomo aureo inter deaſ fuerit in nuptiiſ pelei & thetidiſ ſtatiuſ declarat libro. v. ca/pitulo. ii. ibi Atꝗ adeo hiſ illa tuiſ exorta ſub antriſ Con/ſilio ſuperū/dum pelea dulce maritat/ Pelion. & noſtris iam tunc promitteriſ armis

AGNANIMVM EACIDEM. Statiuſ hic fuit de tholoſa/ciuitate/que in gallea eſt: in qua rhetoricā celeberrime docuit. floruit enim max/imo ingenio tempore imperatoriſ ueſpaſiani: & peruenit ad tempora domitiani fratriſ Titi/q & minor Tituſ ap/pellatuſ eſt: Qui romam ſe tranſferenſ/& plurimoſ poe/taſ intuēſ/in arte poetica/glorie & famē tituliſ/premioꝗ pollere muneribuſ ſe ad artē poeticam tranſtulit. & the/banam hiſtoriam iam longeui temporiſ nube obductam/ & ab omnibuſ iā elapſam memoria/elegantiſſimi ſtili/ſine inuentione nouauit: & fecit iuueneſcere ſeneſcentem: Imi tatuſ Virgilium nobilem pricipem poetarum: & uſꝗ adeo ipſum imitatuſ eſt/ꝙ aliqui eum Virgilii Simiam uocēt: unde ipſe in fine operiſ/opuſ uirgilii glorioſe extollit/ſuū librum alloquēſ: O michi biſſenoſ. Quantum autem fue/rit huiuſ fulmē eloquentie Iuuenaliſ teſtatur. Curritur ad uocem iocundam/& carmen amice/ Thebaidoſ/ letam dum fecit Statiuſ urbē. Materia huiuſ librïſ.. Statii. Thetiſ & achilleſ. quē uſꝗ ad troiam perducit: aliq̄ geſta eiuſ in ſue primordio iuuētutiſ enumerāſ: ut in fine libri patet. Nam geſta eiuſ apud troiam Homeruſ grece facū die elegātiſſimo carmine docuit/ut autor ipſe/narrat: ubi dicit in principio q̄q̄ acta uiri nimiſ inclita cantu Meonio.
Ietentio eſt ut in arte poetica ſe exercēſ adeptā iam fa/mā libri thebaydoſ/eternā poſteriſ faciat/que eſt potiſſi/ma omnium poetarū intētio: ut teſtatur Ouidiuſ: Quid petitur ſanctiſ tantum niſi fama poetiſ? hoc precium certe ſumma laboriſ habet. Et ſic intentio eſt tractare de hiſto ria Achilliſ/ Quomodo Thetiſ mater Achilliſ eū a Chi/

Verſus

Materia

Intentio

Figure 10.2 Statius, *Thebais* (Rome: s.n. ("The Printer of the Statius"), *c.*1470), first printed page, John Rylands 12279.

boards were removed during its rebinding. Leafing through its pages, I had a momentary and dizzying fantasy of Hering's workshop: full of discarded fifteenth-century wooden boards, chains from chained libraries, and incalculably precious evidence of the histories of a thousand books, all of which would be swept out with the rubbish the following morning.

* * *

At the same time, d'Elci was also eager to see what books he could secure *from* Spencer for his own collection. A letter of 16 May 1803 contains a substantial list of his own desiderata, divided into those "of the first importance" and those "less important". At the top of the list was the 1474 Horace printed in Naples by Arnaldus de Bruxella.[16] Spencer himself was also seeking the Horace and d'Elci's list highlights the inevitable competition between the two men, both of whom were collecting in the same field of classical *editiones principes*.

It is a token, however, of Spencer's genuine goodwill towards a fellow collector, as well as his desire to take advantage of d'Elci's sources for books, that he happily helped the chevalier procure several much-desired volumes. One was an early edition of Boethius, in black letter and without either date or signatures, whose procurement d'Elci responded to "with great pleasure and gratitude" in a letter of 20 August 1803.[17] Not all Spencer's attempts were so successful, however, especially not where trades were concerned.

At the Pinelli sale, Reviczky had purchased two intriguing incunables. One was an edition of the Roman poet Propertius dated February 1472 in its colophon.[18] The other was a copy of Propertius's fellow countryman Tibullus, undated but supposed to be the *editio princeps* and a sibling volume to the Propertius.[19] Earlier bibliographers had suggested that, as was often the case, these two Latin poets, together with Catullus, had originally been issued together as a single volume or at least a single edition.[20] While the Catullus might be lacking, Spencer could comfort himself with having both the Tibullus and Propertius.

D'Elci disabused him of this belief. Writing on 25 July 1804, he stated categorically that despite the similarity in typeface, the Tibullus which

Spencer had was *not* the work of the same printer as the Propertius. How did d'Elci know? Because he had found the real companion volume which was not only the true sibling to the Propertius but, quite probably, the true *editio princeps* of Tibullus and thus "preferable to any other". But the road to acquiring this volume would not be easy,

> I do not know if I will obtain it from the owNer, who is an Amateur who greatly values it. This Copy has a defect in the first leaf; that is to say, the last lines are imitated in pen; well traced, but not legitimate. I have tried in vain to extract it from its owner, but it is impossible for me to get it for cash.[21]

Spencer annotated this letter that in his reply he had "begged him to get me the Tibullus belonging to the Propertius of Feb: 1472". D'Elci had played him perfectly. Having first undercut his belief that he already had the correct Tibullus, he then presented the possibility of acquiring the volume which proved to be the right one after all, and then heightened Spencer's apprehensions by anticipating the difficulty of obtaining it.

It is hard not to imagine that these moves were entirely conscious on d'Elci's part. Their immediate effect, however, was to cause several layers of confusion. In his eagerness to secure the Tibullus, Spencer acquired a 1475 edition of Cato's *Distychs*, one of the items on d'Elci's wish list, from Edwards in London and promptly sent it to d'Elci in Vienna as an encouragement towards acquiring the desired volume. But d'Elci wrote back on 20 October that, alas, he had already acquired a copy of this edition some months ago and that in fact the copy in Edwards' shop had been earmarked by Edwards and d'Elci for the Marchese Francesco Taccone (1763–1818) in Naples: "I do not dare to accept it in exchange for other books which I must deprive myself of in order to procure for you, for a fee, the Tibullus."[22]

It was too late, however, for the Cato was already on its way to Vienna. D'Elci kept it temporarily and wrote to Spencer that the whole confusion was due to a complicated three-way arrangement between him, Edwards, and Taccone regarding who was to have first pick when a copy next came on the market, but, regardless, Spencer's attempted buttering up of d'Elci had been spectacularly unsuccessful.[23] D'Elci kept pursuing the Tibullus, but at less breakneck speed, writing on 7 February 1805 that "I have never received a reply again about the Tibullus…I believe, however, that it is being kept for me, but the one who has it is such an indolent man that perhaps he will never reply, unless I myself go into the country where it is; sooner or later I will certainly go there."[24] He had still received no response from the owner in July when he said that he hoped to go into the country to speak to him in person "next year".[25]

It is the last we hear of this volume and the letter in which d'Elci's slow progress was reported is the last he sent to Spencer for six years. We shall return momentarily to the question of this hiatus, but first we must follow the story of these companion volumes through to its end. D'Elci was, unfortunately for Spencer, completely right. The Tibullus which Reviczky had bought at the Pinelli sale is now attributed to the Venetian printer Florentius de Argentina while the Propertius was the work of another Venetian, Federicus de Comitibus from Verona.[26] Moreover, Federicus de Comitibus had, indeed, printed a copy of Tibullus, which must be the elusive volume described by d'Elci.[27] Spencer never did obtain a copy. It is rare (only nine copies are known) and his misfortune is unsurprising.

But what became of the copy belonging to the indolent country gentleman? It was eventually bought by d'Elci himself and now rests, with his other books, in the Biblioteca Medicea Laurenziana.[28] It is an unusual example of a book which Spencer never acquired despite very much wishing to do so.

* * *

We must now return to the abrupt cessation of correspondence between d'Elci and Spencer. Why did our subject not continue to pursue the Tibullus and the other books in which he was in conversation about with d'Elci? The Spencer correspondence in the British Library is vast, almost overwhelming, but as I was reading through it, I soon became aware of an unexpected caesura. There is no correspondence with d'Elci between July 1805 and February 1811, none with della Lena between October 1805 and December 1814, none with Horn between September

1806 and September 1809, and, indeed, next to no bibliophilic correspondence of any sort between the latter part of 1805 and early 1811. What had happened? Letters on the other side of the break regularly refer to long silences, so it was not simply a case of lost documents, but a genuine hiatus, both in Spencer's collecting and his corresponding.

The answer, here as in many other cases, came from Spencer's receipts.[29] I have mentioned these before, but now they deserve their own introduction. In their present form they occupy three enormous elephant folios in the British Library, half bound in red morocco and red cloth, with the Spencer arms on the boards. These are evidently late nineteenth- or early twentieth-century creations. The material within them is loosely organised chronologically and has the appearance of being only one remove from Spencer's working papers. One gets the sense of desk drawers hurriedly cleared and bound together without much thought as to the actual contents of the individual items.

As I studied the receipts, I began to notice patterns which, ultimately, answered the question posed by the correspondence. The numerous booksellers' and bookbinders' bills contained within the receipt volumes generally take the form of a bill together with a receipt indicating that the bill was paid. Through most of the 1790s, as the volume of Spencer's acquisitions, both high- and low-end, continued to increase exponentially, these were paid promptly and in full, but around 1797 this begins to change. Faced with a substantial bill of £454 12*s.* 6*d.* from Payne, Spencer settled it piecemeal with part payment in cash, a £200 draft on Hoare's, his bank, and a sale back to the bookseller of a "Parçel of Books" valued at £100. Overall, it took the better part of a year for him to pay off the full bill.[30]

This exception quickly became the rule and outstanding sums began to be carried over from bill to bill, as when Edwards, settling up at the end of 1799 for purchases that year totalling £516 11*s.* 6*d.*, discreetly pointed out that there was also an outstanding balance from the previous year for £295 9*s.*[31] As early as 1799 there appears an ominous little scrap in Spencer's hand calculating the interest on £5,000 from August to March (it was £146 11*s.* 5*d.*); he was borrowing heavily to keep pace with his expenditure.[32] Despite this, he continued buying, though increasingly settlement came in the form of a mixed and long-delayed smorgasboard of banker's drafts, petty cash, and the sale of other books. By 1803–04, purchases seem a little thinner on the ground and Spencer heroically paid Payne and Mackinlay in full for his May 1804 bill of £278 *6s.*, but this was unusually prompt.[33] When Spencer finally paid off a bill of £387 *19s. 6d.* from Payne on 8 June 1804 it contained items that had been bought as far back as December 1802.[34]

The conclusion is inescapable: Spencer was deeply in debt and running out of money. There were several reasons for this. To be sure, his father had left very substantial debts, which he had paid off in the 1780s and 1790s by selling a number of major estates in the home counties for close to £200,000.[35] At the same time, however, he had spent more than £20,000 substantially rebuilding Althorp and this was only one of many a luxury which he and his wife had enjoyed at the end of the century.[36] Of these, the books were undoubtedly the most expensive and a sense of how far his finances had become straitened over the course of the decade can be seen by the fact that, while in the late 1780s and early 1790s he could, albeit with white knuckles, pay for the full sum of rebuilding of Althorp, by 1802 he was unable to pay his eldest son's gambling debts, amounting to "several thousand pounds" without borrowing heavily.[37]

The effect of his newfound poverty can be seen in the book bills for 1806 through 1811, which amount to only a tithe of his former purchases and from which incunables are notably absent.[38] The lull in his correspondence then proves to be no sudden misanthropy but, we may presume, an attempt, as best he could, to curb temptation and ignore his continental agents lest their offers prove too tempting to resist. For at least some of this time, he could also justify his absence from the field by his brief service as Secretary of State for the Home Department in the Ministry of All the Talents between February 1806 and March 1807, but that was a cover at best and it is tempting to suppose that his retirement from politics after the fall of the ministry had as much to do with his own impoverishment as with any political disaffection.

These lean years would not last forever, though, and even as early as 1807 we can see a new obsession looming on the horizon. In the summer of that year the library of the late John Brand (1744–1806), antiquary and author of a popular book on folk tradition, was sold. Amongst Brand's antiquarian detritus were some very fine things, including "a perfect and fine specimen" of *The Knight of the Toure* (1483), an early product of the press of England's first printer, William Caxton. It was bought for Spencer by Payne, bidding against Spencer's cousin the Marquess of Blandford and was knocked down to him for the heavy price of £111 6*s*.[39] A few months later he repeated this extravagance, paying £105 on 21 December 1807 for Caxton's 1490 *Boke of Eneydos*, which he had found in the shop of the minor London bookseller Machell Stace.[40] These were the beginnings of a decade-long search for the earliest English printing, a search in which he would be aided and abetted by an unexpected new associate.

ELEVEN

"The Roxburghe fight"

"I will frankly confess", rejoined Lysander, "that I am an arrant BIBLIOMANIAC—that I love books dearly—that the very sight, touch, and, more, the perusal"—"Hold, my friend," again exclaimed Philemon, "you have renounced your profession—you talk of *reading* books—do BIBLIOMANIACS ever *read* books?" "Nay", quoth Lysander, "you shall not banter thus with impunity. We will, if it please you", said he, [turning round to me] "make our abode with you for a few days—and after seeing the library of your neighbour, I will throw down the gauntlet to Philemon, challenging him to answer certain questions which you may put to us, respecting the number, rarity, beauty, or utility of those works which relate to the literature and antiquities of our own country."[1]

So begins one of the stranger works of nineteenth-century literature. The Reverend Thomas Frognall Dibdin's *Bibliomania; or Book Madness: A Bibliographical Romance* (1809) is an imaginary conversation between friends, describing, in prose as purple as it is convoluted, the delights of old books and their acquisition. As Dibdin himself informs us, the term "bibliomania", meaning "a passion for possessing books; not so much to be instructed by them, as to gratify the eye by looking on them", had been known since at least 1762 but he made it his own.[2] In *Bibliomania* and in a series of other works, all immediately recognisable by their excessive prose, their lavish illustration, and their fine printing, he more or less single-handedly created, if not the British fashion for book collecting, than certainly the way in which that fashion was understood and articulated for the better part of a century.

Figure 11.1 Henry Meyer, after Henry Edridge, *Thomas Frognall Dibdin* (1816), Blackie House Library and Museum.

This great publicist of the rare book came from a middle-class family in straitened circumstances and after taking his degree at Oxford embarked on an unsuccessful legal career in provincial England (see Figure 11.1). Within a few years, he had abandoned the law for the church and was ordained an Anglican priest in 1805, but his real passion lay in neither field; it lay in bibliomania. Beginning with his generously-plagiarised *Introduction to the Knowledge of Rare and Valuable Editions of the Greek and Latin Classics* (1802), he found his characteristic expression of that passion in print and in the entrée it gave him to the houses of the great collectors. A small, sharp-featured, curly-haired, outgoing man, full of sheer vitality and joy when confronted with early printing, he proved irresistible to (almost) everyone who met him.

One of those was Spencer. In 1802 Dibdin had sent him a copy of his *Introduction to the Classics*, receiving a polite invitation to Spencer House in return, and occasional letters followed but their acquaintance only blossomed towards the end of 1810.[3] As we have seen, Spencer was recovering from a lull in his collecting occasioned both by public office and by debt. At just the right time, Dibdin wrote to Spencer, on 17 November 1810, describing a rare volume of statutes printed by the early London printers John Lettou and William de Machlinia which he had found for 7 guineas (not a bad price) at one of the less fashionable city booksellers.[4] He ended with a flourish, "I have secured it" (i.e. requested it be set aside for him) "and, if your Lordship likes it, the book is your own!"[5]

Dibdin was fishing. He had already found himself acting as a book agent for collectors richer than himself and this was a straightforward bid for Spencer's patronage. Spencer responded, coolly but favourably, on the same day, asking Dibdin to forward the book to Spencer House.[6] By December, he was inviting Dibdin to spend Christmas at Althorp.[7] A bibliophilic friendship had been formed. The fruits of this friendship would be substantial for Spencer, life-changing for Dibdin.

One immediate effect of their closer connection was that Dibdin could now often be found at Spencer House, delightedly working his way through Spencer's collection, at least when its librarian, the long-serving and long-suffering Ocheda, was present to open the doors. The riches he found there caused him to daydream of a new book project. Writing to Spencer in July 1811 he reported that:

> I am meditating the execution of the most beautiful, curious &, I may say, valuable volume of foreign bibliography; devoted to Greek, Italian, Latin & French books, with elegant fac similes of Printers' devices, water marks &c in one thick octavo volume—to be printed in all the luxury of Bulmer's press. I shall send your Lordship a specimen of this work in the course of ten or twelve days.[8]

While Dibdin evidently wanted to use Spencer's library as a key point of reference, his initial conception was what modern bibliographers would now call a "universal" rather than a library-specific catalogue. In the intervening months, however, his ideas began to change and by October he had sent Spencer a specimen of his work in which he had taken the "liberty" of having "inserted your Lordship's name abruptly" upon the title page, i.e. of taking the first step towards making his book, not a study of incunables in general, but of Spencer's library in particular.[9]

Once again, whether by good fortune or close attention to his subject, Dibdin had made exactly the right move. Entering the third decade of his collecting life, Spencer still lacked anything more than a rudimentary catalogue of his library, and though his shelves were evidently in good order, finding books, much less knowing what he had, must have been an increasingly complex and fraught process. He approved of Dibdin's specimen and seems to have granted him even more unfettered access to the Spencer House library than he had previously enjoyed. By 28 October, Dibdin could write that he had been working there three days a week and gave the clearest outline yet of the book which was germinating in his mind,

> I consider a carefully executed 'Catalogue Raisonée' of your Lordship's early and most precious books, accompanied with accurate facsimiles, to form one of the finest foundations imaginable for a General History of Printing; and if it shall please God to grant me health and spirits, such a work—before I am three-score—shall be executed by me.
>
> Another six weeks application in St. James's Place, would enable me to go to press, shortly after Xmas, with that part of the 'Bibliotheca Spenceriana' which comprehends Divinity: my attention hitherto having been chiefly devoted to Bibles. But I will not ask for any favors or indulgences of admission into your Lordship's Library, which may be incompatible with previously established rules.[10]

This was the beginning of what would become the *Bibliotheca Spenceriana*, one of the most lavishly produced, and most bibliographically important, catalogues of a single library ever to be printed. Dibdin, as in all things, was grossly optimistic, however, in imagining that he could produce the theological volume by the beginning of the year. But we may forgive him that and join with Spencer who was delighted with Dibdin's progress and offered to have books put aside so that he could continue work even when Spencer, his family, and Ocheda had departed to Althorp for the winter.[11] Dibdin responded with characteristic enthusiasm and a description of his methods and goals which would guide him over, though he did not yet realise it, a further decade of scholarship:

> Three objects constantly present themselves to my view: 1st: to give a full & accurate account of the books contained in your Lordship's library: 2dly: to illustrate this account by making fac-similes & other ornaments of some of the most curious and early printed books contained in it; and 3dly. to bring together, to bear upon one point, all the bibliographical ~~know~~ learning which appertains to it: thus making the work accurate, splendid and erudite. If I fail, the fault will be my own.[12]

* * *

The catalogue was a project both men delighted in and it brought them closer together than Spencer had ever been with any of his previous agents. The correspondence of Spencer's daughter Sarah, then a spirited young woman in her early twenties and a keen observer of what transpired around her, offers a series of delightful vignettes of Dibdin at Althorp around this time. At one moment, "Papa and Mr. Dibdin have been quite full cry after a new-discovered black-letter book", at another the departure of guests from Althorp has meant that "we are reduced again to our own snug party, little Dibby included; who is become as inoffensive to us from habit, as poor dear Ocheda".[13] We could happily follow the two bibliophiles through their letters and trace in minute detail the gradual evolution of "little Dibby's" project from a simple "'Catalogue Raisonée" to the multi-volume work it would ultimately become, but other, more pressing, events detain us.

The first of these was the resolution of a long-standing peerage case which had unexpected and momentous consequences for the book world. John Ker, 3rd Duke of Roxburghe (1740–1804), was fabulously wealthy, the owner of one of the greatest libraries of his age, and, crucially, unmarried. When he died, the dukedom, its subsidiary titles, thousands of acres of land, Floors Castle, and, of course, the library, passed to his second cousin once removed William Bellenden, a half-pay army captain who must have been stunned by his good fortune. Alas, the elderly Bellenden only enjoyed his new estate for a year before he in turn died childless. A host of kinsfolk then eagerly competed for the title based on all of the more or less intricate claims of priority that could be made in such cases and it was only after an acrimonious battle lasting the better part of seven years that the right to become 5th Duke of Roxburghe was finally settled upon yet another distant cousin, James Innes (1736–1823), a Scottish laird until then best remembered for having sold the ancestral estate which his family had owned since Christmas 1160.[14] Perhaps unsurprisingly, the new duke immediately sought to pay both his legal fees and his pre-existing debts by sending his late cousin's library to the auction block.

And thus, the sale which would subsequently be remembered as the high watermark of bibliomania, began on 18 May 1812, lasting for forty-one days, "Sundays excepted", in the late duke's London townhouse.[15] The collection was outstanding, a library of 30,000 volumes which contained an unparalleled number of rarities: Elizabethan ballads, Arthurian romances, some of the first books printed in England, and about 120 incunabula. Small wonder, then, that its sale attracted immense excitement and was attended, either in person or through representatives, by every major collector in Britain. We have come across some of them before, but it is time to meet these men properly.

Spencer was there, of course, as was his foppish cousin, George Spencer, Marquess of Blandford (1766–1840), then busy bankrupting himself with improvements to his house, White Knights, near Reading, while expanding his own formidable library. He had been recently satirised by James Gillray as possessing "the inexpressible Air of Dignity,—the incomprehensible je-ne-sçais-Quoi of Elegance", i.e. looking as if he had swallowed a lobster.[16]

Richard Heber (1773–1833), the most obsessive of the collecting brotherhood, was also present: small and self-effacing, with a bald head protruding, dome-like, from a fringe of curly hair, seeming to hide behind his spectacles but following the course of every lot.[17] His clothes were elegant, neither the height of fashion nor outdated, his manner polite and friendly yet containing in it something many people did not quite like. His homosexuality, and his unfortunate habit of propositioning young men whilst drunk, would eventually see him in social exile on the continent a decade later.[18]

Lastly, we may mention one of the most striking figures in this room of strong personalities. He had been beautiful once and traces of that beauty remained, but at fifty-two he already looked gaunt and stretched, the bones of his face seeming to push against their skin like Voltaire and his elegant manner marred by thick five o'clock shadow.[19] William Beckford (1760–1844), slave owner, novelist, traveller, would-be architect, and the subject of scandals which put him well beyond the pale of polite society, was high on life. The price of sugar, the main product of his vast Caribbean plantations, was rising and he had money to burn.[20]

These were the key players in an auction immortalised both by its consequences in the book world, which we shall soon see, and by Dibdin's blow-by-blow account of "the Roxburghe fight", a bravura performance, even for him, who lovingly narrated, five years later, how "[t]he shouts of the victors, and the groans of the vanquished stunned and appalled you as you entered" the dining room-cum-auction house.[21] This should be taken with a grain of salt, but a tang of feverish excitement was certainly in the air.

The first day saw a victory for Spencer. Bidding boldly against John Dent, the London bookseller, he secured two of the earliest pieces of English printing, both from the press of William Caxton, for 100 guineas and £140 respectively. Having done so, with consummate suavity he "put each volume under his coat, and walked home with them in all the flush of victory and consciousness of triumph".[22] Spencer's obsession with England's first printer had begun several years before, as we have seen, but now it was in full flower and one can hardly blame him. William Caxton (*d.* 1492) was an English merchant long settled in Bruges who acquired a printing press in the early 1470s, began printing on the continent, and in 1475 or 1476 brought his press to England, the first of its kind. He established a flourishing trade there and by the eighteenth century was widely recognised as the iconic forefather of English printing. Little wonder, then, that he should be an object of fascination for Spencer.[23]

It was a good start, but Spencer did not have everything his way. Another Caxton, the 1480 *Mirrour of the World*, was the subject of hot bidding. 100 guineas, 150, "two hundred guineas!" a voice shouts and an over-excitable audience member lets out a loud whistle of amazement. Up and up the price goes until the hammer falls at the eye-watering sum of £351 15*s*. Who had spent so much? Not Spencer, but a quiet little bookseller named John Nornaville. The major players were baffled but then, "[t]he whisper went round... 'He is bidding for Bonaparte;' and all eyes were turned upon Mr. Nornaville".[24]

This was nonsense, of course. Napoleon, in the midst of preparing his massive and ill-starred invasion of Russia, had better things to do than bid for English bibliographical rarities. Instead, Nornaville was acting as agent for William Cavendish, 6th Duke of Devonshire (1790–1858), Spencer's nephew and another acquisitive collector.[25] That this was not obvious was due in part to the byzantine bidding methods used by these men. Sometimes they would bid in person, as Spencer had for his Caxtons earlier in the day, but as often if not more often, they would delegate the task to one or more booksellers, providing a list of desired lots together with what they were prepared to pay. Deputising a bookseller did not necessarily mean absence from the sale or, indeed, an attempt to conceal the source of the bid; Devonshire, whose connection to Nornaville was unknown to the others in the room, was himself standing behind the chair of another bookseller, Foss, who was quite openly bidding on the peer's behalf, and "occasionally restrain[ing] the impetuosity of his bidding".[26] Heber would sometimes bid against his own commissioned booksellers, though whether this was an attempt to disguise his intent or simply an eccentricity, no one was quite sure.

Reading an annotated auction catalogue, with its lists of buyers, can accordingly present a very strange image of a sale. The annotated copy of the Roxburghe sale catalogue now in the Bodleian Library tells us, for example, that a richly illuminated early sixteenth-century manuscript, the *Romances of the Knights of the Round Table (Romans des Chevaliers de la Table Ronde)*, was purchased for £78 15*s*. by the bookseller Robert Triphook. But Triphook was bidding on behalf of Blandford and the *Romans* accordingly found their way into the latter's library, after a commission was paid to Triphook, of course.[27] On the other hand, Blandford bid in person—with Triphook still in the room—for the *Storye of Frederyke of Jennen*, paying £65 2*s*. for the early Antwerp imprint.[28] The name of the immediate purchaser does not necessarily indicate the final destination of a book under the hammer.

And so the sale continued, day after exhausting day. It is highly doubtful that the great collectors attended with anything like regularity. More likely, with their catalogues in hand, they made their appearances when a particularly desirable or famous lot was in the offing but otherwise allowed their agents to do the work for them. Not every collector had the stamina of Heber, who seems to have attended nearly every day of the auction.

The twenty-seventh day, Wednesday, 17 June 1812, was different. The morning began with torrential rain, splashing London mud onto the boots of the crowds who gathered for the disposal of one of the greatest gems in the Roxburghe collection: the 1471 Valdarfer Boccaccio.[29] Boccaccio's bawdy tales of Renaissance Italy had been a favourite for centuries, read by everyone from dukes to postboys, but why had crowds gathered to see the sale of this particular copy?[30] Bound in "a faded yellow morocco binding" it was not an especially prepossessing volume, "a sound rather than a fine copy" as Dibdin put it, and many another product of fifteenth-century printing which sold that summer attracted little or no interest.[31] But this book, closeted away in the Roxburghe family's library for at least two generations, was universally believed to be the only complete copy of the first printed edition of Boccaccio; a rarity beyond price. "[N]o other perfect copy is yet known to exist", proclaimed George Nicol in his catalogue of the sale, "after all the fruitless researches of more than three hundred years".[32]

Unfortunately for Nicol and the breathless audience, not only was this not the only copy in existence, it was not even the first edition of Boccaccio. Modern scholarship knows of a second complete copy in Milan's Biblioteca Ambrosiana as well as two imperfect copies in the French Bibliothèque Nationale and the British Library respectively but, more to the point, twenty-first-century bibliographers are also relatively confident that Cristoforo Valdarfer's Venice edition of 1471 had been pipped to the post by an undated version, usually called the "Deo Gratias" edition, published probably in Naples and probably in 1470 (in Spencer's day, scholars supposed it to be the third edition and found it accordingly uninteresting).[33]

Hindsight, in bibliography as in all other things, is 20:20. What mattered to the crowd was that they *knew* they were watching the sale of one of the most sought-after books in Europe. One onlooker, the MP Thomas Johnes, reported the rumour that it could fetch as much as a thousand pounds, a price unheard of even in the current environment of febrile bibliomania.[34] We can sense the impatience as Evans doggedly worked his way through the day's sales. The Boccaccio was lot 6,292, but thirty-one lots of altogether less interesting Italian books must be ploughed through before the gem could emerge. One wonders if Heber, who bought fourteen of those thirty-one, did so simply to hurry things along. The perennially over-enthusiastic Dibdin probably prided himself on having purchased the first item of the day, a 1629 Venetian edition of an unreadable, and largely unread, then as now, save by Don Quixote, medieval romance, *Amadis of Gaul*.

During this prelude, Spencer leaned casually against the wall, just to the right of the auctioneer, while his cousin Blandford stood a little further down the room.[35] For all their insouciance, both were tightly coiled springs. At last, Evans proclaimed "lot 6,292" and a hush fell over the room.[36]

"One hundred guineas!" The speaker was a nobody, a country gentleman who seemed embarrassed at breaking the silence. His bravado was lazily followed by further bids up to 500 guineas, "masked and desultory" bids, designed only to flush out the real competitors.

"A thousand guineas". It was Spencer, still leaning against the wall. And "ten" rejoined Blandford.

"You might have heard a pin drop. All eyes were turned—all breathing well nigh stopped." And well they might. The two men were bidding sums which could have set up a man or woman in comfort for the rest of their life. On they went, back and forth, until Evans cried out, "two thousand pounds are offered by the Marquis" (i.e. Blandford). Spencer paused and one could see his determination falter. He stopped for a moment and spoke quietly to his son who was standing nearby. Then,

> "Two thousand two hundred and fifty pounds", Spencer said.
> And "ten", Blandford added.

The silence stretched on and on, every eye fixed on Evans's hammer which hung in the air for an eternity before descending with a crack. "Sold for £2,260 pounds to the Marquis of Blandford!"

Spencer must surely have felt at least as much relief as chagrin at his failure. He had narrowly avoided spending a sum which we might tentatively place as the equivalent of £2.6 million today on the battered volume which lay before them.[37] Just as surely, Blandford must have wondered, "my God. What have I done?"

* * *

The sale of the Valdarfer Boccaccio almost instantaneously became a symbol for something much larger: for the whole ridiculous, exclusive, and bankrupting phenomenon of bibliomania. Newspapers reported the phenomenal sum paid with mingled outrage and ridicule, while the punch-drunk bibliomanes, Spencer and Dibdin prominent among them, had a dinner in celebration, what would become the first meeting of the still-extant and still-august Roxburghe Club, now the oldest and most exclusive society dedicated to book collecting. Their first toast: "The cause of Bibliomania all over the world" (we may be confident that this was Dibdin's formulation).[38]

But what of Spencer himself? He had missed the Boccaccio this time but could console himself with many substantial and outstanding purchases. His two victories on day one were John Mirk's *Liber festivalis*, printed by Caxton about 1491, and *The Chastysing of Goddes Chyldren*, a small devotional pamphlet then attributed to Caxton but now recognised as being the production of his assistant and successor, Wynkyn de Worde (*d.* 1534/35), about 1494.[39] His best acquisition, however, came when he was still reeling from the narrow escape of the Boccaccio. He had bought the lot following the Valdarfer Boccaccio, a much less impressive 1516 Venetian edition of the same work which cost him £7, but that must have been a mere automatic response. Sixty lots later he returned to the fray and paid the stiff price of £215 5*s.* (the sixth highest price fetched by any book at the sale) for Caxton's *Blanchardyn and Eglantyne*, a late medieval romance printed about 1490.[40] For once, the catalogue was correct in saying that "there is no other copy known to exist". This remains true; only two further stray leaves are known in other collections.

Whether Spencer would have taken home his new Caxton and examined it with anything approaching calm seems doubtful, but we may do so from our own, less interested, vantage point and in so doing catch a flavour of the Duke of Roxburghe's magnificent library. *Blanchardyn* is an elegant quarto, bound in crushed red morocco with rich late eighteenth-century gold tooling and the duke's arms in the centre of each board; this was the most luxurious binding you could get in England if you were a member of the previous generation.[41] It is only when we reach the flyleaf, however, that we find a note in Spencer's hand explaining his willingness to pay so much for this volume and, perhaps, the fond memories it evoked.

It had, he wrote, previously been owned by the writer and collector George Mason (1735–1806) whose library was dispersed in several sales over the years 1798 and 1799.[42] As Spencer recounted it, the old Roxburghe and the still youthful Spencer had agreed not to oppose each other at Mason's sale (a sensible move to keep prices down) but both desperately wanted the *Blanchardyn*. Accordingly, when it came onto the block, they tossed a coin to see who would bid for the volume, and Spencer lost. It must have been a considerable satisfaction to recover it a little over a decade later.

The book as it now comes down to us has been "sophisticated" to the hilt (see Figure 11.2). Not only does it possess Roxburghe's luxury binding, an engraving of Caxton and a manuscript title page have been added as have numerous manuscript quasi-facsimile pages, red ruling, and other, we might say, "gussying up" such that the original type of Caxton is in many places drowned by well-meaning intrusions.

* * *

The fact of the matter was that early English printing was now more expensive than it had ever been. A good Caxton could reasonably be expected to fetch well over £100 and the works of his successors, Wynkyn de Worde and Richard Pynson, did not fall far behind.[43] Casting our minds back to the previous decades, we can see that these were exorbitant prices compared even to what Spencer had paid for the earliest incunables in the 1790s. Why? The simplest answer is a question of supply

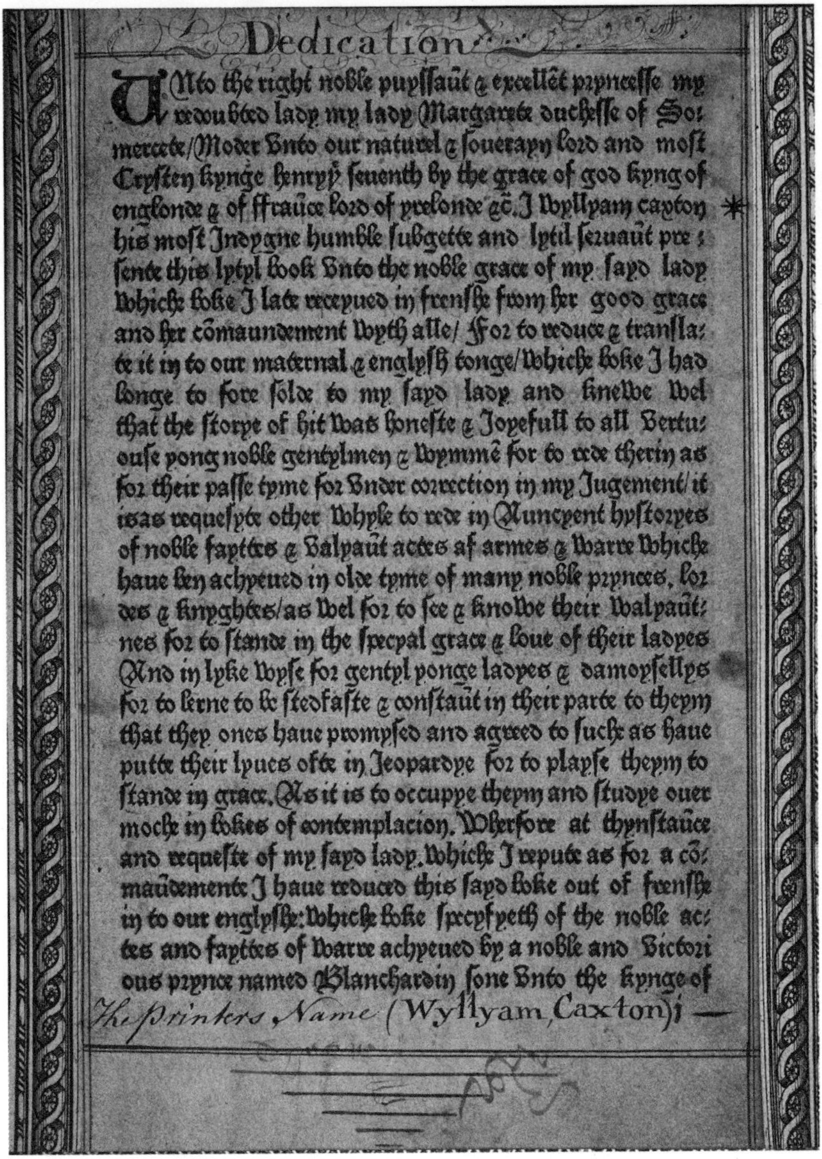

Dedication

Unto the right noble puyssaũt & excellẽt pryncesse my redoubted lady my lady Margarete duchesse of Somercete/Moder vnto our naturel & souerayn lord and most Crysten kynge henry ye seuenth by the grace of god kyng of englonde & of ffraũce lord of yrelonde &c. I wyllyam caxton his most Indygne humble subgette and lytil seruaũt presente this lytyl book vnto the noble grace of my sayd lady whiche boke I late receyued in frensshe from her good grace and her cõmaundement wyth alle/ For to reduce & translate it in to our maternal & englysh tonge/ which boke I had longe to fore solde to my sayd lady and knewe wel that the storye of hit was honeste & Ioyefull to all vertuouse yong noble gentylmen & wymmẽ for to rede therin as for their passe tyme for vnder correction in my Jugement/ it was requesyte other whyle to rede in Auncyent hystoryes of noble fayttes & valyaũt actes af armes & warre which haue ben achyeued in olde tyme of many noble prynces, lordes & knyghtes/as wel for to see & knowe their walyaũtnes for to stande in the specyal grace & loue of their ladyes And in lyke wyse for gentyl yonge ladyes & damoysellys for to lerne to be stedfaste & constaũt in their parte to theym that they ones haue promysed and agreed to suche as haue putte their lyues ofte in Jeopardye for to playse theym to stande in grace. As it is to occupye theym and studye ouer moche in bokes of contemplacion. Wherfore at thynstaũce and requeste of my sayd lady. which I repute as for a cõmaũdemente I haue reduced this sayd boke out of frensshe in to our englysshe: whiche boke specyfyeth of the noble actes and fayttes of warre achyeued by a noble and victorious prynce named Blanchardin sone vnto the kynge of

The Printers Name (Wyllyam Caxton)i —

Figure 11.2 *Blanchardyn and Eglantyne* (Westminster: William Caxton, *c.*1490), dedication recto, John Rylands 15027.

and demand. The great English collectors, Spencer among them, were fascinated by their own country's typographical history and ardently desired examples, better yet, long series, of that history but, as a rule, very few copies of these items had survived. Accordingly, not only did they fetch eye-watering prices at auction, but other, more creative, means were required to source unobtainable imprints.

One option, just as on the continent, was to see what might be gently pried loose from institutional collections, but in England such an action had to be undertaken with considerably more circumspection. On 6 October 1811 Spencer wrote to Dibdin that:

> I have had a great piece of black letter fortune within these few days, having added to my collection of Caxtons the three following, viz., the first edition of the *Game of Chess*, a perfect and very fine copy; the *History of Jason*, perfect and pretty good as to condition; and the *History of Reynart the foxe*, perfect and very fine. All acquired from the same quarter, and at the same time.[44]

So far so good, but Spencer was not going to trust to paper the knowledge that this "same quarter" had been the Chapter Library of Lincoln Cathedral.[45] They had formed part of a bequest to the cathedral in 1681 from Michael Honeywood, Dean of Lincoln, and their sale, had it been made public, would likely have raised eyebrows at the very least.

Dibdin was not slow to take the hint, but he lacked Spencer's discretion. Over the course of 1813 and 1814 he embarked on delicate negotiations with the dean and chapter of Lincoln for the acquisition of three more Caxtons and a series of other early books, writing to Spencer, with very questionable truthfulness, that "I have no wish to make money by them—but may reasonably hope that the expenses of myself and family (somewhere about £35) might be defrayed by this adventurous & spirited offer."[46] This was nonsense and Spencer probably knew it, though he chose not to say so.

On 7 October 1814 matters were concluded and Dibdin bought the nineteen items, bound in six volumes, which he had been negotiating for, offering the large sum of £525. Dibdin had given a promissory note payable at eighty-five days, meaning that he had a little under three months to find the money with which to pay the clergy at Lincoln.[47] He had to act fast and it was probably this pressure which led him to the inadvisable decision of publicly advertising his acquisitions under the equally inadvisable title of *Here begyneth a littel tome and hathe to name the Lincolne Nosegay: beynge a brefe table of certaine bokes in the posession of Maister Thomas Frognall Dibdin clerk. Which bookes be to be sold to him who shal gyue the moste for ye same*. It was not Dibdin's finest moment and his efforts at sixteenth-century prose composition are painful to read.

Fortunately for him, while Spencer was initially hesitant, by 31 August 1814 he had come round to purchasing four of the six volumes for £575 10*s*., giving Dibdin a clear profit of £50 as well as whatever he could make off the remaining two items.[48] His single largest purchase was Caxton's 1480 *Cronicles of Englond* and *Discripcion of Britayne*, described in Dibdin's cod-Tudor English as "perfait and meruelouslye clene copies of these moste rare bokes, and are bounde in one tome", for which he paid £210.[49] While Dibdin made his money back, the printed *Lincolne Nosegay* did not go away and its fame spread disproportionate to the small number of copies actually printed. Writing a generation later, the collector and bibliographer Beriah Botfield echoed what seems to have been a general condemnation of the whole affair, thundering that "the guardians of the temple slept, and Mammon prevailed".[50] Doing his best to be impartial, Botfield noted that:

> The loss thus sustained by the ancient Library of Lincoln Cathedral by the sale of the volumes thus inconsiderately, and in my opinion unjustifiably, detached, was compensated in some degree by the purchase of other books with the proceeds, and the addition to the original Collection of the books thus purchased... Much as I am inclined to disallow the right of any corporate body to alienate the property bequeathed to it by any such process of commutation, I think it right to annex a full account of the books purchased, that the reader may be enabled to form his own judgment upon the literary discretion of the Dean and Chapter.[51]

The reader could hardly disagree with Botfield as the long list of modern books so acquired contained rather too much ephemeral bulk (e.g. "the Gentleman's Magazine from its commencement in 1731 to 1816") and too little which could justify "the sacrifice of books which it is nearly impossible to replace".[52]

Holding the Caxton *Cronicles* in my hands and puzzling through its own complicated provenance (it has been sophisticated to make it appear to be the 1480 edition, but is really the 1482 with a false colophon), I could not help but compare this incident with so many similar acts of "purchase" or "exchange" undertaken by Spencer's continental agents. There, any risk of bad publicity was minimal, if not non-existent, and there was no danger of public censure like that which Botfield visited upon Dibdin and his collaborators at Lincoln. To a very real extent, this remains the case, but does the morality of such a transaction really change simply because one holding institution is continental and Catholic while another is British and Anglican? I do not think it does. We shall—indeed, we must—return to this question in due course.

TWELVE

Missteps

Rarely did Spencer make a misstep in his collecting. His sharp focus, his ready willingness to say no to unwanted items, and his deep pockets combined to make for a collector who was not easily swayed but who, when he wanted something, would move heaven and earth to get it. In the case of the Alchorne collection, however, Spencer made a misstep not once, but twice: first by not buying the library, then by buying it.

This requires some explanation. The imposingly named Stanesby Alchorne (1733–1800)—his given name was the surname of his grandfather Thomas Stanesby, a well-known London woodwind maker—rose from a relatively humble background as an apothecary to the posts of Assay Master at the Royal Mint and "Demonstrator of Plants" at the Chelsea Physic Garden.[1] He was also a collector with a discriminating eye and a taste for incunables, especially English ones. His was a small library, only one hundred and twenty books, but few libraries, large or small, could boast, as Alchorne's could, of nine books printed by William Caxton.

Alchorne gave his estate to his niece Sarah, who had looked after him in his old age, and she rapidly disposed of the library to the ever-present Thomas Payne.[2] In 1806 Payne offered the entire collection to Spencer for £1,200, a substantial but hardly unreasonable sum given the apparent quality of the books it contained. But Spencer, having, as Dibdin wrote, "just entered upon the important situation of Secretary of State for the Home Department…had absolutely no time either to consider the proposition, or, if considered, to examine the books out of which such proposition grew".[3] So he turned it down. Knowing what we do of his financial situation in 1806, he couldn't have afforded it anyway (which was probably the real reason for him declining to entertain Payne's proposal). By the time he began to have second thoughts, it was too late; Payne had sold Alchorne's books to Thomas Johnes of Hafod, a bibliophilically-inclined Welsh gentleman whose country house, including his library, had just been destroyed in a fire.[4]

There the matter rested for seven years. Thomas Johnes happily rebuilt his house at Hafod, buying more books as well as a lot of rather gaudy household furnishings from William Beckford's Fonthill Abbey sale in 1807, and incorporating the "Bibliotheca Alchorniana" into his own collection.[5] But running a private press, buying books, and beautifying his estate were all expensive propositions and after the death of his beloved daughter Marianne in 1811, Johnes lost the will to keep going. "I am an extinct collector", he wrote, "for although I enjoy what I have…for who am I toiling"? This led him, in January 1813, to write to Dibdin outlining the plan of selling his library and gingerly enquiring whether Spencer, who he well knew had refused the Alchorne books before, might be inclined to buy them now. But this came with a sting in the tail. Johnes was no fool and clarified that "as books since I bought it have risen so amazingly, [would] Lord Spencer…give me *three* times what I paid"?[6]

£3,600 was an enormous sum by any calculation, but Spencer had been prepared to pay £2,250 for the Valdarfer Boccaccio alone in the previous year, so it was clearly not out of the question. Dibdin instantly sprang into action, communicating the contents of Johnes's letter to Spencer on 23 January and even going so far as to "cut up my handsomely bound copy of the Catalogue of the Hafod Library, in order that no time may be lost, and that your Lordship, from a perusal of the enclosed, may be better enabled to make up your mind…on the prudence of the purchase".[7] "Prudence" was the watchword here and Dibdin, pleased though he was by the idea that the Alchorne collection might "become a tributary stream to that of the SPENCER" was cautious, counter-offering 3,000 guineas to Johnes.

Letters flew thick and fast between Dibdin and Johnes, with Spencer proposing sums in the background. Already, however, Dibdin was sounding a note of worry, first about the number of duplicates in the Alchorne collection which would need to be sold subsequently and second about the condition of the books. By 26 January, he had written to Johnes seeking reassurance that some of the key items in the collection were perfect (i.e. containing all leaves as called for without damage, facsimiles, etc.) and especially whether "the Caxtons, unless otherwise expressed, were presumed to be perfect".[8]

Johnes's answer was decidedly unsatisfactory. "I cannot answer your queries as to the books", he wrote, "but they are precisely in the very same condition (which was excellent) that I received them in…in truth the moment I was forced to determine on parting with them, I took the whole of them down, and nothing now will make me look at them again."[9] As Dibdin confided to Spencer when reporting this, "his answer…to my queries…makes me very fidgetty, if not tremulous". Worse still, Johnes had somehow talked himself up to £4,000 as a reasonable price for the collection, with Dibdin returning with £3,500 and cautioning Spencer against any further compromise: "I should certainly advise you not to extend your offer."[10]

Negotiations continued between Kensington and Hafod. The lack of a much-desired red-printed colophon to Johnes's copy of the *St Albans Chronicle* led to the knocking of £100 off the proposed £3,500, but finally, on 9 February, Dibdin was able to write that "the negotiation is concluded; and the Alchorne Collection may on Friday be on its way to St. James's Place".[11] While not explicitly stated, £3,400 seems to have been the agreed-on sum.

But all was not well on more than one front. First, a postscript in a letter from Dibdin on 3 February makes it clear that Spencer had, so far, been concealing the negotiations from his family.[12] It had not been long since his heavy purchases at the Roxburghe sale and the family's finances were still sufficiently straitened that this impulsive expenditure of over three thousand pounds was evidently not (or not yet) for the ears of Lady Spencer and the children. Second, and perhaps even worse, the books still remained an imperfectly known quantity, at least where condition was concerned. Writing after the fact with uncharacteristic acidity (he normally treated Spencer as something halfway between a beloved older brother and a minor deity), Dibdin recalled that:

> I proposed visiting Hafod for the sake of examining the books; but his Lordship thought such an undertaking, at such a time of the year, perfectly unnecessary; and thanking me for my zeal thus manifested on the occasion—and trusting to his own supposed perfect recollection of the *condition* of the books in question—he consented to the terms.[13]

Caveat emptor. When the books reached London in mid-February, "the memories of all parties, including even that of Mr. Payne, turned out to be somewhat *treacherous*". We can imagine the crestfallen faces of Dibdin and Spencer as they opened the boxes from Wales only to find that the books, which had cost so much and had been so long awaited, "were dirty, and eke defective, copies—and the duplicates were manifestly numerous". All nine Caxtons were already present in Spencer's collection and only one was a clearly better copy. Meanwhile, almost all of the early Latin incunables were also duplicates such that of the one hundred and twenty items in the Alchorne collection, no fewer than forty-five were inferior duplicates of items already in Spencer's library.[14] Aside from one Caxton, a Boethius which we shall meet presently, the few successes of the purchase were some early items from the presses of Caxton's successors Wynykn De Worde and Richard Pynson as well as the *St Albans Chroncicle* which had worried Dibdin (it turned out to be entirely lacking the colophon).

A sale to make good at least some of Spencer's losses was therefore imperative. Dibdin had been planning one almost from the beginning and was keen that it should be rushed forward quickly, "not an hour must now be lost; and the Stanley fever must not be suffered to abate, before the Alchorne infection takes place".[15] Unfortunate metaphor aside, Dibdin was referring to the keenly anticipated sale of the library of the Lancashire MP Colonel Thomas Stanley at the end of April and beginning of May 1813.[16] If they could ensure that the Alchorne rejects entered the market while collectors were still riding the high of the

Stanley sale, which promised to be the next major auction after the Roxburghe, they could hopefully be assured of good results.

Spencer, no doubt smarting from his error, bid modestly at the Stanley sale, though he could not quite resist commissioning Dibdin to obtain for him the first, undated edition of the collection of medieval Italian literature known as the *Cento novelle antiche* (or simply *Il Novellino*) for the stiff price of £59 17*s.*[17] A few weeks later, on 22 May, the remainder of Alchorne's library together with other duplicates which had been building up in the Spencer collection was sold in the course of a single day.[18]

Cutting through the morass of purple prose, there was no doubt that Dibdin was worried. "I will not dissemble the sensations I felt before and during the sale", he wrote. "Having been in a great measure instrumental to the 'striking of the bargain'... I was naturally and necessarily anxious that [Spencer] should, on no account, be a loser in the end!" Bidding began slowly and good books in the opening lots went for modest, uninspiring sums. But this was still close to the high-water mark of bibliomania and there were men in the room whose pockets were at least as deep as Spencer's: Thomas Grenville, the insatiable Richard Heber, the almost equally insatiable Mark Masterman Sykes (1771–1823), and the young Duke of Devonshire. All made substantial purchases, nowhere more so than amongst the Caxtons, none of which went for under £50 and the most expensive of which, *The Book named Cordyale*, was knocked down to the Royal Library for £127. Devonshire commanded the field, acquiring three Caxtons and many of the other best pieces. All in all, Spencer made £1,769 off the sale.[19]

Writing after the fact, Dibdin claimed that:

> it was found, upon adding the amount of the *Alchorne Articles* in the *sale*—to that of the sums allowed, and liberally allowed, for the articles, from the same library, *retained*—that his Lordship had 'brought himself home' within about 25*l.* Thus nice was the calculation, and thus fortunate the result![20]

While it seems implausible that Dibdin would have lied outright in a public forum (this claim is found in his *Bibliographical Decameron* of 1817), it is also hard to reconcile this claim with even the most basic of calculations. Dibdin seems to be saying that the seventy-five items retained from the Alchorne library were collectively valued at about £1,700–1,800, an average, at the high end, of £24 per volume. This is generous at best and it is tempting to imagine that both Dibdin and Spencer were using this calculation to make themselves feel a bit better about what, more pragmatically conceived, had been a rather bad mistake.

Buying the Alchorne collection for Payne's 1806 price of £1,200 would have been an undeniably good bargain, regardless of duplicates; buying it for £3,400, getting only a few good items from it and then reselling the duplicates for half that sum seems, by any measure, to be a very doubtful prospect, but perhaps we should reserve our judgement until we, unlike Spencer in January of 1813, have actually looked at some of the books.

One good example is an early Caxton, Boethius's *De consolatione philosophiae* of about 1478.[21] The binding is a modest but not unpleasing russia (leather, often calf, tanned with willow and curried with birch bark extract, which was originally a distinctive product of northwestern Russia, hence its name) with a gold-tooled border of snails and insects, probably commissioned by Alchorne himself, and his engraved bookplate appears, as was his slightly eccentric custom, on the rear pastedown (the half of the endpaper which has been pasted onto the inside of the board) of the volume. I confess, having read Dibdin's account beforehand, I was prepared for a truly foul book, but by the standards of modern bibliographers it is actually a pleasingly unsophisticated copy, a little dirty, a little stained, and full of scribbles (see Figure 12.1), but hardly contemptible. All the same, it is not in the condition to which Spencer was accustomed and, given that the title itself is not tremendously rare, was hardly an outstanding catch.[22]

If Spencer had cared about provenance, he would have found it a much more exciting volume. It is full of writing in multiple hands, some, rather surprisingly, in Spanish, as well as the names of numerous sixteenth- and seventeenth-century owners: Francis Shewarde, Ambrose Niclas, Nicholas Morgan, and Hugonis Mercator (presumably a Latinising Hugh Merchant) amongst others. Such rich traces of former owners are now immensely precious to bibliographers, but that attitude is far

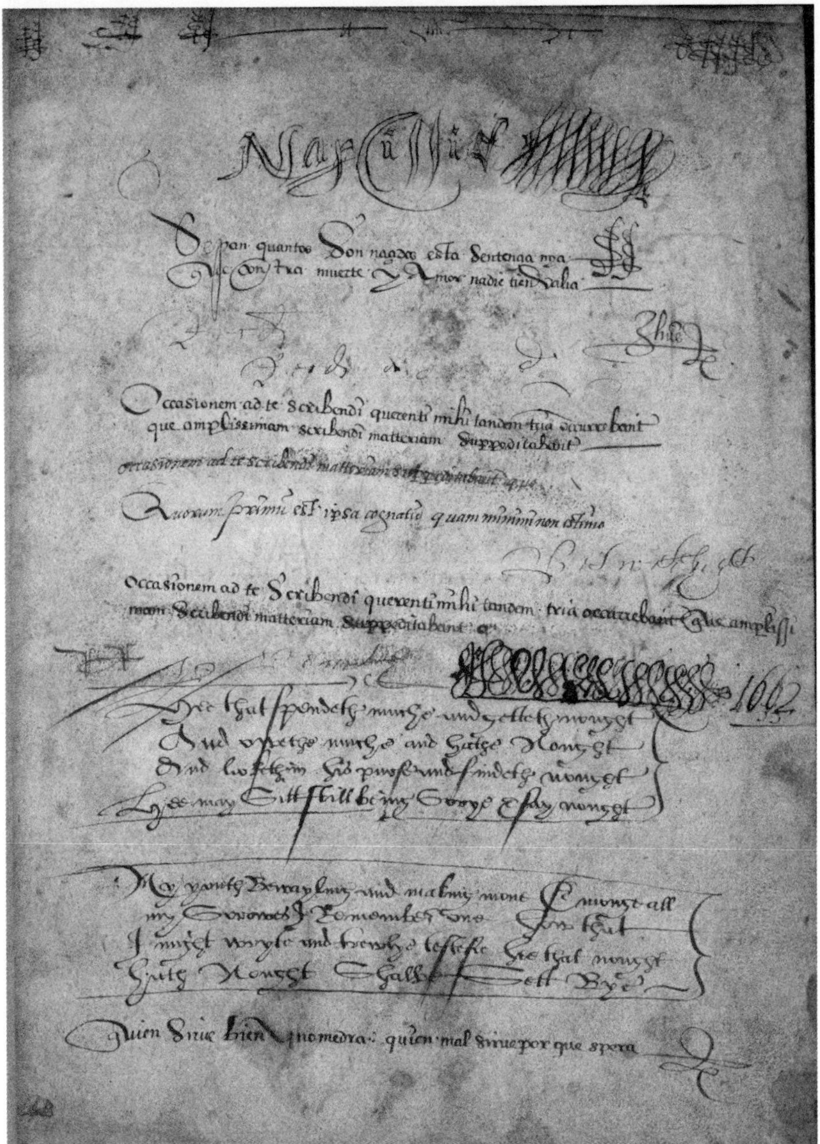

Figure 12.1 Boethius, *De consolatione philosophiae* (Westminster: William Caxton, c.1478), front flyleaf recto, John Rylands 15388.

removed from Spencer's and we can, even if only intellectually, join with him and Dibdin in their disappointment at finding their new purchase to be such a ratty, well-used volume.

Indeed, this proves to be the rule amongst the Alchorne books, and one more example may suffice for the whole. It is none other than Alexander Barclay's 1509 translation of Sebastian Brant's *Ship of Fools* with which this book began.[23] It is bound in russia identical to the Boethius and with the same snail and insect tooling, suggesting these bindings were commissioned by Alchorne himself, and is similarly messy inside. The initial leaf, a bold, full-page woodcut of the printer, Richard Pynson's, coat of arms, has been badly worn and its edges damaged. At least three ownership inscriptions are visible, though only one, "John Taylor", is legible. The final leaf contains further provenance—"Doctor Rydley", "D Gardyner", "J: G: 1621"—and the leaves are often stained and dirty at the edges, with more than one ancient grubby fingerprint visible, the ghost of a page turned hundreds of years ago. Most delightfully, there is a large ink stain on one of the pages describing the Book Fool. Again, it is a book that tempts a modern far more than it would have Spencer.

* * *

If the Alchorne books proved disappointing, there were other more important matters to keep both Dibdin and Spencer occupied. Dibdin had been patiently working on the ever-expanding project of Spencer's library catalogue since 1811. The original plan of "an octavo volume of some 500 pages" had long since gone by the board and by April 1812 he was publicly advertising it in the *Gentleman's Magazine* as a substantial two-volume work in super-royal octavo (i.e. closer to the size of a quarto than an octavo). This was soon expanded to three volumes, now costing seven guineas to subscribers or eighteen guineas on large paper, steep prices for a new book, though Spencer, who had enthusiastically approved the expansion into three volumes, felt that "the price proposed is by no means high".[24] Even this, however, proved inadequate and by 22 November 1813 "a <u>fourth</u> Volume seems a <u>settled</u> thing!"[25]

The first three volumes, having been in the press for some time, were issued in January 1814 and Dibdin, in his *Reminiscences*, could not resist recalling their success with satisfaction:

> Never did the bibliomaniacal pulse of the British public beat with a livelier throb. The Allies had just then, in a manner, taken possession of Paris. The bells had scarcely ceased to ring, and the guns to be fired. A dozen hackney coaches, in all directions, were filled with the Spencerian tomes... Before sunset on that same day, I have reason to *know* that a copy of this work—although obviously in an imperfect state—was sold for 12*l.* 12*s.*; and before that day three months a copy had reached the sum of 15*l.* 15*s.* As to the Large Paper, the price galloped up quickly to *Forty Guineas*; just double that of the publication.[26]

Dibdin was still worried about the substantial sums of money he had invested in the work and he had good reason to be. By the time the final volume, containing the all-important indices, was issued in 1815, he was dealing with increasing numbers of booksellers returning unsold copies, or, worse, demanding that he buy them back at inflated prices.[27] By 11 November 1815 Dibdin was, or so he claimed,

> sometimes tempted to "sink or burn and destroy" the remaining 60 or 70 copies in hand of Vol. IV: as there seems no immediate chance of disposing of them, and as it would serve those booksellers right who refused taking them—and thus render their imperfect copies nearly useless, and give additional value to the perfect ones.[28]

This is probably just Dibdinian persiflage and it is unclear whether Spencer took it particularly seriously or, if he did, whether he cared (he kept himself largely aloof from Dibdin's increasingly involved financial affairs). What we do know is that in early December 1815 a finely-bound large paper copy of all four volumes reached Spencer at Althorp. He reported with pleasure to Dibdin that:

> [it] is arrived quite safe, & makes so brilliant an appearance, that it has excited the Admiration of every one here, & has even made Ocheda quite eager to place it in its Class where it may be most conspicuous.[29]

For many a bibliographer, the monumental accomplishment of the first four volumes would have been more than adequate, especially given the risky financial status of the project, but Dibdin could neither control his spending nor not be writing a book. Having completed his massive three-volume *Bibliographical Decameron; or, Ten Days Pleasant Discourse upon Illuminated Manuscripts, and Subjects Connected with Early Engraving, Typography, and Bibliography*, an expansion *ad nauseam* on the dialogic conceit he had first deployed in *Bibliomania*, at top speed, by 1817 he was already scheming a plan for another Spencerian project. While visiting Spencer at Althorp for Christmas 1816 they had apparently discussed the possibility of a volume describing the house and its contents, half-guidebook, half-collection catalogue. By 8 September 1817, he could write that he was enclosing "a rough announce" of the work, imagined as a companion to the *Bibliotheca Spenceriana* and likely to "be acceptable to a larger class of readers".[30] Spencer approved and by 5 December Dibdin happily presented a revised prospectus for the work, now titled *Aedes Althorpianae; or, a Descriptive Catalogue of the Pictures and Library of Althorp*.[31]

The events which will be described in Chapters 14 and 15, however, meant that Dibdin only turned to the project in earnest in 1821, four years after he had issued his prospectuses. Much had changed in the meantime. Volume I, which described the principal rooms, their pictures, and a small selection of the books, together with a lengthy account of the Spencer family's history, seems to have done reasonably well. Volume II, which was framed explicitly as a "Supplement to the Bibliotheca Spenceriana" and contained bibliographical descriptions of a further 313 incunables acquired since the publication of the original four volumes, did not. As Dibdin put it in his *Reminsicences*:

> To speak the truth, the second volume was a sort of drag-chain to the first. The public "gan tire" of *Fifteeners*; by which I mean books printed in the fifteenth century…Had not the proposals been absolute and irrevocable, by the advance of *one-third* of the money due upon the *two* volumes, the second might have more judiciously made its appearance [later][32]

Somewhat contradictorily, he was also aggrieved that space and finances did not permit the stuffing of yet more books from the Spencer collection into volume two, particularly those issued from the Aldine Press or previously owned by the Renaissance bibliophile Jacques-Auguste de Thou.[33] Regardless, the *Aedes* seem to have been one of Dibdin's worst financial failures, with 28 August 1825, three years after their publication, finding him selling the remaining 120 unsold copies of the edition to Payne and Harding at the steeply discounted price of £3 10*s.* a copy (the subscription price had been £6 6*s.* for small paper copies) to pay off outstanding debts incurred by their publication.[34]

The *Aedes* was not only a financial disaster, it strained relations between Dibdin and Spencer himself. Dibdin had apparently been working at breakneck speed in the latter part of 1821 and when he sent a substantial clutch of proofs to Spencer on 11 December he was more honest than diplomatic when writing that "of course, I expect many inaccuracies to appear, & many hiatuses to be filled up".[35] This remarkably cavalier attitude, brought about, perhaps, by the friendly relations he had enjoyed with his patron for so many years, led to a lengthy response from Spencer on 13 December in which his frustration with the situation was only too visible.

"The haste with which you are proceeding in your work", he wrote, "affords me so short a time to give it that attention which appears to be absolutely necessary." In the past, he had examined Dibdin's proofs simply as a friendly corrector of "mere typographical errors",

> but in the present instance, when the title of the work itself, & the nature of its contents, according to your present plan of it, connects it so intimately with myself, I feel a much greater degree of responsibility as to what it may contain, & a much stronger desire that it may contain nothing which shall draw upon me the imputations to which such a description of my habitation, & in some instances of the habits & life of myself & my family, living as well as dead, are too liable.

More than anything, Spencer hated that the whole production might seem, to outside observers, simply a monument to his own vanity (an interpretation to which Dibdin's effulgent and genuflecting prose could too easily lead). Accordingly, Spencer went over the proofs with a fine-toothed comb, apologising that "I have been very liberal of erasures", but even in his attempts to politely soften the blow, he was unable to conceal his anger at what he felt was Dibdin distinctly overstepping his bounds. "[I] must enforce in the strongest manner", he wrote,

> my injunctions to you to stop short, as soon as you have traced down the owners of Althorp to the present Owner; as it was not in my contemplation when I consented to your giving a Catalogue Raisonné of my books & pictures, to constitute you, or any one else, my Biographer, or that of any part of my present family; and I have a decided & mortal aversion to that sort of thing which is called living biography, as it must either be fulsome panegyric, or offensive satyre, & very often in attempting to be neither the one nor the other, produces an effect on the object of it, as distressing & disturbing & disagreeable as either of them could be.[36]

Rarely do we see Spencer so vulnerable as in this letter. One could easily be forgiven for not wanting one's life history penned by an author as given to bathos and malapropisms as Dibdin, but Spencer's terror here is much more visceral; a deep nerve had been touched. That that nerve should be connected to the writing of his biography is particularly striking given, as we have seen before, how oddly self-effacing Spencer could be in the midst of his collections. Far from his larger-than-life sister, the Duchess of Devonshire, he was so often simply a shadow cast amongst his bookcases. This letter suggests that absence was not unintentional.

Dibdin responded in a flutter, clearly worried about the mounting cost of proof corrections and eager to cater to Spencer's wishes as soon as possible, but the damage had been done. From here on their friendly closeness of the 1810s was increasingly marred by unease and frustration, largely centring around Dibdin's inability to manage money.

Nonetheless, his labours in the collection at Althorp continued and the sizeable acquisition detailed in Chapter 15 led to a seventh and final Spencerian volume, *A Descriptive Catalogue of the Books Printed in the Fifteenth Century, Lately Forming Part of the Library of the Duke di Cassano Serra, and Now the Property of George John Earl Spencer, K.G. with a General Index of Authors and Editions Contained in the Present Volume, and in the Bibliotheca Spenceriana and Ædes Althorpianae*.

It was finished in May 1823 and Dibdin had evidently learned from his misadventure with the *Aedes*. The preface contained praise for Spencer and his library in Dibdin's usual superlative-laden prose, but this time it came guarded round with its author's protestations. "I cannot give up, without a struggle for their retention", Dibdin wrote,

> those passages, or sentiments, in which your Lordship, as connected with your Library, is, I submit, properly and fairly mentioned: and those passages must, and will, be considered by the world, as having been penned in the most free & unbiased manner—and without the knowledge & participation of your Lordship.[37]

How far he succeeded in convincing Spencer is unclear; we have only the final version, not the proofs which accompanied this letter. That some trimming occurred seems likely from the highly circumspect language of the final preface. "I have done everything in my power", Dibdin wrote,

> to establish, on a firm foundation, the celebrity of a LIBRARY, of which the remembrance can only perish with every other record of individual fame. I will say nothing of the high and honourable character of its NOBLE OWNER, either in his public or private capacity; but I may be permitted to remark, that, it is even possible for the names of COLBERT and HARLEY to be forgotten, as Ministers, while they will be for ever remembered as Collectors of MANUSCRIPTS and PRINTED BOOKS.[38]

And so, twelve years after its inception, the project of publishing a catalogue of Spencer's library reached its conclusion (see Figure 12.2). Even then it was by no means comprehensive.

In all, 1,715 incunables were described as well as the several hundred post-incunables listed in volume one of the *Ædes*. But by the time this series of publications was finished, the library as a whole consisted of over 20,000 volumes; the catalogues represent, at best, only about 10% of the whole and they did not even cover all of the incunables. One of the finding aids inherited by the John Rylands Library is a thin quarto, heavily used and now shedding leather dust like thistledown, which describes itself as "A Catalogue of some Books which are in the Althorp Library which were Printed in the Fifteenth Century. But are not Described in

Figure 12.2 The seven volumes of the *Bibliotheca Spenceriana* and *Ædes Althorpianae*, Blackie House Library and Museum.

Dibdin's Bibliotheca Spenceriana".[39] It itemises perhaps a further 250 incunables not noticed elsewhere.

Partial as it may be, the *Bibliotheca Spenceriana* remains one of the great milestones in the history of library catalogues. While its entries often seem egregiously long and filled with pointless detail to a bibliographer with the internet at her fingertips, the unprecedented level of detail, the notes on other copies, and the careful attention to the history of typography made it an important reference work for several generations of bibliographers, despite the inevitable Dibdinian errors.

They are also beautiful books. If nothing else, Dibdin was very good at ensuring his productions were generously margined, pleasingly printed, and full of woodcuts and engravings illustrating their subject. Published in imperial octavo, large paper copies are almost folios in size and their heavy paper stock makes them as thick as dictionaries—it is a monumental set in every sense of the word.

In following the torturous history of this great catalogue, however, we have run far ahead of our story. It is still 1814 and Europe must endure the violence of the Hundred Days before the Napoleonic Wars will finally reach their end on the field of Waterloo. And for Spencer some of his greatest acquisitions still lie in the future.

THIRTEEN

The passing of a generation

"I congratulate Your Lordship and the World on Bonaparte's wretched End", Horn wrote to Spencer.[1] After Napoleon's brief return to power in the summer of 1815, he had been decisively defeated at the Battle of Waterloo and exiled to Saint Helena. For the first time since 1789 Europe could breathe a sigh of relief as the Treaty of Paris was signed on 20 November and the Napoleonic Wars were finally brought to an end.

For bibliophiles, and for all Britons, it marked a dramatic shift away from two decades of isolation, largely cut off from the continent and from continental markets, to a world in which they could not only easily trade with France, Germany, or Italy, but could visit them as well (both Spencer and Dibdin did so in due course). It also marked a re-energising of Spencer's long-standing collaborations with men like della Lena, d'Elci, and Horn as letters could more easily find their way across the newly peaceful map of Europe.

The now elderly Abbé della Lena could still be found in his ancestral town of Bagni di Lucca. He had turned sixty-eight in 1815 and would die three years later, but in his old age continued to offer books to Spencer. This was no doubt in large part due to his melancholy situation. The bankruptcy of a merchant "has taken away from me almost all of my inheritance", he wrote, and he spent the last year of his life trying, with increasing desperation, to sell several books to Spencer, most likely items from his own collection.[2] Chief amongst these was the 1478 edition of Torquemada's *Meditationes*, the same book whose first edition Spencer had so desperately attempted to obtain through Horn a decade before. While Spencer initially refused and the book, "a beautiful copy…exceptionally rare and not to be found in all of Italy", was still being offered in della Lena's final surviving letter, dated 25 March 1817, the abbé's predicament seems to have eventually softened the earl. We cannot be absolutely certain, but the copy of the 1478 *Meditationes* now in the Rylands bears a Spencer accession number from about this period and is likely identical with that offered by della Lena.[3]

By contrast, peacetime found the Chevalier d'Elci happily ensconced in Vienna and continuing to build one of the few collections which could rival Spencer's. But here too changes were afoot. With the final defeat of the French, he returned, at least part of the time, to his beloved Florence and in 1818, now well into his sixties, made the most dramatic decision a bibliophile could make. He announced to Spencer in a letter of 7 June 1818: "I have made an act consigning all my books to the Biblioteca Laurenziana…*inter vivos* as a mark of my attachment to my Fatherland."[4] The formal act of donation was dated 15 July and the books eventually followed, though the lavish printed catalogue which marked the donation only appeared in 1826, two years after d'Elci's death.[5] It is in very large part due to d'Elci's donation that the great Florentine library, the Biblioteca Medicea Laurenziana, is now such a rich storehouse of incunables. A neo-classical rotunda named after him still forms part of the library buildings and was used as a reading room until the latter half of the twentieth century.

A postscript to d'Elci's letter of 1818 came nine years later, after the posthumous publication of his catalogue. On 6 April 1827, Giovanni degli Alessandri, sometime director of the Uffizi in Florence, wrote a flowery note to Spencer begging him to accept a copy of the d'Elci catalogue, courtesy of the Grand Duke of Tuscany, in the hopes that his long-standing acquaintance with d'Elci would make the gift all the more agreeable.[6] Spencer's collection is frequently referred to as a point of comparison throughout the catalogue and the *Bibliotheca Spenceriana* is regularly cited. In this presentation copy, Spencer returned the favour: he went systematically through d'Elci's catalogue and marked every book which he also owned, giving his own shelfmark and occasionally an additional reference. Even after d'Elci's death, Spencer was comparing his collection with that of his principal rival.

If the changes in della Lena's and d'Elci's lives led to any reflections on the fleeting nature of life, the certainty of death, or the impossibility of taking one's possessions with one when the time came on Spencer's part, we do not have them. Instead we have evidence of a renewed passion for collecting which extended across the decade and saw a series of major purchases as he filled gaps or traded up at the highest possible level. Some of these came from auctions, some from that never-failing source of otherwise impossible-to-find rarities, Father Horn.

After a several-year lull in correspondence, letters between the two men began to pick up again in 1815. Horn had been in Prague, had visited London in 1812, stayed for a time in Stuttgart, and was now in Frankfurt. More surprisingly, he was now married. His wife was the Baroness Sophie von Gumppenberg, the daughter of an old Bavarian noble family who had been a canoness in the Marienstift Bedburg in Kleve.[7] The Marienstift had been secularised in 1802 and by 1805 she was living in Regensburg when she sheltered Horn for over two years while he was on the run from the French.[8] Whether the marriage occurred then or later is not clear, but they were certainly husband and wife by 1813–14 when she and her lady companion, a maiden daughter of the English Catholic Lord Falkland, were mentioned as living with Horn in Prague.[9] Lest we imagine some unduly romantic flight from a nunnery to her dashingly bibliophilic lover, we should remember that when Baroness von Gumppenberg sheltered Horn in 1805 she had already obtained her fiftieth year; whatever romance connected the two, it was undertaken in the judgement of maturity.[10]

However else marriage may have affected Horn's estate, it made him no less eager a searcher out of books across Germany and advisor to Spencer on the European book market. In the circumstances, he even returned to old challenges, hoping that the redrawn map of Europe might shake loose books which had previously been carefully guarded by their owners. Foremost amongst these was the long-desired 1467 edition of Torquemada's *Meditationes* at Nuremberg. Having failed a decade before, he returned in hopes of better success:

> on my Arrival here [I] first offered 50 Louis which were politely declined, and afterwards 100. but the Answer to my last Proposal was that the Town not being in Want of Money, the Book would not be surrendered, if ten Times that Price was offered, in short, under no Consideration whatever.[11]

Once more the Nurembergers held tight to their treasure, but just as all seemed lost, a second copy of that book, so long "considered as unique", "burst into my Hands like a Shell".[12]

There was a sticking point, however. As Horn explained with a certain degree of embarrassment, if he had obtained the Nuremberg Torquemada, he would have considered himself duty-bound to immediately sell it to Spencer, having been commissioned by him to obtain this item. The new copy, however, had been bought as part of a consortium between Horn and the venerable London bookseller, George Nicol (*c.*1740–1828)—who had made his name as dealer to both the late Duke of Roxburghe and George III—and so it was not, Horn lamented, entirely in his hands, though he assured Spencer that Nicol was a reasonable man and would let him have "the Book on fair and easy Terms".[13]

It is unfortunate that we do not possess Spencer's response to this letter, though his notes towards it—scribbled on the back of Horn's initial epistle—simply indicate that he had met with Nicol, they could not agree on a price, and that if Nicol and Horn proposed "a very extravagant Price I will have nothing to do with it".[14] The final letter must have been couched in rather more incendiary terms than the summary as it provoked a complete breakdown on Horn's part. "I cannot say", Horn wrote, in his reply of 14 July,

> that I felt myself happy on reading the Contents [of Spencer's last letter] and I do most seriously regret that I ever took up the Idea of collecting old Editions because I fear that instead of obliging I run the risk of making Enemies... Had I been at Liberty to act for myself there would never have been any Difference and if your Lordship will look back for more than 20 Years, I do not believe that I ever gave you Reason to be

> displeased...As this unfortunate Business, which I only entered into in order to pass the Time with doing something, is likely to cast some Shade on my Character, I beg Leave to assure your Lordship that I never cared for money, always lived within my Revenue, and even when employed abroad and living for 4 years at Inns I lived with my 2£ a Day and never put down a farthing but for my Posthorses...should I run the Risk of forfeiting the good graces of a Nobleman whom nobody in England respects more, or is more faithfully attached to, I could wish never to have seen an old book in my Life.

In a final pitch of despair, no doubt intended to convey the most overwhelming depression, but sounding a touch bathetic, even to sympathetic modern ears, Horn concluded that "[i]ndeed this Idea has so greatly distressed me that since the Arrival of your Letter on Friday last, I [have] not looked into" any bibliographical reference works.[15]

Spencer was genuinely upset, as was Horn, and their correspondence foundered for three months before Spencer wrote a mollifying reply on 20 October. When Horn returned the favour, he was fulsome in his reconciliation, "for I beg Leave to assure you Lordship that only a few Things could happen to me in this World, which I would compare with the Misfortune of losing the Esteem and Favour of a Nobleman whom all that know, and have only heard of him, so universally respect and revere".[16] By then, Spencer had received the book itself from Nicol, probably for the "proper Price" of £200 which the two dealers had communicated to him earlier in the summer.[17]

By the time he took it home with him in autumn 1816, Spencer had been trying to obtain a copy of the 1467 *Meditationes* for eighteen years. What made it so remarkable? And—the elephant in the room—where had Horn suddenly located a second copy of a book so long supposed to have been unique?

The second question is harder to answer than the first, despite what seems a straightforward provenance. Unusually amongst Spencer's books, it retains its old—perhaps seventeenth-century—vellum binding and has not been washed or otherwise tampered with. As a result, the bold inscription "Ad Biblioth: aul: Eystettensem" on its front flyleaf is as clear as when it was first written.[18] This was the "Bibliotheca aulica

Eystettensem", the court library of the Prince-Bishops of Eichstätt in Bavaria. When Eichstätt was secularised in 1806, the old library of the prince-bishops became the core of what would eventually become the modern University Library in Eichstätt, but this volume escaped in ways we do not understand.[19]

In Chapter 9 I explained the desirability of the *Meditationes* as the first illustrated book printed in Italy. When one finally opens it, though, it is hard to avoid being a bit disappointed. Yes, it's printed in a pleasing, open textura with headings in red, but the woodcuts themselves are hardly the best, certainly not up to the standards of the Bamberg *Vier historien*. The first shows Christ blessing some animals: a rather bored deer, an attentive leopard, and a pupilless elephant who seems not to have noticed what's happening and is facing in the opposite direction; this is not exactly Dürer. The other woodcuts in the series, which largely depict the life of Christ, follow this model, with the most successful being that of his baptism (see Figure 13.1). Two angels stand to one side holding towels, looking patient and a touch distracted, while on the other side John the Baptist, who has a genuinely craggy wisdom to him, empties a bowl of water over Jesus's head. Jesus, in the centre of the woodblock, stands, solid and muscular with flowing locks and a slightly pointed beard, his right knee slightly bent and his hands clasped together, a stoic Viking. Its value never really lay in the quality of its art, though, but always in its position of primacy, its place in the larger history of the spread of printing, and it is undoubtedly for that that Spencer had so long and so badly desired its possession.

This was to be one of the last major acquisitions facilitated by Horn. The two men continued to correspond until the spring of 1819 but something seems to have happened to Spencer's letters to Horn in February or March of that year. It was probably an accident of the post, but Horn wrote an intemperate letter to Ocheda—not knowing he had left Spencer's service—suspecting that the lack of a response meant "that somebody must have been endeavouring to blacken me in his Lordship's Opinion". And he knew who. "It can only come", he added, "from a sneaking fellow who wishes to remain unknown, such as that equally arrogant and ignorant Mr. Dibdin who in attempting to ruin my litterary

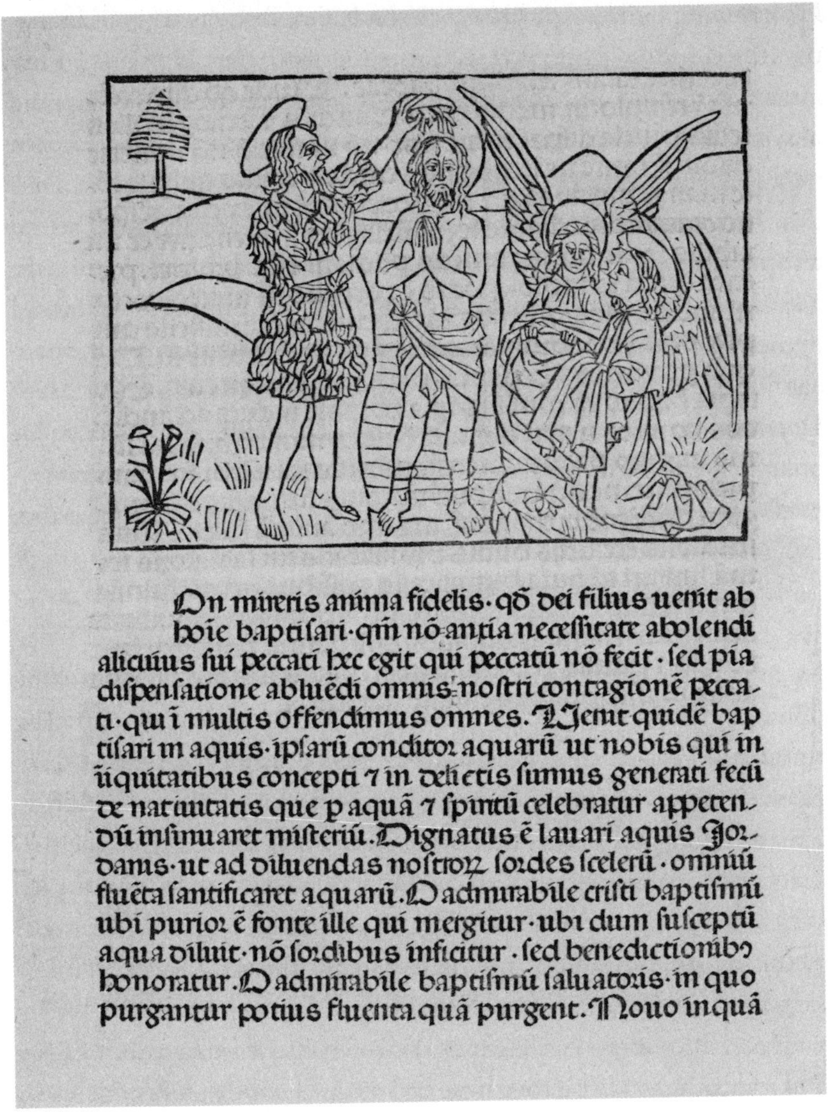
On mireris anima fidelis· qđ dei filius uenit ab
hoie baptisari· qm̄ nō an̄tia necessitate abolendi
alicuius sui peccati hec egit qui peccatū nō fecit · sed pia
dispensatione abluēdi omnis nostri contagionē pecca-
ti· qui ī multis offendimus omnes. Venit quidē bap
tisari in aquis· ipsarū conditor aquarū ut nobis qui in
īiquitatibus concepti ⁊ in delictis sumus generati fecū
de natiuitatis que p aquā ⁊ spiritū celebratur appeten-
dū insinuaret misteriū. Dignatus ē lauari aquis Jor-
danis· ut ad diluendas nostroꝝ sordes scelerū · omniū
fluēta santificaret aquarū. O admirabile cristi baptismū
ubi purior ē fonte ille qui mergitur· ubi dum susceptū
aqua diluit· nō sordibus inficitur · sed benedictionibꝰ
honoratur. O admirabile baptismū saluatoris· in quo
purgantur potius fluenta quā purgent. Nouo inquā

Figure 13.1 Juan de Torquemada, *Meditationes* (Rome: Ulrich Han, 1467), fol. [11]v, the baptism of Christ, John Rylands 17251.

[*sic*] Character lost his own."[20] This was followed by a circumstantial account of Dibdin's inaccuracies in the *Bibliotheca Spenceriana* and how they had negatively affected Horn's reputation in Germany.

The letter was received, not by Ocheda but by Spencer himself, who docketed it as "Mr Horn to Mr Ocheda, R[eceive]d 6 Ap[ril] 1819".

He never responded and that was the end of a quarter century of correspondence and collaboration between the two men. Horn had been intemperate, but I cannot help but feel that Spencer's decision to ignore him was cold. Surely, after so long, he deserved a second chance? Horn only survived another year. Having been exiled from Regensburg since 1813, he requested permission from the Bavarian foreign minister to return in a letter of 2 March 1820. It was granted, but he never lived to see his old home and died on the road on 16 April.[21] The necrology of his old monastery at Regensburg—which had miraculously survived the general wreck—records under that date "our Father Maurus Horn".[22] Mark Dilworth, the twentieth-century Scottish Benedictine chronicler of his order in Germany piously hoped that this indicated Horn had been reconciled with his sometime brothers before his death.[23] I hope so too, though I doubt it.

* * *

After spending the majority of his life caring for Spencer's books, in 1818 Tommaso de Ocheda finally retired to Italy for his health, supported by a generous pension from Spencer, and spent a further happy decade in Florence, regularly corresponding with his former employer.[24] Reading Spencer's daughter Sarah's letters, it is clear that Ocheda, even if the children tended to treat him with a certain sympathetic condescension, was very much a member of the family and one can imagine that they were genuinely sad at his departure. A few years before, in 1809, Sarah had sketched a little caricature of Ocheda and Spencer having "a Bibliographical discussion" (see Figure 13.2) which is by far the most engaging and sympathetic portrait we have of Spencer (and the *only* portrait we have of Ocheda).[25]

Dibdin, who had an ambivalent relationship with Ocheda (after all, he wanted his job) nonetheless remembered him fondly in a pen-portrait which must date from around this period:

> On rising from table, after dinner, it was almost my constant practice to resort to the "Raffaelle Library" for the purpose of half an hour's agreeable chat with [Ocheda]. I used to draw him insensibly into a long discourse,

Figure 13.2 Lady Sarah Spencer, *A Bibliographical Discussion* (1809), reproduced in *Letters from Sarah, Lady Lyttleton, 1797–1870* (London: Spottiswoode & Co., 1873). Photo © the Author.

and copious off-hand quotations from Lucretius and Virgil. Mr. Ocheda's memory was great. I used ordinarily to find him close to a lamp, with one of the "FATHERS" before him. He had read them ALL twice through. His reading was prodigious; but I do not think that his intellectual receiver digested the enormous quantity of food introduced into it. He read walking, sitting, and standing. He was a native of Tortona, and his recitations of the Italian poets—especially of Dante and Tasso—were beautifully impressive.[26]

A similarly fond portrait from a decade later was painted by the French travel writer Antoine-Claude Valery, who had shared an *auberge* in Florence with the now elderly Ocheda in the late 1820s. He "was a little old man, pale with study, but still vigorous and lively... working twelve to fourteen hours a day [and] regularly beginning his year by reading Homer". Valery was fascinated by his conversation and was convinced that Ocheda might have been a great scholar, but "amidst the vast libraries in which he had spent his life, reading had become Ocheda's sole passion, and he had sacrificed to it the reputation he would certainly have earned through his writings".[27]

Spencer found himself in an unfamiliar position upon Ocheda's departure. Who would fill the post he had so long occupied? It was not until September or even October 1818 that he wrote to Dibdin, then on a continental journey which we will turn to in the next chapter, with a "'proposition' connected with the departure of Mr. Ocheda".[28] Unluckily, the letter went astray and Dibdin found himself mystified (though, one also suspects, elated) upon finding an obscure allusion to the "proposition" in the next letter of Spencer's which did reach him. He said, yes, unsurprisingly, and was at Spencer House and in post, Spencer's librarian at last, by November.[29] Alas for Dibdin, he would not enjoy the same lengthy tenure as Ocheda. For the moment, however, he could revel in his good fortune and enthusiastically bid for Spencer at the last great British book auction of the 1810s: the sale of the White Knights Library in June 1819.

* * *

We have already met the profligate Marquess of Blandford. Having bought the Valdarfer Boccaccio, he continued to collect aggressively, if not wildly, acquiring the Bedford Hours, an exceptionally beautiful fifteenth-century manuscript book of hours now in the British Library, from James Edwards's sale in 1815 for £687 and engaging in plant collecting, gardening, and estate planning on an immense scale.[30] As early as 1812 his estate of White Knights in Berkshire had been mortgaged for £45,000, an indication of the scale of his debts, and these continued to increase.[31] In 1817 he succeeded his father as 5th Duke of Marlborough, but he had borrowed such vast sums against his father's death that this did little to alleviate his financial situation (by one estimate, that year found him owing as much as £600,000).[32] The crash inevitably came and the only surprise was that it had been so long in coming. The books went in June, followed in rapid succession by the wines, the paintings, the furnishings, and eventually White Knights itself.[33]

Spencer bought heavily at Blandford's sale and accounted for many of the highest prices paid. His was John Bellenden's translation of Hector Boece's foundational *History of Scotland*, one of the earliest books printed in Edinburgh, for £64 1*s*.[34] His the exceptionally rare Caxton, John Russell's *Propositio ad Carolum ducem Burgundiae* (the only other known copy is that from Holkham Hall, now in the British Library), for £126.[35] And his, at long last, the Valdarfer Boccaccio, for £918, the second highest price ever paid for a book, though a long way short of what Spencer had almost spent in 1812.[36]

We have no words of Spencer's describing his emotions upon acquiring the Boccaccio, but they must have been intense. Knowing its history, I could not help but feel moved when I walked from my chair to the issue desk at the Rylands and asked, casually, for shelfmark 17659. The attendant passed it across to me, my heart rate rising, my hands a trifle sweaty, and began to chat pleasantly about it and the surreality of handling such exquisitely rare and precious items. I had to interrupt him. "One moment, while I put the book down", I pleaded, for fear I would stain it with my sweat or accidentally drop it on my feet in a climax of bibliographical clumsiness.

Thankfully, it survived my nerves. Let us begin, as I did, with the binding (by Charles Lewis; see Figure 13.3).[37] It is truly princely: dark green straight-grained morocco with a faux sixteenth-century design of interlocking gold-tooled bands, forming ever more elaborate shapes around the central gold-tooled arms of the Dukes of Marlborough. As with other Lewis bindings, the doublures are at least as richly tooled as the boards. Here the Roxburghe arms take centre stage with more strapwork and floral tooling framing them, including some of minute intricacy.

Figure 13.3 Binding by Charles Lewis to Boccaccio, *Decamerone* (Venice: Christophorus Valdarfer, 1471), upper board, John Rylands 17659.

The flyleaves, again as with other Lewis bindings, are vellum with narrow double gold-tooled borders around the facing pages. At the bottom of the front flyleaf verso is the discreet morocco label of the "Bibliotheca Spenceriana".

When I first saw the Boccaccio, I presumed that the binding had been commissioned by Blandford—why else would his arms, rather than Spencer's, be present on both boards? But a closer examination of the binding reveals multitudes of little 'S's surmounted by earl's coronets. The binding, then, was Spencer's, but designed such that his ownership appears only as an afterthought to the distinguished libraries in which it had previously resided. There is something quite touching about this; it is one of the many small things that make me like Spencer, sometimes against my better judgement.

The textblock, which no writer on this volume has ever paid much attention to, is a trifle ordinary for such an outstanding book. The printing is competent, though the letters are a touch too rounded and close-set for my taste, and there's a simple but pleasant spray of illuminated foliage in purples, blues, greens, and golds on the opening leaf of the main text; otherwise there is only sparing rubrication of the simplest kind and some later chapter headings in a seventeenth-century hand. But, as with many of the books we have now seen, after a certain point its desirability became less about the book itself and more about the *idea* of the book. After 1812, the Valdarfer Boccaccio became a dream, a kind of bibliomaniacal fantasy of the rarest possible volume; its reality as a moderately well-printed Italian incunable receded into the distance. It is perhaps always this way with such books, though I think that the Gutenberg Bible or the Mainz Psalter, to name two others whose names have quite obscured their physical realities, stand up better under scrutiny than does the Valdarfer Boccaccio.

FOURTEEN

Dibdin on the hunt

"Here, I shot two birds, in the shape of black letter tomes, the first morning, before breakfast."[1] Such a mangled metaphor could belong to none other than Dibdin and it reached Spencer from the former's lodging in Caen on a May morning of 1818. What was Dibdin doing in Normandy? The latter part of the decade had not been kind to him. His lavish *Bibliographical Decameron* had brought in less income than he had hoped, the *Aedes Althorpianae* was dragging on without an end in sight, and Spencer's (quite reasonable) refusal to buy Dibdin's bibliographical reference library en masse and for a high price had left him with no choice the previous year but to endure the public humiliation of its sale by auction.[2] He was, however, nothing if not resilient and, having learned very little from his previous disasters, was soon scheming to undertake and subsequently publish an account of *A Bibliographical, Antiquarian, and Picturesque Tour in France and Germany*.[3]

The Treaty of Paris in 1815 had brought profound changes to a Europe inured to war for almost a generation. As we have seen, one of these, small in the grand picture but of great moment for bibliophiles, was the sudden resumption of tourism: English men and women could once more travel on the continent and, perchance, buy a book or five on the way. They were not slow in doing so and Dibdin was, as he himself ruefully admitted, rather behind the curve in planning his own tour three years after the peace. "[F]ortunate it had been for me", he later wrote, "on the score of further book-acquisitions, had I carried my wishes into effect about a year or two *earlier* than I did... I was earnest and sincere in the wish."[4] Be that as it may, the opportunities of a tour, both for seeing and for buying, must have seemed particularly attractive in the wake of his financial crash in 1817. He was soon planning and it rapidly became clear that a mainstay of the voyage, both in directing his steps and buoying him up financially, would be his role as an agent for Spencer.

And so, Dibdin found himself in Normandy, accompanied for part of the journey by his son Frank and for all of it by the bookbinder Lewis's brother, George Robert Lewis, a talented painter and engraver, whom Dibdin had hired to take sketches as they went.[5] As with many of Dibdin's business partnerships, this one ended in acrimony.[6] With great pleasure he rambled through Normandy, from Dieppe to Rouen to Caen, and by June he was established in Paris.[7] All the time he was buying books, mostly for Spencer. After lingering in Paris for over a month, he proceeded to Strasbourg and from there into Germany, still recovering from the chaos of the previous decades, and it is here that our interest, like Spencer's, becomes focused.

Spencer had obtained the *editio princeps* of Virgil, a beautiful folio printed by Sweynheym and Pannartz at Rome in 1469, as early as 1797, buying it from Edwards who had, in turn, obtained it in dubious circumstances from the Augustinians of Santa Maria del Popolo in Rome in the midst of the Napoleonic invasion.[8] What he lacked, however, was the even rarer second edition of 1471, also printed by Sweynheym and Pannartz, and another of the same year, printed in Venice by one Adam of Ambergau. Virgil was one of the authors who stood at the centre of Spencer's classical collection and it is not surprising that the lack of these two editions was a thorn in his side.

But where might he find them? One copy of Ambergau's Virgil was in the British Royal Library, and so clearly out of the picture, one of the 1471 Sweynheym and Pannartz was owned by d'Elci, but Spencer's correspondent was not about to let it go, and another, equally inaccessible, was in the Hunterian Museum in Glasgow, having been brought into Britain the previous century by the bibliophile and physician William Hunter.[9] Prospects looked bleak. It must have been particularly galling to know that, of the handful of collections and collectors who owned these *desiderata*, one, the public library in Stuttgart, owned copies of *both*. As Dibdin recalled, this came up, inevitably, in conversation before his departure for the continent. "I was reminded by his Lordship", of these volumes, he wrote, "but, rather with a desire, than any seriously-grounded hope, on his part of possessing them."[10] Dibdin had no doubt of his goals, "that I should gain possession of these long sought after treasures: but in fair and honourable combat: such as beseemeth a true bibliographical Knight".[11]

Dibdin reached Stuttgart, "a thoroughly dull place", at the end of July and within three hours of his arrival was visited by the librarian, Karl Friedrich Lebret.[12] "[A]mong his full cheerful topics of conversation (for he is a very merry soul)", Dibdin reported to Spencer, "he said—in French—'Well, my Lord S. has not *yet* got our second Roman Virgil'.—'No, Mr. Professor, but depend upon it he will possess it within 48 hours'—Ça reste a sçavoir'—was his reply."[13] "I thought this a good beginning", Dibdin added. The following day, he was confirmed in his hopes, when, he went to the Public Library and

> found, on my arrival, the worthy Head Librarian, seriously occupied in a careful estimate of the value of the Virgils in question—and holding up *Brunet's Manuel du Libraire* [one of the standard guides to the price and rarity of early books] in his right hand—"Tenez, mon ami", exclaimed he, "vous voyez que la seconde édition de Virgile, imprimée par vos amis Sweynheym et Pannartz, est encore plus rare que la premiére".[14]

And so the negotiations commenced. As well as quoting Brunet on the edition's rarity, Lebret also pointed out the repeated and unsuccessful attempts by Horn to obtain the same volumes (Dibdin noted this with a certain relish in his account—he knew well enough that Horn was his competitor for Spencer's favour). In the end, they settled that, if the Virgils were to be sold, they would be sold by exchange, with new English books to a certain value offered in return. Further negotiations resulted in an agreement that that value would be the price realised for the second Roman Virgil in the La Vallière sale (about £220), a reasonably favourable outcome on Dibdin's side, one might suppose, for a higher price would have likely been obtained had it gone to auction in 1818.[15]

Reaching an agreement with the jolly Lebret, who, then or subsequently, had "partaken of a trout and veal dinner with me, and shared in one bottle of *Fremder Wein*, and in another of *Ordinärer Wein*...in short, become quite sociable", was only half, and the lesser half, of the battle, for a book to be sold out of the Public Library required the consent of the king himself.[16] This, in the still newly-constituted kingdom of Württemberg—the Napoleonic successor state of the old duchy of Württemberg—was the young King Wilhelm I, who had only succeeded his father two years previously, and Dibdin solicited an audience through the local British chargé d'affaires. Wilhelm's father, the immensely fat Friedrich I, had been Horn's stumbling block, "having been *furiously* obstinate upon the *keeping* of these volumes", in Dibdin's words, but the son was another matter. An invitation was issued on Friday for Dibdin's attendance at the royal "cercle", a kind of reception, on Sunday evening and after a fretful weekend he found himself within the royal palace. The room was thronged "and I began to despair of having even 2 seconds to tell my tale", but he had his turn nonetheless and the briefest of conversations led to the amiable king stating that "he saw no obstacle to the arrangement". Victory had been achieved. Dibdin, with his usual ingenuousness, admitted to Spencer that during the course of this conversation he had, "I will frankly confess", been mostly staring at the queen's breasts and "upon the most stupendous & superb diamond necklace human eyes ever alighted upon", adding that "I could not but think how much *more* precious were those *gems* manufactured by Messrs Sweynheym & Pannartz & Adam!"[17]

Dibdin hastened to meet Lebret when the royal reception ended. "It was about half past nine only, but that philosophical bibliographer was about retiring to rest."[18] Nonetheless, Lebret received him "with open arms" and "told me that I might now depart in peace from Stuttgart—for that 'the affair might be considered as settled'".[19] The reality, of course, was not so simple. In a letter of 1 September Dibdin itemised to Spencer the various pieces of high-end British printing requested by Lebret, including his own *Bibliographical Decameron*, totalling £181 10*s*.

in value.[20] He added, however, "that all this supposes that matters are left in *status quo*", recognising that nothing could be considered quite certain until the deal was fully accomplished. "If once, I *catch hold* of them", he wrote of the Virgils, "whether at Nuremberg, or at Manheim, I shall hold them *tight*."[21]

There could be no doubt that Dibdin was nervous. Affairs might still miscarry, even at this late date, and, having spent September in Vienna, he wrote to Spencer from Nuremberg that he very much hoped to find a letter from Lebret and, better yet, the books, in Mannheim upon his arrival.[22] When he reached that city he found only the former, a "very long" and "prosing" letter such that "'till towards the conclusion, it was hardly possible to draw any *correct inference* as to the exact state of the negotiation". We can imagine Dibdin's nervous impatience in the face of Lebret's cheerful bombast, hurriedly scanning for the key phrase, "4500 francs—*plus*, le Decameron". In many ways, this greatly simplified matters. No longer would a costly and complex shipment of books have to be ferried from London to Stuttgart; instead, the matter could be transacted in ready cash.[23] The only sticking point was Dibdin's own work. Where might he find a copy of his *Bibliographical Decameron* in southern Germany? Fortunately for him, the long-established book dealers and publishers, Artaria & Fontaine of Mannheim, happened to have a copy in stock, "in blue morocco binding", which he acquired later on the day of his arrival.[24] Still moving at breakneck speed, he tasked his valet Rohfritsch with the task of posting from Mannheim to Stuttgart—"35 good heavy leagues"—to seal the transaction and "with an injunction *not to return without the books*!" The "very comely, creditable young" Rohfritsch acquiesced, and began the arduous journey, departing Mannheim at three the following morning and making straight for Stuttgart. There he met Lebret, exchanged the *Decameron* (and a promise of the payment of the 4,500 francs) for the two Virgils, and then posted straight back to Mannheim, arriving around two the following morning, twenty-three hours after his departure. "I had told him", Dibdin wrote, "that, at whatever hour he arrived, he was to make his way to my chamber" and so Rohfritsch did, proclaiming 'Les voila, Monsieur!!!'

Here then they are—within 5 feet of my elbow!"[25] Though it may be a later, literary elaboration, the account in Dibdin's printed *Tour* ends with the Sancho Panza-esque Rohfritsch wryly commenting, "faith, sir, this is a droll affair. I've travelled I don't know how many leagues for two old books not worth, it seems to me, a third of a Napoleon". "I readily forgave him all this saucy heresy", Dibdin added, "and almost hugged the volumes... on finding them upon my table."[26]

* * *

This is not the place to enter into a minute and exhaustive listing of Dibdin's many continental acquisitions for Spencer, of which the affair of the two Virgils may stand *pars pro toto*; suffice it to say, the tour bore better fruit for his patron than it did the impecunious bibliographer. We cannot quite leave Dibdin just yet, however, without taking some notice of his other two great acquisitions for Spencer: the 1497 Greek *Hours* and the books of the Salzburg Benedictines.

Spencer had been searching for Aldus Manutius's 1497 Greek Book of Hours for at least two decades. It is not now thought to be a terribly rare book (thirty-one copies are known in public collections) but for Spencer it had proved maddeningly elusive. In 1798 Horn had been negotiating for a copy in Ingolstadt but this quickly fell through.[27] In 1802 Horn found another copy, this time in the possession of Joseph Weber, a priest and professor of philosophy at Landshut, but Weber fell ill and once more the deal collapsed.[28] Aldines had long since been established as a particularly collectible sub-category of early printing, with many continental collectors eagerly assembling long runs of works from Aldo Manuzio's press, and it is likely that competition closer to the source had stymied Spencer's attempts before.

What must have been Dibdin's delight, then, to learn from one of the librarians at the Munich library that a certain bookseller dwelt in the town, "chiefly devoted to the purchase and sale of *Aldine* volumes", and that he "had even a copy of the" *Hours* themselves? The librarian hastened to add that the bookseller would never sell it, despite the importunity of "both the Prince Royal and our Public Library" but, as with the Virgils, Dibdin was undeterred. "Having been instructed from early youth", he recollected, "never to take that for *granted* which remained to be *proved*", he proceeded straight away to the home of Munich's "vendor of Aldine tomes". This was one Maximilian Joseph Stöger, "a short, spare man, with a sharp pair of dark eyes, [who] speaks French with tolerable fluency".[29] Dibdin probably did not know that Stöger was an important link in the chain with saw duplicate incunables and other rare printed works sold out of the Munich library, whence they had been gathered in the looting of the Napoleonic period, often for bargain prices.[30] For us who possess this knowledge, however, it suggests that the Munich librarian, one M. Bernhard, may not have been entirely financially detached from the transaction which seemed to be in the offing.

Our suspicion that Dibdin was being played increases as we read the bibliographer's account. "One of the Librarians" he had already met, he wrote, "introduced me—adding as [Stöger's] door opened, 'remember, he has the *Horae* of 1497—the only *disponable copy* in the world: but both the royal library and that of the Prince Regent have made overtures for it & it is *in vain* to think of buying it at *any* price'." With this bait in his mouth, Dibdin entered into a friendly bibliographical conversation with Stöger, who complimented the *Bibliotheca Spenceriana*, adding, rather implausibly, that "he had read [it] through". It did not take long for him to come to the point. Stöger "found, he said, that [Spencer], like the great Collectors in Italy (mentioning their names) was in want of that wonderfully rare book, the Horae of 1497: 'that book, Sir, (says he in French) is in *yonder drawer*—but it is *sacred*!'—& he then gave three strides across the room". Dibdin was hooked:

> I waited till his fit of grandeur and bibliographical inspiration had ceased—and then quietly told him it was both *cruel* and *absurd* to keep it from your Lordship—adding reasons, which I will not here repeat. He told me all solicitation was *unavailing*—that he had entered it (as he really had) in the MS. catalogue of the Prince Royal's Alduses—and that it was as sacred... [*sic*] "but come" (says he) what will Lord S. offer for this treasure, which cost me 200 leagues travelling to possess?!

And so, somehow, Dibdin found himself buying, not only the *Horae* (for the price of 550 florins) but ten other books, mostly Aldines, to the combined tune of £61 12*s*.[31] Fortunately for Dibdin, Spencer's desire for the *Horae* was such that he did not balk at the cost and so all parties, including, no doubt, both the bookseller and his librarian friend, were satisfied.

Where had Stöger come by this treasure? Dibdin, though he was evidently taken in at the time, subsequently had doubts as to whether his contact was really the "bibliopola honestissimus" he was advertised as being and seems not to have taken seriously the claim that Stöger had travelled two hundred leagues, almost seven hundred miles, to obtain it. Instead, he suspected, he had bought it from a rather lower-end bookdealer in Augsburg named Christoph Kranzfelder, for "peradventure only the *hundredth part* of the sum which he" subsequently received.[32] Certainly the volume had an older Augsburg provenance, with one inscription at the bottom of the first leaf reading "F. Gregorius prior ad S. Vdalricu[m] Augustæ" and another on a stub, probably taken from a previous flyleaf, which gave Father Gregorius's ownership again together with the truncated date "An. Dn. XCV" (probably 1595). If it had been owned by the prior of the Benedictine Monastery of SS. Ulrich and Afra in Augsburg, it is probable that it suffered the same fate as the remainder of that monastery's collection at secularisation in 1802, was confiscated, looted, or otherwise dispossessed and so found its way into the possession of the local bookdealer Kranzfelder. As with so many of the books we have seen here, the circumstances are suggestive but definitive evidence is lacking.

I can speak with more authority about the book itself (see Figure 14.1a–b).[33] It now rests in a black buckram box within a grey archival box; only the Mainz Psalter has been accorded a similar box-in-box treatment amongst the Rylands volumes we've looked at so far. The tiny volume inside is mounted like a ring in a jeweller's display, surrounded by protective foam. It is minute, even for a 16mo, the size of an old-fashioned cigarette case. The Aldine anchor and dolphin are gold-tooled on both boards and the page edges are intricately gauffered (gilded and then decorated with heated finishing tools) with a flowing, pseudo-Renaissance vegetal design. Gingerly opening the boards—my hands feel like giant's paws by comparison—one sees spectacular red morocco doublures with Spencer's monogram. The book is so small that the Rylands bookplate takes up almost the entirety of the facing page. Unsurprisingly, the binding is by Lewis.

Figure 14.1 [*Greek Book of Hours*] (Venice: Aldo Manuzio, 1497), fols. a1v–a2r, John Rylands 19202.

The first page of the old textblock gives the title, in both Greek and Latin, in fine orange-red printing with Father Gregorius's slightly shaky ownership inscription below. Turn the page and your eye (my eye, at least) is immediately arrested by a graceful little woodcut of the Annunciation. Mary kneels, hands clasped to her breast, at a lectern and

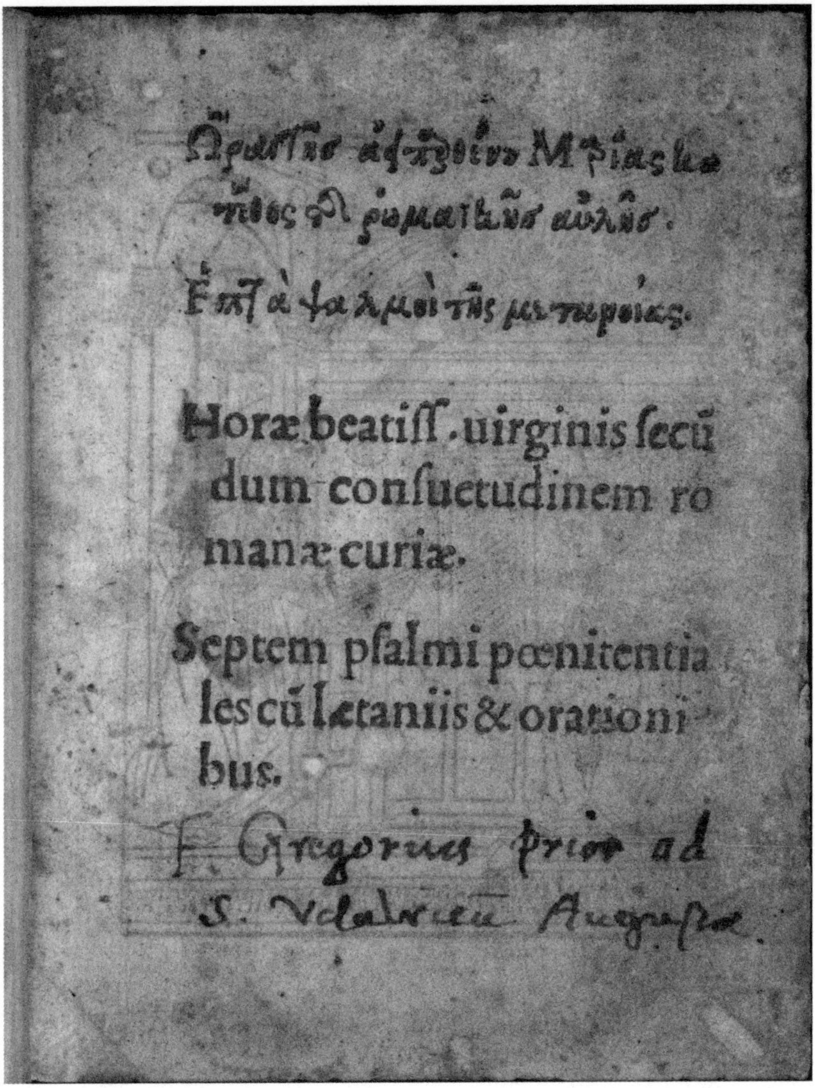
Ὧραι τῆς ἀειπαρθένου Μαρίας κα-
τὰ ἔθος τῆς ῥωμαϊκῆς αὐλῆς.

Ἑπτὰ ψαλμοὶ τῆς μετανοίας.

Horæ beatiss. uirginis secū
dum consuetudinem ro
manæ curiæ.

Septem psalmi pœnitentia
les cū letaniis & orationi
bus.

F. Gregorius prior ad
S. Vdalricū Augustæ.

Figure 14.1 Continued

Gabriel copies her gesture on the floor nearby. Behind is a vaguely classical building, a glimpse of rolling hills, the Holy Spirit, flapping dovelike in the middle distance and, at the top left corner, God looking on, rather jealously, I can't help but think. It probably is not copied from one, but it has the distinct feel of an Orthodox icon.

As with almost every Aldine I've seen, I cannot help but admire Aldus's black printing, which is gorgeous, deep, and even. His red printing is not above reproach, though, and is at times over-inked and blotchy. I can understand Dibdin's slightly dismissive comment in the *Aedes Althorpianae* that "[t]he present work, interspersed with red printing, is by no means among the happiest specimens of the Aldine press. It appears to have been struck off in haste".[34] A human note is added at signature 5r where a missing epsilon has been added by hand in an ink which, if intended to be red, has now turned a dusty orange. What a rather intimate and almost awkward little volume to have evoked such surges of desire and greed!

* * *

By comparison, Dibdin's transaction with the Benedictines of S. Peter's in Salzburg was substantial in every sense of the word. In September Dibdin, with "no letter of recommendation; but, taking my valet [Rohfritsch of the two Virgils] with me", knocked at the gate of that venerable institution, this being his "first appearance in a fraternity of Monks". He was politely received and passed, with evident amusement, some "athletic young Benedictins [*sic*]" playing skittles in one of the quadrangles of the monastery, before being admitted to the presence of the abbot, Albert Nagnzaun, whose powerful, gloomy figure impressed Dibdin considerably. There he was made welcome and told to return the following day to meet the librarian, Corbinian Gärtner.

When he did, he found himself presented to "a somewhat venerable Benedictin [who] was walking, apparently to and fro, with a bunch of keys in one hand, and a thick embossed quarto under his other arm". This was the ageing Father Gärtner, in his time a well-known jurist and rector of the University of Salzburg, but now enjoying a quiet retirement at S. Peter's.[35] "Anon, one of the larger keys in this said bunch was applied to a huge lock, and the folding and iron-cramped doors of the library were thrown open." It was small, the windows were open, and it was raining heavily outside, but Dibdin was not deterred and scrambled up "a few slight ladders" to leave no shelf unturned. After several hours of largely fruitless searching in the cold, damp library room, he was in a bad mood and inclined to find the whole project pointless, but "he is a bad sportsman who does not hit *something* in a well-stocked cover" and he nonetheless managed to select a pile of works which he hoped the monastery would part with "for a valuable consideration". When he reached Vienna he found a letter from Father Gärtner, genially agreeing to a deal and proposing 440 florins for the lot.[36] Writing to Spencer, he could barely contain his incredulity, "the Abbot foxed his own price—£42 Sterling for the whole!!"[37]

Dibdin had reason to be pleased. His Salzburg haul contained twenty-eight volumes, most of them incunables, and many of them exceptionally rare.[38] His low spirits at the time evidently owed more to the rain than to the quality of books he was examining. Looking at them now, though, they are far removed from the dim monastic shelves of S. Peter's. To take one example, a particularly tempting Sammelband (the bibliographic term for a group of separate texts, printed or manuscript, which have been bound together) contained, besides two more substantial works, a life of S. Jerome in eight leaves printed in 1473 at Naples by Sixtus Riessinger, a peripatetic printer who was active in Rome, Naples, and Strasbourg, and who had become an increasing obsession of Spencer's.[39] Coming to it now in the Rylands I find it detached both from its companions and whatever delectable old monastic binding it may once have been sheltered by and, instead, squeezed into a restrained red morocco binding by Hering. Provenance has been removed and only Dibdin's own account, here and in the *Aedes Althorpianae*, allows us to connect it to Salzburg. It is, at least, unwashed (the printing, if you were wondering, is rather poor, blotchy and badly set, like much of Riessinger's work).[40] Looking at it in its Regency gaudery it is difficult not to feel sad.

* * *

The preceding pages may have given the impression that Dibdin's tour was unremittingly triumphant, a juggernaut of bibliomaniacal acquisition rumbling across the continent, leaving nothing but well-filled purses and empty shelves in its wake. This is not quite true. Even Dibdin's fast talking and ready payment could not dislodge every book he desired. In the same letter of 12 September 1818 in which he joyfully announced to Spencer his acquisition of the Salzburg books, he added that:

> I have inspected *another* monastic library, about 8 miles up the Danube from Vienna: and have seen *wonders* here *before unknown*. This very day I have written to offer 2000 florins for [here follows a long list of incunables]. Such copies I never before saw—not in France or Germany—those scored under are quite *gigantic* & beautiful—worth £49 or £50 apiece. Your Lordship shall have the *entire pickings* of them.[41]

The unnamed monastery was Klosterneuburg, the magnificent Augustinian abbey above the Danube to the north of Vienna, still in the midst of its Baroque rebuilding. Dibdin, Rohfritsch, and Lewis the artist had had a pleasant drive along the riverside road, and were not particularly impressed by the inchoate reconstruction, but nonetheless took the step of postponing dinner in the interests of tracking down the librarian. Unlike Dibdin, the librarian Maximilian Fischer was enjoying *his* dinner, but Augustinian hospitality dictated that he rose immediately from table to attend to his importunate guests, though "[a]s he did not understand a word of French, it became necessary again to brush up my Latin". Dibdin waved aside Fischer's attempts to interest him in a Hebrew Bible printed under the patronage of the abbot, and "begged that I might have a sight of the *Incunabula Typographica* of which I had heard a high character":

> He smiled, and said that a few minutes would suffice to undeceive me in this particular. Whereupon he placed before me . . such a set of genuine, unsoiled, uncropt, *undoctored*, ponderous folio tomes . . as verily caused my eyes to sparkle, and my heart to leap! They were, upon the whole—and for their number—*such* copies as I had never before seen.[42]

Alas for Dibdin, and for Spencer, his proposal of 2,000 florins was met with a polite Latin letter from Fischer advising that their sale was quite impossible, being both against the law and the wishes of the monks.[43] It is tempting to consider the counterfactual: what if Dibdin *had* acquired the incunables of Klosterneuburg? The answer, most likely, would have been a loss similar to the losses of context, provenance, and binding associated with his Salzburg acquisitions. Although he wrote rapturously of one volume "[i]n its first binding of wood", and another "in its original wooden binding", it seems doubtful these would have survived the knives of Hering and Lewis with all the losses that might entail.[44] As it was, the library remained—and remains—untouched, its remarkable collection of nearly a thousand incunables in the same state as they were when first seen by Dibdin. A detailed catalogue was published in 1920 and the abbey library is today an active centre of scholarly bibliographical research.[45] We should, I think, be glad of Dibdin's failure and add to our stock of counterfactuals by wondering what other abbey libraries might be like Klosterneuburg's today had it not been for Dibdin, Horn, Van Praet, and their contemporaries?

* * *

By November, Dibdin was back in England and anticipating "the unpacking of the Dover Chest at Spencer House", when his continental spoils could be displayed and "when I may be said to make my 'first appearance' in the character of your Lordship's Librarian".[46] Spencer could congratulate himself on his friend and agent's success. Long-desired rarities such as the two Virgils and the Greek *Horae* had now found a place in his collection and dozens of other valuable, if less longed for, volumes had come in their train. Indeed, the reality of a continental book-buying tour had so far outshone its potential that it was only a matter of time before Spencer would decide to remove the middleman, however able, and undertake a tour himself.

FIFTEEN

Thirty thousand Neapolitan ducats

On 15 November 1474 a printer from Brussels named Arnaldus (really Arnaud or something similar, but we are in a Latin world here) had just finished printing an edition of Horace on his press at Naples.[1] It was not the first edition of Horace to see print—that had already issued from a Venetian press a few years before—nor was it a reading from an important manuscript, nor a particularly beautiful piece of printing, nor, frankly, anything much of note. A poet like Horace, central to the Renaissance educational curriculum, would see untold thousands of editions produced in the ensuing centuries. All that was really going for Arnaldus de Bruxella's Horace is that it was quite early—several editions of the poet were issued around 1474 or 1475 but Arnaldus's was certainly one of the first half dozen or so printings—and, eventually, very rare. By now, we can guess what effect great, almost unobtainable, rarity would have on Spencer.

But before we get to Spencer, we need to have a sense of how *he* knew about Arnaldus's book and why he wanted it, as he did, quite so badly. In 1794 the second volume of the German bibliographer Georg Wolfgang Panzer's enormous *Annales typographici* was published in Nuremberg (Spencer had bought his copy while he was posted to Vienna later that year).[2] In enumerating the early output of the Neapolitan press (a *terra incognita* to most northern European scholars) Panzer relied heavily on previous bibliographical works and on the first-hand observations of Jacopo Morelli, his contemporary and the librarian of the Biblioteca

Marciana in Venice. Morelli, Panzer wrote, had seen a copy of Horace printed by Arnaldus in Naples in 1474 which had never before been known to bibliographers.[3] This was, of course, the book we have been considering.

Once knowledge of its existence, however ambiguous, entered the world of bibliomania, its discovery assumed an entirely disproportionate importance. On 11 May 1801 Horn had written to Spencer that he had "for these 3 or 4 years past" been bargaining with Joseph von Stubenberg, the Prince-Bishop of Eichstätt, for an early Horace in his possession, which Horn judged to be "either the Edition of Arnoldus de Bruxella or an unknown one printed certainly between 1470 and 73".[4] Spencer was predictably interested, but the Prince-Bishop dithered, "in order as he says", Horn wrote in exasperation, "to make me hasten the return of a Telescope Glass, of Ramsden's making, which he broke and which I sent about 6 weeks ago to London…[to] have another made for him".[5] When he finally succeeded in wheedling it out of the Prince-Bishop's hands a year later it proved to be "an absolutely unknown Edition, about 1470–72"; a prize, certainly, but not Arnaldus's work.[6]

For a decade or more, there was no whiff of Arnaldus's Horace, but then it came to Spencer's notice that a copy might be in the hands of a Neapolitan bibliophile, the imposingly titled Luigi Serra, 4th Duke of Cassano, 4th Marquis of Rivadebro, 5th Marquis of Amendralexo, 6th Marquis of Strevi, and patrician of Naples, Genoa, Spoleto, and Camerino (1747–1825), who we briefly saw in action, enriching his collection during the Napoleonic invasion of Italy, in Chapter 6. But who exactly was this rival collector? Cassano Serra came from an old and wealthy Neapolitan noble family, studied widely, had an early love of books, and while still a young man married the strong-minded Giulia Carafa Cantelmo Stuart, a fellow Neapolitan noble whose connections to the Scottish royal house were, despite her name, entirely imaginary. Luigi Cassano Serra was a reformer, often in tension with his conservative Bourbon monarchs, a freemason, and a supporter of the short-lived Parthenopean Republic, an attempt to establish a republican government in Naples in the first half of 1799 during the chaos of the Napoleonic invasion. His wife gained legendary status as one of the "mothers of the nation" during the brief life of the ill-fated state and their son Gennaro, one of its leaders, was executed when the Bourbons returned to power that autumn. The duke and his family were forced into exile, but returned a few years later and flourished under the new Bonapartist regime; he indulged in his love of rare books—easily obtained in an era of confiscations, secularisation, and warfare across southern Italy—and remained a leading figure in Naples until the 1815 Bourbon restoration.[7]

I have said he was a bibliophile, but what did he buy and how? Predictably, Luigi Cassano Serra liked incunables and classical texts; they bulk large in his 1807 library catalogue. Also predictably, his library was rich in early Italian printing, especially printing from Naples and the surrounding area. Where did these books come from? The answer by now is probably obvious: religious houses. Secularisation, sequestration, and looting were the order of the day in southern Italy during the chaotic decades of declining monarchy, bloody republic, enforced Napoleonic overlordship, and Bourbon restoration and the Duke of Cassano made the most of the opportunities presented.[8] Lacking a detailed archive and with many of his volumes washed and rebound, it is difficult to recover details but telling examples give a sense of the whole: Laudivio Zacchia's *Epistolae magni Turci* (Naples, 1473), from the library of the Capuchins of the Immaculate Conception in Naples, *Quaestiones* on the *Metaphysics* of Aristotle (Naples, 1475), from the monastery of Santa Maria Donnaregina there, and Diogenes Laertius's *Lives of the Philosophers* (Naples, 1472), from the Benedictine house in the same city.[9] Further afield a copy of St. Augustine's *Confessions* (Milan, 1475) retains the ownership inscription of the convent of San Nicola da Tolentino at Nembro.[10] These tantalising connections are thrown into violent clarity by what can be recovered of Cassano's correspondence with none other than Spencer's old friend d'Elci. Writing in 1791 about an edition of Dante (Naples, 1477), then in the library of a seminary at Fiesole, he made no bones about the actions needed:

> How are we going to get it out of the hands of these peasants [i.e. the seminarians]? Fuck, there's nothing else to do but have it stolen! But

> how? Think, dear Friend, think how to help me. The thing is worth any expense, any sacrifice, any inconvenience; I would go there in person even at the cost of taking that Provost as a Confessor: and show that I have converted.[11]

D'Elci obliged, somehow.[12] Whether a theft actually occurred or not, there seems to be little doubt that Cassano would happily have supported one if it brought him the lusted-for book. We cannot rule out the possibility—indeed, the probability—that this interchange was not an exceptional one in his collecting career.

We do not know where or when the Duke of Cassano discovered his copy of Arnaldus's Horace, but it must have been some time between 1807 and 1815, when his star was in the ascendent in Naples.[13] Around the time of the monarchy's restoration, when he must have known that the Neapolitan political situation could only turn against him, he proposed selling his library for the equivalent of £10,000. Spencer was tempted and commissioned Dibdin to prepare an itemised estimate, but even Dibdin's enthusiasm "could not", as he wrote, "push to more than between £6 & 7,000".[14] Spencer was not a man to lightly buy an entire library, as we have seen, and the matter dropped.

But having now twice failed to secure a copy of the Horace, the idea of it began to haunt him. Around the same time that he entertained the idea of buying the Cassano Serra library, Horn had finally picked up the scent of a second copy. Writing on 12 March 1815 he was optimistic: "[y]our Lordship seems to despair of the Horace by Arnald du Bruxella [but] as long as I know where he is I do not despair, tho' I have nothing to add on the Subject for the present".[15] The now-anthropomorphised book was on Horn's radar, as it were, and the hunt was afoot. By 29 April, its acquisition seemed almost certain. The Bruxella Horace, Horn triumphantly announced, "has been formally promised: but when you will receive him, I cannot yet tell".[16] But then Horn's brother fell ill and other concerns distracted him. A year later he still hoped to obtain it, but his negotiations came to nothing. It is in this final letter, of 20 June 1816, that he at last revealed the location of the book: "The Horatius by Arn. de Bruxella at Admont, your Lordship shall have for the Price I get it at; as I there consider myself as acting as your Commissioner."[17]

The Benedictine abbey of Admont in Styria, founded in the eleventh century, but architecturally a baroque masterpiece, was—and is—home to one of the great European monastic libraries and is rich in incunables. What it does not now contain, however, is a copy of Arnaldus's Horace. What had happened? Was Horn in error? Possibly. It is intriguing to note, however, that the Biblioteca Nazionale di Napoli acquired a copy of the Horace, the *only* other copy now known, in 1973. It contains no earlier provenance, but it is tempting to suppose that it may once have rested on the shelves at Admont.[18]

Be that as it may, the end of the decade found Spencer still without a copy of this absurdly rare book, all of his previous efforts having met with failure. That this should have aggravated him is understandable, but it must also be set within the context of his collection as it stood at the end of the decade: there were very few early editions of classical texts which he did *not* have. Amongst the handful of exceptions which were occupying him at this time, the Horace undoubtedly came first, followed close after by other equally elusive volumes: Sixtus Riessinger's edition of Terence's comedies, probably the second or third to be produced, which had been printed in Rome about 1469, and the *editio princeps* of Juvenal's satires, printed by Ulrich Han, also in Rome and about the same time. The King of Württemberg had a copy of the Terence, but Dibdin's success on that front was unlikely to be replicated, and d'Elci had the Juvenal but could under no circumstances be convinced to part with it.

There was, however, one man who had copies of all *three* desiderata: Cassano Serra. When Spencer and his wife decided to holiday in southern Italy during the winter of 1819–20, therefore, we can be entirely justified in assuming that his goal was something more than warm Neapolitan air. As soon as they arrived in Naples in December 1819, d'Elci was writing from Vienna, planning out Spencer's introductions to leading collectors, especially "le Duc de Cassano mon ami" and Spencer evidently lost no time in taking up the leads offered, making the rounds of Naples' private libraries.[19] On 10 January 1820 Dibdin, then ensconced in Spencer

House working on the interminable *Aedes Althorpianae*, wrote to his employer:

> allow me to express both pleasure and pain upon the perusal of the contents of the Neapolitan letter: pleasure, that your Lordship saw so many delightful things, with shape of books, in the libraries of C. Melzi, M. Trivulzio, &c... and pain, that your Lordship does not appear to have made any very first rate acquisitions. The Ulrich Han Terence & the Naples Horace of 1474 are doubtless the most material: and I am almost sanguine in believing that if a train be laid, the result will be propitious.

What, he added, of the Cassano Serra library? "Is any portion of it meltable?"[20]

This same question was preoccupying Spencer himself. Writing to his friend and fellow collector Thomas Grenville on 18 January, he lamented that "I have as yet done nothing here worth mentioning in the way of acquiring Books, indeed there seems to be nothing of that kind worthy of notice that could be obtained." The Duke of Cassano's library remained a temptation but:

> as he persists in his Notion of selling it altogether, or not at all, and has most extravagant Ideas of its Value, I fear I will fail in my hopes of getting the two or three Articles belonging to him which would have been an acquisition to my Collection worth making any Sacrifice for; I mean to try him with a pretty stout offer for those Articles before we part, but am not sanguine about succeeding with him.[21]

When Spencer proposed "a pretty stout offer" he meant what he said. It must have been around the end of January or beginning of February, sitting in Naples with the long-desired books filling his mind, that he either offered, or almost offered (the evidence is ambiguous), the sum of 1,000 guineas for the Horace and Juvenal.[22] While less than half the price of the Valdarfer Boccaccio, this is a staggering sum, all the more so considering the circumstances. While the Boccaccio realised its unique price in a context of intense auction room competition, this was an offer made more or less in cold blood to an owner who was financially struggling and clearly needing to sell one way or another. Spencer wanted these books more, perhaps, than he wanted anything in the world.

But, for better or for worse, this was not how the sale went. The ageing Neapolitan duke, though he may have needed the money, was determined that his collection should be sold in its entirety and, eventually, Spencer agreed. Sometime in February he made a proposal, which was accepted, for the purchase of the majority of the library.[23] This was only the third library he had ever purchased whole—the first two being Reviczky's and Alchorne's—and by far the most expensive. Dibdin, though "breathless with delight" at news of the acquisition, was evidently worried that Spencer might have paid too much in his eagerness to secure the collection and reminded him that:

> some five or six years ago, I made a very minute valuation of the Duke of Cassano's library—for which £10,000 was asked—but which, upon a very liberal allowance, I could not push to more than between £6 & 7,000 [later in the letter he corrects this to the more precise figure of between £7,140 and £7,440]: and I would venture to guess that your Lordship has not much exceeded two fives and two noughts.[24]

Did Dibdin guess correctly? We know that the transaction was conducted in the local currency and that Spencer paid Cassano Serra the, for southern Italy, astronomical sum of 30,000 Neapolitan ducats.[25] This equates to about £4,970 assuming Spencer and Cassano Serra were following the exchange rates of the period, so it would appear that Dibdin's £5,500 was not wide of the mark.[26]

Nonetheless, £4,970 was the largest lump sum Spencer had ever spent on books, singular or plural. What did he get for such a vast amount? The inescapable conclusion one reaches is that, in the moment at least, he didn't really know. What he wanted was the Horace, the Juvenal, and the Terence; everything else was just icing on the cake. What he received, however, was something in the region of 600–700 volumes, mostly incunables or sixteenth-century imprints, with a particular strength, as might be expected, in southern Italian printing.[27] Having made his purchase, Spencer leisurely proceeded to Marseilles, sending the books ahead of him, while Dibdin impatiently awaited "the arrival of the great bibliographical cargo from Naples".[28] Both men understood from the outset that the purchase would inevitably involve the acquisition of many duplicates and that, as in previous moments, an auction would be organised to dispose of these.

Accordingly, Dibdin leapt into action. He would make a catalogue with the aim of having the sale take place towards the end of May, while buyers would still be in town, or, failing that, sometime in January. "The selection of the duplicates subject to such particular exceptions as your Lordship may inspect", he added self-importantly, "may, I think, be safely trusted to myself." Enthusiastic as he was, he still fretted about the economic sense of the purchase, hoping that once separated out, Spencer's desiderata would not have proved inordinately expensive. Neither, he thought, could really be worth more than £50 or £100. Like so many Dibdinisms, this strikes one as rather tone deaf when directed to the man who had spent almost £5,000 essentially to acquire just these books.

Even Grenville was sceptical and Spencer wrote from Marseille, on 17 April, acknowledging that he was probably right without quite admitting that he had made a bad deal:

> I suspect that I shall have paid pretty dear for the possession of nearly every object in my line of Collection which remained a desideratum; for if you are correct in your Opinion of the diminished Estimation of old Classicks, the load of duplicates with which I have been obliged to encumber myself will not come to a good Market though there are many of them which ought to be tempting to collectors of that sort of stuff.[29]

Meanwhile, despite Spencer's efforts to keep the purchase quiet, *The Times* reported that "Lord Spencer, during his stay at Naples, purchased the superb library of the Duke de Cassano: it has been put on board an English vessel, to be conveyed to London."[30] When it reached the docks it was met by Dibdin and by mid-April Spencer's librarian had secreted it away in Spencer House, enjoining George Appleyard (*d.* 1855), the former admiralty clerk who had become Spencer's secretary in 1817 and would eventually replace Dibdin as librarian, to show the new books to no one.[31] The level-headed Appleyard, who reported the books' successful unpacking at Spencer House on 15 April, wrote that he and Dibdin had compared key Cassano duplicates with the same items in the existing collection "and the latter were I think invariably preferable" with one or two exceptions; trading up would certainly not be the rule.[32]

Dibdin soon began to collate and organise the new books, though he remained distracted by the *Aedes* and lamented that "The Aldine Volumes, and the Cassano Collection, will make 100 additional pages" (a few days before this calculation he had plaintively asked Spencer, "Need all the Aldines be mentioned?"; Dibdin was clearly flagging).[33] Accordingly, much remained to be done when he joined Spencer in Paris in mid-May. A spring sale was out of the question and only a "rough proof" of the catalogue had been prepared by the latter part of the summer.[34]

From the start, Dibdin had a clear idea of how to sell the duplicates to best advantage. When Spencer objected that his catalogue drafts dwelt over-long on minute imperfections, Dibdin countered that this had been "done with a view to foreign purchasers—for the Catalogue, I hope, will be at Paris, Munich & Vienna three months before the sale".[35] When the catalogue was finally finished that winter and the sale firmly set for the beginning of March 1821, he wrote to Spencer that "I will undertake to write letters to Paris, Strasbourg, Stuttgart, Munich, & Vienna accompanying several copies of the Catalogue if your Lordship will undertake the Florence, Milan, & Bologna packets." "I am in great hopes", he added, "that, at Munich, they will bite" in the name of adding to the still new national collection there.[36] By 28 December, he had posted twenty-eight copies of the freshly-printed catalogue abroad and a further dozen or more around Britain, targeting not only leading book sellers but major collectors like d'Elci and Heber.[37]

When the sale began, on 2 March, it enjoyed every Dibdinian puff which could be given. "It may with truth be affirmed", Dibdin pronounced in the preface, "that, since the sales by auction of the Askew and Pinelli Libraries, there has not appeared, in our own country, any Collection like the present—submitted to public competition."[38] But did Dibdin's hopes of a high-profile, truly international auction succeed? It is difficult to gauge the international scope of the bidders as most acted through London booksellers (the private bidders were all English and were predictably dominated by Heber). What we can gauge, however, is the financial success of the sale and here, alas, Grenville's cautionary note proved only too true. To be sure, some lots realised very substantial prices. The most expensive was Boccaccio's *Teseide* (Ferrara, 1475), allegedly the first copy to be sold since the Askew sale in 1775, which realised £117 12*s*.[39] Not too far behind came a 1462 Bible (£94 10*s*.), a 1471 Sweynheym and Pannartz Ovid (£73 10*s*.), and a 1469 imperfect Sweynheym and Pannartz Virgil (£63), but these were exceptions.[40] Most of the books, even those which would have been considered highly desirable by the standards of the period, went for very little. The 1465 *editio princeps* of Lactantius, which also was generally reputed to be the first book printed outside of Germany, made only £12, despite being a large copy, "superbly bound in (foreign) red morocco".[41] Less famous and less well-bound incunables barely sold at all. A 1479 *Fasciculus temporum* in half calf only realised 2*s*. 6*d*., a 1482–83 Juvenal in calf only 3*s*., and a "very indifferent" 1496 Pliny went for a single shilling.[42] In total, the 463 duplicates—a mixture of discards from Cassano Serra and discards from Spencer's existing library where Cassano Serra volumes represented upgrades (contrary to Appleyard's initially pessimistic estimate)—realised £1,750 7*s*., about a third of what Spencer had paid for the collection as a whole. While no straightforward calculation of value and expense can be made for such a complex process of acquisition, trading-up, and sale, there is little doubt that Spencer paid dearly for his three classics.

* * *

With that in mind, let us turn to the books themselves. What *were* these so-coveted objects? We cannot help but start with the Horace, which Dibdin more enthusiastically than accurately described as, "beyond all doubt, the rarest classical volume in the world" (see Figure 15.1).[43] It is surprisingly small. Although printed in folio it is closer to the size of a quarto and rather dumpy in shape. The present binding is plain, almost crude, red morocco with a simple double wavy gold rule around the

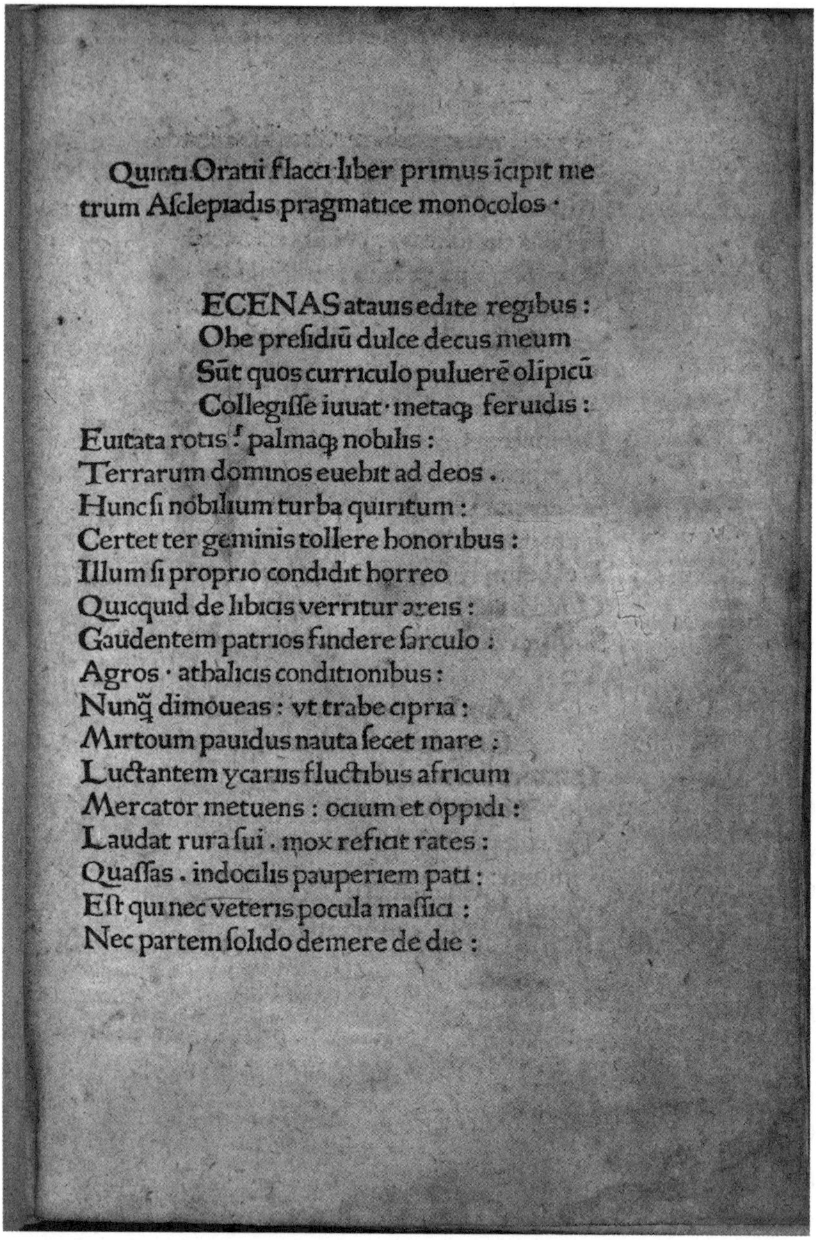

Quinti Oratii flacci liber primus icipit me
trum Aſclepiadis pragmatice monocolos ·

ECENAS atauis edite regibus :
Ohe preſidiū dulce decus meum
Sūt quos curriculo puluerē olipicū
Collegiſſe iuuat · metaq; feruidis :
Euitata rotis : palmaq; nobilis :
Terrarum dominos euehit ad deos .
Hunc ſi nobilium turba quiritum :
Certet ter geminis tollere honoribus :
Illum ſi proprio condidit horreo
Quicquid de libicis verritur areis :
Gaudentem patrios findere ſarculo :
Agros · athalicis conditionibus :
Nunq̄ dimoueas : vt trabe cipria :
Mirtoum pauidus nauta ſecet mare :
Luctantem ycariis fluctibus africum
Mercator metuens : ocium et oppidi :
Laudat rura ſui . mox reficit rates :
Quaſſas . indocilis pauperiem pati :
Eſt qui nec veteris pocula maſſici :
Nec partem ſolido demere de die :

Figure 15.1 Horace, *[Opera]* (Naples: Arnaldus de Bruxella, 1474), first printed leaf, John Rylands 19045.

edges of the boards and (now) an incongruous Rylands monogram in the middle. The spine is a bit sunned, the raised bands slightly angling down to the right and the gold rules setting them off appearing equally crude and lumpish. A simple green morocco label on the spine gives the title, date, and place of printing.

In other words, this is not high-end binding. The colour of the goatskin (a kind of reddish ochre) makes me strongly suspect it is Italian, probably southern Italian, and, I presume, applied to this book at the order of Cassano Serra. His hand is present elsewhere. Shadowy as they are, one can easily spot the remains of early humanist annotation throughout the margins and the verso of the final leaf contains a lengthy Latin poem in a neat fifteenth- or sixteenth-century hand. These have, of course, all been washed and Dibdin, presumably on good authority, says that this was done "by its late owner by means of pure water; so that, with the exception of a few tender places, the volume may be considered sound and desirable".[44] I cannot share his enthusiasm.

But let us look past the binding to the text block. Despite the washing, the paper is rather brown and unprepossessing and the printing adequate if uninspiring: an even, slightly heavy Roman type with blocky capitals which seem sometimes to have been set slightly squint. There is space for rubrication but no evidence any was ever applied; this was a scholar's copy, not a collector's.

You can probably guess my judgement from what I've written so far, but let me hold off on any pronouncement until we have turned our eyes to the Horace's companions. First, the Juvenal.[45] Dibdin described it as being in "foreign red morocco binding" when he prepared the Cassano volume of the *Bibliotheca Spenceriana* (one imagines a binding similar to that of the Horace), but since then it has been rebound, most likely in Lewis's workshop though the present characteristically rich Regency red morocco is unsigned. Opening the volume, we are presented with the same conundrum as has appeared so often in these pages: a washed leaf with tantalising remains of an ownership inscription at the bottom. Alas, I cannot read it; all we know of this volume's provenance is that it was in Cassano Serra's library by 1807.[46] Unlike the Horace, the Juvenal has been illuminated with quite attractive white vine capitals that harmonise nicely with the otherwise squat Roman of Ulrich Han. As with the Horace, there are shadows of extensive humanist annotation, once again "taken out by pure water".[47] It is an attractive enough piece of fifteenth-century printing, though hardly exceptional on aesthetic grounds.

Finally, the Terence.[48] It is the most substantial and the most attractive of the three volumes. Dibdin describes the binding as foreign and I think I believe him. The deep green (possibly Scheele's green) morocco is elegantly tooled with a wide decorative border which looks French, or just possibly Italian. The wide inner dentelles repeat this pattern and give an impression of just how striking a colour it would have been when first bound. This is later work, though—eighteenth or nineteenth century—and conceals a more complicated story. Opening the volume, the first thing you notice is that the entirety of the outer margin is gone and has been skilfully inlaid with paper; this volume must have been in truly appalling shape when it was first discovered by a bibliophile: gnawn by rats, thumbed to pieces by scholars, partially burnt in a fire or some similar fate. Accordingly, the text block was drastically trimmed and then made good by inlaying. All in all, it is quite a good job, though the freshness of the modern paper jars with the dark brown of the original. Like the other two it has also been washed, but not very well. Ugly brown blotches mark where extensive early annotations have been removed. It is simply rubricated with pleasing red and blue capitals and did I mention that the whole text block has been ruled in red, line by line? This was part of the conservation job that saw the inlaying and is a massive intervention to the original appearance of the pages, but I can't deny it looks nice.

I said it was simply rubricated, but I must except the opening page (see Figure 15.2). Here there is a refulgent white-line S whose vegetal tendrils spread around most of the text block, a two-colour rather modernist P and, perhaps most interesting for our purposes, the coat of arms of the fifteenth-century worthy who paid to have this volume rubricated. They are quite simple, at least by the standards of subsequent ages: a red goat on a white field, the arms of an obscure Florentine family, the Giorgini.[49]

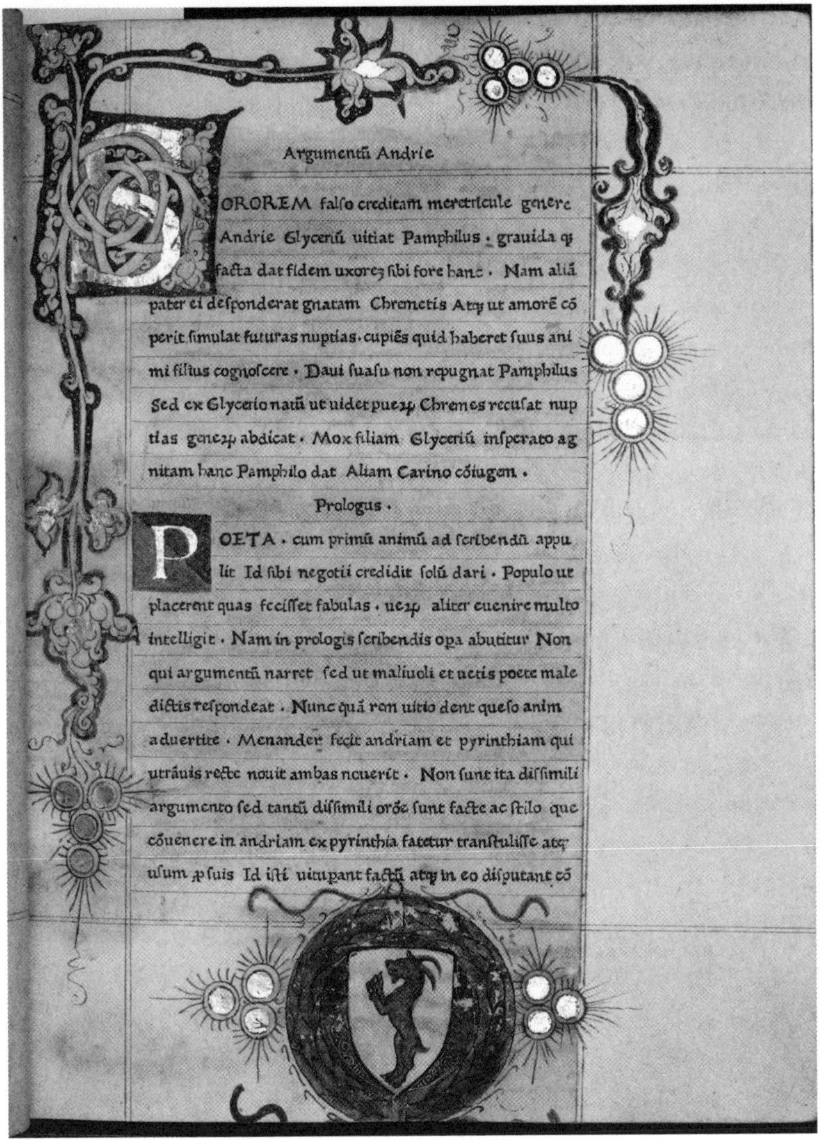

Figure 15.2 Terence, *[Opera]* (Rome: Sixtus Riessinger, *c.*1469), fol. 3r, John Rylands 18028.

What I hope is clear from these descriptions is that none of these are particularly exciting books within the context we have been exploring. They are relatively workaday printing, have all been extensively annotated and sometimes battered over the course of their lives and bear no especially remarkable bindings or illuminations or provenances to set them outside the common herd. All they have is *rarity*, if that (the Juvenal is now known in seven copies). There is a concept in psychology named "set completion". In its crudest form: people like to form complete "sets" of things, however you might define that.[50] I have already expressed my doubts as to how far academic psychology can explain the kind of collecting Spencer was doing, but it is also hard to avoid the conclusion that, in the case of the Cassano Serra library, he paid an absurd sum of money to obtain three items which he needed to complete a set: his collection of incunabular classics. Of course others remained in the wild, but Spencer could still say, in a very real sense, that with the acquisition of the Cassano Serra books, Reviczky's dream of a perfect collection of early classics had, in essence, been achieved.[51]

Spencer was sixty-one and had been collecting for thirty years (if we take his fateful meeting with Reviczky as a starting point): almost exactly half his life. During that time he had amassed something nearing twenty thousand volumes and created what by any standards was the greatest private library of his age and one of the greatest the world has ever seen. But can we reach any kind of measured assessment of such a remarkable accomplishment and its place in the history of libraries and of books?

SIXTEEN

The judgement of history?

George John, 2nd Earl Spence`r, died in Althorp at 2.25 in the afternoon on 10 November 1834.[1] He was seventy-six years old (see Figure 16.1). On the nineteenth the funeral procession wended its way from the house, through the estate, to the Church of St. Mary the Virgin in Great Brington, a mile away. It was, a contemporary observer wrote, "remarkable only for the immense concourse of persons assembled to witness it" (Spencer had requested a minimum of pomp), but all the same, "the lengthened and melancholy train, as it wound along the avenues of the noble park, had a very imposing appearance".[2] At Great Brington he was laid to rest amongst his ancestors and near his younger son Robert, whose unexpected death in 1830, followed soon after by Lavinia, his wife of fifty years, in 1831, had cast a shadow over the final era of his life.[3]

Contemporary assessments of Spencer were almost universally positive. According to his obituary in the *Times* "he commanded universal respect";[4] the *Annual Biography and Obituary* averred that his "private life...was not less entitled to our admiration than his political career" and that "inheriting a splendid fortune, he spent it generously and rationally";[5] the *Gentleman's Magazine* found him "calm, gentle, dignified, but not unbending...with Earl Spencer *gentility* as well as *title* seemed to be hereditary".[6] It is, however, very doubtful that any public announcement of his death would be less than celebratory given the social mores of 1830s England.

Figure 16.1 An older Spencer among his books. Jacob Thompson, *George John, 2nd Earl Spencer*, John Rylands PCF8.

Dibdin immediately wrote a prolix obituary for his local *Bury and Norwich Post and East Anglian* and his *Reminiscences*, written around this time, were predictably full of praise,

> It may be permitted an humble individual, like myself, to notice his love of letters and patronage of learned men; his pure political principles as a constitutional whig; his unbending attachment to church and state; his love of order; or moral worth; and of all those endearing qualities which move in the train of CHRISTIAN CHARITY.[7]

But there is an unspoken edge to this praise. Dibdin's own financial situation had gone from bad to worse; in 1831 he had become caught up in the bankruptcy of the bookseller Robert Triphook, his country living was sequestered, and by 1833 even his London living, the rectory of St. Mary's, Bryanston Square, was facing a similar fate. His attempts to borrow money—attempts which had been repeated over the years—were finally too much for Spencer who, while not fully breaking with Dibdin, kept him increasingly at arm's length, refusing what he described as Dibdin "borrowing without the smallest prospect of keeping your engagements" and preferring the far more reliable George Appleyard as his librarian to the scatterbrained Dibdin.[8] There was more than a little bitterness in Dibdin's reference to "Christian charity" (Dibdin long outlived Spencer, growing ever poorer and finally dying, more than a little crazed, in 1847).[9]

The final era of Spencer's library, which may be broadly dated from Appleyard's increasing involvement around the time of the Cassano Serra sale up to Spencer's death, was a quiet one, focused more on organisation than acquisition. Appleyard, good naval clerk that he was, was full of ideas for how best to organise and catalogue the libraries and also substantially contributed to the two "sheaf catalogues" at Althorp, essentially loose proto-card catalogues of the collection (one of these is now in the Rylands, the other is at the Grolier Club in New York).[10]

All in all, Spencer seems to have acquired about three thousand more books in the last decade and a half of his life. Many are modern, many more filled the remaining small gaps in his collection of incunabula, and a small handful pointed towards what seems to have been a late interest in Hebrew printing. Books printed by early Jewish printers like Gershom Soncino had cropped up before, but they increase in number in these years. It was, perhaps, the only part of the incunabular landscape that he had not yet conquered. The last (at least by acquisition number) incunable he acquired, only weeks or days before his death, was a 1475 Paduan *Quaestiones de tribus principiis rerum naturalium* printed by Laurentius Canozius.[11] It has not been rebound (its present binding of very parsimonious quarter calf and black-speckled brown paper is rather ugly), is not particularly well printed, and has, quite honestly, nothing in it of great interest. I doubt it would fetch £10,000 in today's market—probably just a few pounds in the 1830s. As an *envoi* it hints at the extent to which Spencer already had everything worth having; what was left were the dregs.

In Spencer's lifetime the incunables and the Aldines were all kept at Spencer House, while the "great bulk" of the rest of the library was

Figure 16.2 Edward Blore, *Interior of the Long Library at Althorp* (1822), from *Aedes Althorpianae*, i. facing 20, Blackie House Library and Museum.

kept in the ever-increasing number of book rooms at Althorp (see Figure 16.2).[12] Subsequently his books were concentrated in Althorp, looked after by the ageing but still spry and dedicated Appleyard until his death in 1855.[13] Then, they seem to have slept in the latter part of the nineteenth century, sitting quietly on their shelves during the lives of Spencer's sons John Charles, 3rd Earl Spencer (1782–1845) and Frederick, 4th Earl Spencer (1798–1857), and his grandson, John Poyntz, 5th Earl Spencer (1835–1910).

It was during the fifth earl's tenure at Althorp, however, that the books made a final, momentous move. John Rylands (1801–1888) was a wealthy Manchester textile merchant, one of a long tally of now more or less forgotten northern industrial magnates of his day. He was, to be sure, a philanthropist, as were many of his peers, but even this is unlikely to have bought him any lasting memory beyond Manchester itself.[14] It was, instead, his fateful third marriage in 1875 to the much younger,

Cuban-born Enriqueta Augustina Tennant (1843–1908), which would lead to his enduring fame. Having been born a Catholic, Enriqueta Rylands had converted to Congregationalism and directed her husband's philanthropy towards religious ends. After her husband's death, she determined to memorialise him with a theological library in Manchester, but this initial plan was utterly transformed in 1892 when she purchased the entirety of the Spencer library at Althorp, in a single stroke making the new John Rylands Library one of the great research collections of the British Isles and ensuring that her husband's name would be perpetuated *ad aeternam*, albeit amongst bibliographers rather than devout Congregationalists.[15]

Why did the earl sell? The answer was straightforward: rural Britain was in the midst of an agricultural depression and he needed the money. When news of the likely sale first reached public ears in June 1892, the presumption was that it would be broken up and auctioned (*The Times* piously hoped that "at least... not all, and not the best" books would be bought by "New York, Paris, and Berlin") and this certainly seems to have been John Poyntz Spencer's initial intent.[16] Enriqueta Rylands, however, recognised the opportunity the library's sale presented, acted immediately, and by the following month had agreed the purchase of more or less every book in Althorp—amounting to something over 40,000 volumes—for a grand total of £210,000.[17] Some of these she gave away, some she kept for her own use, but most went to the library founded in her husband's name and most of those—excepting those dispersed in the ill-advised 1988 sale discussed in Chapter 3—still remain there. Against all odds, Spencer's great collection has now survived for two centuries largely intact. As I was writing this book, the incunables were in the process of being re-catalogued to a much higher level, making them increasingly accessible to a new generation of scholars.

* * *

Spencer's library was the greatest private collection of books ever formed in Britain—not the biggest, but certainly the best, at least where early printing was concerned. It was, by any standards, a remarkable achievement. But we must confront its dark side too, as even his adulatory obituarists did, albeit obliquely. A jarring note is sounded in the otherwise conventional praise of the *Gentleman's Magazine* when we read that:

> It is impossible to contemplate [Spencer's] library—the achievement of one individual—without emotions of the deepest admiration. It is not that the books are, uniformly, in as beautiful condition without, as they are intrinsically attractive within; but that, in their acquisition, the noble owner never once descended to any mean or unworthy act. It was, from beginning to end…one unvaried course of liberal feeling, and of downright hearty enjoyment in the objects before him.[18]

Why did Spencer's honesty as a collector need such emphasising? Precisely because it was in doubt and with good reason. The fact of the matter is that many, if not most, of the key items in Spencer's collection were either directly or indirectly obtained through means, sometimes illegal, often immoral.

I do not mean to suggest that Spencer himself stole books; that would be absurd. What I *do* mean to suggest—and what I have shown throughout this volume—is that he took systematic advantage of the instability, confiscation, and looting occasioned by the Napoleonic Wars to acquire books which would never have been sold in ordinary circumstances. This seems like a relatively minor sin, taken in the abstract, but in considering what Spencer's purchases truly entailed we need to consider here, first, the *means* by which he acquired many of his books; second, the *impact* those purchases had upon their source libraries; and third, the *results* of his ownership for the books themselves.

The means by which Spencer acquired books varied both by individual situation and by the preferred tactics of the book agents, booksellers, or other middlemen with whom he was dealing. We may, however, broadly divide them into five categories. The smallest of these are the rare cases where we have clear evidence of Spencer purchasing stolen goods, as with the papal indulgence stolen from the University of Louvain library (see p. 124) or the Dante removed by d'Elci and Cassano Serra from the seminary at Fiesole (see pp. 210–211). A somewhat larger set of cases are those where we may entertain a reasonable suspicion that books have been stolen, but where proof is lacking; these include, most significantly, Spencer's Gutenberg Bible (see pp. 68–81).

The majority of the incunables which Spencer bought from continental sources fall into neither of these categories, however. Instead they were purchased, via a book agent, for a more or less fair market value, but from individuals and institutions in extremis, men and collections which were facing existential threats to their way of life. In other words, Spencer's agents were simply taking advantage of a larger existing situation. In the case of many of them, Horn especially, they did so both knowingly and ruthlessly (see, for example, his comments on how the threats facing Bavarian monasteries would yield a better crop of sales at p. 117). Rather less often, sums were offered which were simply large enough to appeal to the cupidity of otherwise secure institutions, as in the case of Lincoln Cathedral's sale of its Caxtons (see pp. 164–166).

It needs to be reiterated, though, that many other early books in Spencer's library were purchased perfectly legitimately and without any hint of undue pressure or foul play. In this category we may include those bought at auctions like the Pinelli sale (auctions after 1789 are more suspect and dependent on the sources of the books there sold) as well as the thousands of new books bought each year from London dealers.[19]

These were his means, but, given that almost all of his earliest books were purchased from the representatives of other collections, what impact did these purchases have on the collections in which they had formerly resided? In considering this, we need to face the overwhelming source of his incunabular purchases head on: monasteries. Spencer and his contemporaries, including (perhaps especially) the French government, participated in the single largest violent re-distribution of books that Europe has ever seen. The losers were the French aristocracy, to a considerable extent (see the discussion of the revolutionary book depots at pp. 78–80), but, more than anyone, the religious institutions—monasteries, nunneries, seminaries, and religious colleges—across continental Europe which saw not only their libraries but their very existence snuffed out by the draconian actions of the French, German, and Italian states during the course of the Napoleonic Wars.[20]

On the one hand, it would be foolish to blame Spencer, or even English bibliophiles as a group, for a much larger international catastrophe, but by the same token his purchases *did* directly result in the spoliation of collections and the overall impoverishment of continental, and especially German, book culture. This was recognised by contemporaries. As early as 1803, the Bavarian bibliographer Georg Wilhelm Zapf had little doubt as to who was to blame. "How many" incunabula, he wrote,

> can have been snatched from our sight in this long period of time, through ignorance, neglect, self-interest, bigotry or envy...and in wars through plunder! Germany has lost many of its treasures through several travellers [*Reisende*] and through other scouts [*Kundschafter*] who have been put to this purpose; some of these have migrated to England and some to Russia, and many went to the National Library in Paris during the last war.[21]

Zapf correctly identified book agents, working for Spencer and his peers, as the principal marauders leading to the loss of precious early printing from German libraries. A generation later, Heinrich Joachim Jäck, a former Cistercian monk who later become Bavarian Royal Librarian, could name names. It was the "infamous robbers" Alexander Horn and Jean-Baptiste Maugérard whose thefts could be traced in many a monastic library in Bavaria and he pointed out moments which saw them depriving a Franciscan collection "of its most beautiful early imprints" or "taking advantage" of a Carmelite librarian, removing from his care "a Bible printed on parchment and other valuables".[22]

Nor can any faint defence be mounted in the name of the old anti-Catholic canard of "rescuing" books from "ignorant monks". The men who were forced by circumstances to sell their precious treasures were enlightened scholars and bibliographers. We may consider here Michael Seuffert, the Carmelite librarian at Bamberg (see p. 102), Sigismund Hogl, the Premonstratensian librarian at Rot an der Rot (see p. 119), and Franz Krismer, the Carthusian librarian at Buxheim (see p. 134), among many others. These were scholars who understood and valued early books just as much as Spencer or Dibdin. They sold, not because they knew no better, but because they had no choice.

We may also approach the issues of the effects of Spencer's purchases upon collections by considering a counter-factual: what does a monastic library which has not been looted, purchased, and/or secularised look like? Good examples include the Benedictine Abbey at Admont in Styria (see p. 212) and the Augustinian Abbey at Klosterneuburg near Vienna (see pp. 205–206), both of which have retained most of their incredibly rich medieval and early modern collections. Are they sticks in the mud? Inaccessible, old-fashioned book dungeons? No. They are incredibly important, historically rich, and thriving centres of research in the present day.[23] We may pause for a moment to imagine what the equally or even more significant libraries at Buxheim, Bamberg, Regensburg, or Eichstätt might have looked like today if they had had the similar good fortune to escape unscathed.

Even in cases such as Lincoln Cathedral Library, where most of the collection has survived, the impact of selling a dozen of the best books has still been significantly detrimental to the collection as a whole and was already perceived as such by contemporaries (remember Beriah Botfield's 1849 denunciation of the Lincoln clergy—"the guardians of the temple slept, and Mammon prevailed"—at p. 165).

If both means and institutional impact seem not to tell in Spencer's favour, can we at least find favourable results stemming from his acquisitions? At first, this might seem to be an easy case to make. Seeing the books' current situation in the Rylands, we might reasonably assume that all's well that ends well: they are safe, accessible, and (aside from those sold in 1988) in a stable, open, long-term home. This is all true *now*, but the immediate results of their acquisition by Spencer were very different.

Until his finances or his energy or both were finally overwhelmed at the time of the Cassano Serra purchase, Spencer consistently and at great cost pursued a systematic policy of sending his books for rebinding by the major London bookbinders. Where earlier annotation—usually, given the age of the books, annotations by fifteenth- or sixteenth-century

Humanist readers—was present, the books were disbound and washed to remove any extraneous marks before rebinding. Where provenance was present, it was systematically crossed out, scratched out, cut out, or otherwise defaced, either by Spencer's agents, his binders or—just possibly—Spencer himself. Because of these processes, the books which went through the Spencerian mill have lost a very significant proportion of their overall cultural value as we would now understand it. Bindings, many of which would have dated to the same period as the printing itself, offer precious information about previous artistic and bibliophilic practice, annotations help us recover the mental world of earlier readers, and provenance helps us understand the trajectory of a book through time. Shorn of these crucial elements, many a book in Spencer's library is simply an empty husk of print in a whited (or azured or rubrified) sepulchre of goatskin. Its ability to communicate to future generations has been essentially crippled.

Beyond this, there was also a major loss occasioned simply by taking them out of their previous contexts. Buxheim offers a pertinent example. The incunable donations of Hilprand Brandenburg (1442–1514) could have told us far more when they still sat side by side on the monastery's shelves than they do now when scattered across multiple continents (see p. 232. Just as books from Spencer's own collection have richer layers of meaning when they can be consulted and engaged with alongside their siblings in the Rylands than if they had been dispersed at auction after all in 1892, so books from the many monastic and other libraries which were Spencer's hunting grounds could have told us much more had they simply remained where they were.

I have marshalled these points in such detail because I am, I regret to say, moving towards a painful conclusion. It is undeniable that Spencer's collection is magnificent, in every sense of the word. Looking at the pictures of the library rooms in Althorp, before the move to Manchester, gives the most vivid sense of this. They present such an overwhelming quantity of such excellent, indescribably beautiful books. They are, in fact, as close as one could reasonably get to the realisation of every bibliophile's dream. Nor was his achievement a purely aesthetic one. Spencer assembled a genuinely unparalleled collection of early printing and so created a resource which could be—first through the medium of the *Bibliotheca Spenceriana*, later through the presence of the books themselves in the Rylands—deployed by generations of scholars to better understand the history of the printed word in Europe.

And on a purely personal level, I still can't help but *like* Spencer. I see too much of myself in him, in this quiet, slightly awkward, determined, erudite man who filled his life with his passion (admittedly, Spencer was an extremely wealthy peer and I am a not-at-all-wealthy writer, but the resemblance remains).

But none of this changes the essential fact: Spencer's collecting was awful. It was, in fact, a crime against the common European cultural heritage which can never be undone. The removal of books from their centuries-old homes, the destruction of their bindings and annotations, the defacing of their provenance, these in themselves are terrible crimes in the world of the book. But they are only part of the story. The truly painful conclusion I've reached in writing this book is that Spencer ruthlessly took advantage of a largely harmless, frequently intellectual, and occasionally holy group of men—the inhabitants of the great European monasteries—to line his shelves with books, destroying incalculably precious evidence of those books' histories in the process.

Nor was he alone in this, as we have seen. His is simply a particularly vivid case study of a generation of English collectors who delightedly pillaged the war-torn continent for their own ends, creating collections which are now, in many cases, the foundations of the modern research libraries of the Anglophone world. Where Spencer stands out among his contemporaries, aside from the quality of his library, is its ultimate fate. Most of his fellow collectors—Blandford, Heber, Sykes, Beckford—built libraries which were dispersed at or before their deaths.[24] Their books can now be found in public institutions (and private libraries) from New York to Tokyo. Spencer and his friend Thomas Grenville (whose books now form a core part of the British Library's early printed collection) were exceptions to the rule.[25] As such, their collections present some of the moral conundrums I have outlined above in particularly acute forms.

* * *

Where does this leave us? Knowing what we do about how Spencer and his contemporaries acquired so many of their books, what relationship ought we to have to them? These are not the Parthenon Marbles; we have no Greece to return these volumes to. Instead, they come from an Atlantis sunk as surely as any. What secularisation did not achieve in 1806, twenty-first-century secular society has, and only a tiny handful of the monasteries and other religious institutions from which Spencer took his books still exist today, and even those survive in drastically altered circumstances.

So I am not proposing restitution, that increasingly common answer to thorny problems of cultural looting.[26] Nor do I think I would find much support if I did. The damage has been too great, it is too poorly documented, too old, and—this I find the most shocking part, but I know it carries considerable weight—committed against a too unfashionable sort of people (white, male, European religious) for anyone to seriously consider it as an option.

Nor, however, do I think we can afford to ignore what happened. As the inheritors of Spencer's books and others like them, today's research libraries have also inherited the weight of their histories and the damage done, as well as the collections formed, by the men of Spencer's generation. If we want to be honest with ourselves, and do justice to history, we need to hold in the balance our pleasure at having so many of the world's oldest books at our finger tips in Manchester, in London, in New York, in California, and our knowledge that they are there because of a great and unrightable historical wrong, committed against institutions which, for over a thousand years, had been the memory keepers of the western world until war, greed, and obsession cruelly tore that inheritance away. It is an uneasy balance to hold in mind and an uncomfortable burden to carry, but it is the only morally right thing to do.

I cannot end, however, without returning once more to our—hero? anti-hero?—Spencer. He was the Book Fool *par excellence*, the great collector, in all its light and dark shades. If we go back to November 1834, I wonder if he died content? Somehow I doubt it. Not because of any pangs of conscience at his collecting practice—I do not think he gave that a moment's thought—but because true collectors are not content people. They are always striving, groping blindly in the dark for the realisation of an impossible dream: of placing every desired object within the magic circle of personal ownership. No, I do not think contentment was a natural condition for Spencer. I do suspect, though, that he was not unfamiliar with joy. Maybe we can do worse than leave him, not as an old man looking back in 1834, but as a young man looking forward in 1789, unpacking Reviczky's newly-acquired library and dreaming of all the beautiful, ancient, rare, irresistible books he was still yet to buy. In that moment, I think, he knew joy.

Notes

FRONT MATTER

1. *A Miscellany Containing Richard de Bury's Philobiblon...* (London: George Routledge and Sons, 1888), 21.
2. John Ferriar, *The Bibliomania, an Epistle to Richard Heber, Esq.* (London: Printed for T. Cadell, and W. Davies, 1809), 3, ll. 1–2.
3. BL Add MS 76300, fols. 735–736.
4. This and subsequent equivalents, together with some of the methodological substructure of this note, are derived from measuringworth.com.
5. https://grants.fnl.org.uk/archbishop-mortons-copy-quintilian-institutiones-oratoriae
6. https://www.christies.com/en/lot/lot-6311800

PROLOGUE

1. The history of panegyrics focusing on Spencer and his collection begins with Thomas Frognall Dibdin, whose many works are cited *passim* in this volume. Subsequent important, but inevitably brief and partial, additions to this tradition can be found in Edward Edwards, *Libraries and Founders of Libraries* (London: Trübner and Co., 1864), 392–447, and Seymour de Ricci, *English Collectors of Books & Manuscripts (1530–1930) and Their Marks of Ownership* (Cambridge: At the University Press, 1930), 72–78.
2. Kristian Jensen, more than anyone, has been my predecessor in the study of Spencer and his collecting, particularly in his *Revolution and the Antiquarian Book: Reshaping the Past, 1780–1815* (Cambridge: Cambridge University Press, 2011). I am indebted to his pioneering work in the Spencer archive, though I have not always reached the same conclusions. David McKitterick's *The Invention of Rare Books: Private Interest and Public Memory, 1600–1840* (Cambridge: Cambridge University Press, 2018) is an invaluable study of larger trends in the book market during this period, but Spencer himself appears only occasionally. My debt to Eric Marshall White's tireless and detailed studies of the trade in early printed books stretches far beyond the subject of his *Editio Princeps: A History of the Gutenberg Bible* (Turnhout: Harvey Miller Publishers, 2017) to include his articles and book chapters, especially those in which Alexander Horn is concerned.

CHAPTER I

1. Thomas Jefferson, *The Writings of Thomas Jefferson*, 10 vols., ed. Paul Leicester Ford (New York and London: G. P. Putnam's Sons, 1892–1899), i. 122.
2. J. Neumann and J. Dettwiller, "Great Historical Events that were Significantly Affected by the Weather: Part 9, the Year Leading to the Revolution of 1789 in France (II)", *Bulletin of the American Meteorological Society* 71 (1990): 33–41 at 39.
3. John Nichols, *Literary Anecdotes of the Eighteenth Century*, 6 vols. (London: Printed for the Author, 1812–1816), v. 324.

4. G. E. Bentley, Jr., "The 'Edwardses of Halifax' as Booksellers by Catalogue, 1749–1835", *Studies in Bibliography* 45 (1992): 187–222 at 197.
5. *Bibliotheca Pinelliana: A Catalogue of the Magnificent and Celebrated Library of Maffei Pinelli, Late of Venice... Sold by Auction, on Monday, March 2, 1789, and the Twenty-Two Following Days...* (s.l.: s.n., 1789), viii.
6. David McKitterick, *The Invention of Rare Books: Private Interest and Public Memory, 1600–1840* (Cambridge: Cambridge University Press, 2018), 219.
7. The printed catalogue indicated that the sale would commence on 2 March, but a notice in *The Gentleman's Magazine* 59 (1789): 70, makes it clear that the library's delayed arrival in England meant that the sale only commenced on 20 April, with the second part of the collection being sold first.
8. McKitterick, *Invention*, 222.
9. Charles Spencer, *The Spencer Family* (London: Viking, 1999), 171.
10. Michael O'Sullivan, "A Hungarian Josephinist, Orientalist, and Bibliophile: Count Karl Reviczky, 1737–1793", *Austrian History Yearbook* 45 (2014): 61–88 at 61.
11. The adverb is from Thomas Frognall Dibdin, *The Bibliographical Decameron; or, Ten Days Pleasant Discourse upon Illuminated Manuscripts, and Subjects Connected with Early Engraving, Typography, and Bibliography*, 3 vols. (London: Printed for the Author, by W. Bulmer and Co., 1817), ii. 349, and probably derives from Spencer's own account of their meeting.
12. Rylands 3205; Thomas Frognall Dibdin, *Bibliotheca Spenceriana*, 4 vols. (London, 1814–15), ii. 238–239; Censimento Nazionale delle Edizioni Italiane del XVI secolo ("EDIT16") 37448.
13. If you want to learn more, the standard guide is Philip Gaskell, *A New Introduction to Bibliography* (1972; Oxford: At the Clarendon Press, 1979).
14. G. A. Olivier, *Travels in the Ottoman Empire, Egypt, and Persia* (London, 1801), 227–229; J. J. H., "Turkey Red. - Manufacture of Morocco Leather", *The Patent Journal, and Inventors' Magazine* 2 (1847): 782.
15. *The Art of Tanning and of Currying Leather* (Dublin: Printed by S. Powell, 1773), 206ff.
16. Olivier, 228–229.
17. John Hannett, *Bibliopegia; or, the Art of Bookbinding*, 4th ed. London: Simpkin, Marshall and Co., 1848, 52, 55.
18. Colin Mackenzie, *One Thousand Experiments in Chemistry* (London, 1822), 607; *The Technical Educator: An Encyclopaedia of Technical Education*, Vol. III (London: Cassell & Company, Limited, s.n.) 87–88.
19. Dibdin, *Bibliographical Decameron*, ii. 349.
20. Penny Jenkins, "Printing on Parchment or Vellum", *The Paper Conservator* 16 (1992): 31.
21. Paul Needham, "Book Production on Paper and Vellum in the Fourteenth and Fifteenth Centuries", in *Papier im mittelalterlichen Europea: Herstellung und Gebrauch*, ed. Carla Meyer, Sandra Schultz, and Bernd Schnedmüller (Berlin: de Gruyter, 2015), 247–271.
22. Thomas Frognall Dibdin, *Bibliomania; or Book-Madness; A Bibliographical Romance* (London: Henry G. Bohn, 1842), 520.
23. Dibdin, *Bibliomania*, 520.
24. Pindar, sig. 16iiiir, Rylands 3205.
25. See Martin Lowry, *The World of Aldus Manutius: Business and Scholarship in Renaissance Venice* (Ithaca: Cornell University Press, 1979), more recently Oren Margolis, *Aldus Manutius: The Invention of the Publisher* (London: Reaktion Books, 2023), and, for his Greek publications in particular, Konstantinos Sp. Staikos, *The Greek Editions of Aldus Manutius and His Greek Collaborators* (New Castle, Del.: Oak Knoll Press, 2016).

26. Spencer's subsequent participation in the culture of Aldine collecting is discussed in Martin Lowry, "Boyars, Bishops and Bibliophiles: An Aldine Network in Revolutionary Europe", in *Libri, tipografi, biblioteche: ricerche storiche dedicate a Luigi Balsamo* (Florence: Leo S. Olschki, 1997), 473–491.
27. Dibdin, *Bibliographical Decameron*, ii. 349.
28. Douglas F. Bauer, "Problems in the Aldine Pindar", *Princeton University Library Chronicle* 76 (2015): 419–446 at 443.
29. The dialogue comes from Lord Glenbervie's diaries and came to him via the recollections of Edwards; see G. E. Bentley jun., 'The Bookseller as Diplomat: James Edwards, Lord Grenville, and Earl Spencer in 1800', *Book Collector*, 33 (1984), 470–85 at 484–85.
30. BL Add MS 76016, Reviczky-Spencer, 24 June 1789.
31. BL Add MS 76016, Reviczky-Spencer, 24 June 1789.
32. BL Add MS 76016, Reviczky-Spencer, 24 June 1789.
33. BL Add MS 76016, Spencer-Reviczky, 26 June 1789.
34. BL Add MS 76016, Reviczky-Spencer, 29 June 1789.
35. Count Reviczky (pseud. "Periergus Deltophilus"), *Bibliotheca Graeca et Latina... editio altera* (Berlin: typis Joannis Friderici Unger, 1784), xiii–xiv.
36. Reviczky, *Bibliotheca, editio altera*, xvi.
37. Reviczky, *Bibliotheca, editio altera*, xvi.
38. BL Add MSS 76017–76019.
39. BL Add MS 76016, Reviczky-Spencer, 15 July 1789.
40. BL Add MS 76016, Reviczky-Spencer, 11 August 1789.

CHAPTER 2

1. Amanda Foreman, *Georgiana: Duchess of Devonshire* (London: HarperCollins, 1999), 4.
2. Foreman, *Georgiana*, 4.
3. Joseph Friedman, *Spencer House: Chronicle of a Great London Mansion* (London: Zwemmer, 1993), 38.
4. Friedman, *Spencer House*, 34.
5. Friedman, *Spencer House*, 70.
6. Friedman, *Spencer House*, 39–40.
7. Charles Spencer, *The Spencer Family* (London: Viking, 1999), 115–116; Friedman, *Spencer House*, 41.
8. Sir Denis le Marchant, Bt., *Memoir of John Charles, Viscount Althorp, Third Earl Spencer* (London: Richard Bentley and Son, 1876), xviii–xix.
9. Friedman, *Spencer House*, 54–55.
10. Foreman, *Georgiana*, *passim*.
11. See the portrait of John (*c.* 1763) by Thomas Gainsborough and that of Georgiana (*c.* 1764) by Pompeo Batoni, both now at Althorp.
12. Friedman, *Spencer House*, 33–34. For Althorp, see Charles Spencer, *Althorp: The Story of an English Country House* (London: Viking, 1998).
13. Friedman, *Spencer House*, 34.
14. Friedman, *Spencer House*, 38–39.
15. Foreman, *Georgiana*, 12.
16. Brian Connell, *Portrait of a Whig Peer: Compiled from the Papers of the Second Viscount Palmerston, 1739–1802* (London: Andre Deutsch, 1957), 51.
17. Connell, *Portrait of a Whig Peer*, 46.

18. Connell, *Portrait of a Whig Peer*, 51.
19. Garland Hampton Cannon, *The Life and Mind of Oriental Jones: Sir William Jones, the Father of Modern Linguistics* (Cambridge: Cambridge University Press, 1990), 11.
20. Marchant, *Memoir*, 6.
21. Cannon, *Life and Mind*, 12–13.
22. John and J. A. Venn, *Alumni Cantabrigienses: A Biographical List of All Known Students, Graduates and Holders of Office at the University of Cambridge*, 10 vols. (Cambridge: Cambridge University Press, 1922–1954), pt. 1, i. 38; *The Letters of David Garrick*, 3 vols., ed. David M. Little and George M. Kahrl (Cambridge, Mass.: Harvard University Press, 1963), ii. 426.
23. J. Cradock, *Literary and Miscellaneous Memoirs*, 2nd ed., 4 vols. (London: Printed for the Author, 1826), i. 195.
24. Sir William Jones, *The Letters of Sir William Jones*, 2 vols., ed. Garland Hampton Cannon (Oxford: At the Clarendon Press, 1970), i. 66.
25. Cannon, *Life and Mind*, 12–13.
26. Cannon, *Life and Mind*, 18.
27. Jones, *Letters*, i. 14.
28. Jones, *Letters*, i. 16.
29. *Letters of David Garrick*, ii. 656; Spencer, *The Spencer Family*, 123.
30. Cradock, *Memoirs*, iv. 240; John and J. A. Venn, *Alumni Cantabrigienses*, pt. 1, i. 38.
31. Foreman, *Georgiana*, 12; Jones, *Letters*, i. 19.
32. Jones, *Letters*, i. 21.
33. Jones, *Letters*, i. 28.
34. "Earl Spencer, K.G.", *The Gentleman's Magazine* NS 3 (1835): 89–93 at 89.
35. Jones, *Letters*, i. 28.
36. Jones, *Letters*, i. 30–31.
37. Jones, *Letters*, i. 31–35.
38. Jones, *Letters*, i. 49, 58.
39. Jones, *Letters*, i. 64.
40. Jones, *Letters*, i. 66–68.
41. Jones, *Letters*, i. 71.
42. Jones, *Letters*, i. 176–177.
43. William Jones, "Solima, An Arabic Eclogue, Written in the Year 1768", in *Poems Consisting Chiefly of Translations from the Asiatick Languages* (Oxford: At the Clarendon Press, 1772), 4–5.
44. W. T. J. Gun, *The Harrow School Register, 1571–1800* (London: Longmans, Green and Co., 1934), 32.
45. John and J. A. Venn, *Alumni Cantabrigienses*, pt. 2, v. 604.
46. See Angela Rosenthal, *Angelica Kauffman: Art and Sensibility* (New Haven and London: Yale University Press, 2006) and Angelica Goodden, *Miss Angel: The Art and World of Angelica Kauffman* (London: Pimlico, 2005).
47. Foreman, *Georgiana*, 73; *The Gentleman's Magazine* 51 (1781): 146; Rose E. McCalmont, *Memoirs of the Binghams*, ed. C. R. B. Barrett (London: Spottiswoode & Co. Ltd., 1915), 115.
48. Sir William Jones, "The Muse Recalled, An Ode; Occasioned by the Nuptials of Lord Viscount Althorp and Miss Lavinia Bingham, Eldest Daughter of Charles Lord Lucan, March 6, 1781", *An Asylum for Fugitive Pieces, in Prose and Verse* (London: Printed for J. Debrett, 1785), 269–276.

49. Foreman, *Georgiana*, 73.
50. Castalia, Countess Granville, ed., *Lord Granville Leveson Gower (First Earl Granville): Private Correspondence, 1781 to 1821*, 2 vols. (London: John Murray, 1916), ii. 352.
51. Werner Muensterberger, *Collecting—An Unruly Passion: Psychological Perspectives* (Princeton: Princeton University Press, 1994), chs. 1–2.
52. William D. McIntosh and Brandon Schmeichel, "Collectors and Collecting: A Social Psychological Perspective", *Leisure Sciences* 26 (2004): 85–97 at 86.
53. G. Thomas Tanselle, "A Rationale of Collecting", *Studies in Bibliography* 51 (1998): 1–25 at 14.
54. Tanselle, "Rationale", 7.
55. Jones, *Letters*, i. 139–140.
56. Cannon, *Life and Mind*, 14 and *passim*; Michael O'Sullivan, "A Hungarian Josephinist, Orientalist, and Bibliophile: Count Karl Reviczky, 1737–1793", *Austrian History Yearbook* 45 (2014): 61–88.

CHAPTER 3

1. Walter Benjamin, "Unpacking My Library: A Talk about Book Collecting", in *Illuminations*, tr. Harry Zorn (London: Pimlico, 1999), 61.
2. BL Add MS 76016, Reviczky-Spencer, 15 July 1789.
3. Mark Purcell, *The Country House Library* (New Haven and London: Yale University Press, 2017), 211.
4. The literature about Gutenberg is vast. For Gutenberg's life a good starting point is Albert Kapr, *Johann Gutenberg: The Man and His Invention*, tr. Douglas Martin (Aldershot: Scolar Press, 1996) and for the great Bible itself, Eric Marshall White, *Editio Princeps: A History of the Gutenberg Bible* (Turnhout: Harvey Miller Publishers, 2017).
5. Rylands 3140; Thomas Frognall Dibdin, *Bibliotheca Spenceriana; or a Descriptive Catalogue of the Books Printed in the Fifteenth Century, and of Many Valuable First Editions, in the Library of George John Earl Spencer, K.G.*, 4 vols. (London: Printed for the Author, by W. Bulmer and Co., 1814–1815), i. 304–305; ISTC ic00575000; GW 6921. Keen readers of footnotes who may not be bibliographers will probably want to know what these latter two citations mean. The Incunabula Short Title Catalogue (ISTC), begun in 1980, is an international database (https://data.cerl.org/istc/_search), currently hosted by the Consortium of European Research Libraries, which provides bibliographical data for every known book printed up to 1500. The Gesamtkatalog der Wiegendrucke (GW), begun in 1925, is the German equivalent, run out of the Staatsbibliothek in Berlin, and exists both online (https://www.gesamtkatalogderwiegendrucke.de/gwen.xhtml) and as a series of printed volumes. The two catalogues provide slightly different information and it is customary to cite both when referring to an incunable. By citing the ISTC and GW references I avoid having to provide the otherwise lengthy bibliographical description which would be needed to make it clear which particular edition I am discussing.
6. For the illumination of incunabula a useful starting point is Lilian Armstrong, "The Study of Hand-Illumination and Woodcut Illustration in Italian Incunabula, 1960s–2020: Historiography and a Memoir", *Bulletin du bibliophile* (2021): 9–36. For rubrication, see Margaret M. Smith, "Red as a Textual Element During the Transition from Manuscript to Print", in *Textual Cultures: Cultural Texts*, ed. Orietta Da Rold and Elaine Treharne (Woodbridge, Suffolk: Boydell & Brewer, 2010), 187–200.

7. Christopher de Hamel, *The Posthumous Papers of the Manuscripts Club* (London: Allen Lane, 2022), 264; David McKitterick, *The Invention of Rare Books: Private Interest and Public Memory, 1600–1840* (Cambridge: Cambridge University Press, 2018), 209.
8. De Hamel, *Posthumous Papers*, *passim*.
9. *Catalogue des livres de la bibliothèque de feu m. le duc de la Vallière*, tome I (Paris: Chez Guillaume de Bure fils aîné, 1783), lot 2275. For prices I have referred to the copy at Bibliothèque Nationale de France 31540262.
10. Rylands 3148; Dibdin, *Bibliotheca Spenceriana*, i. 330–331; ISTC ic00654000; GW 6742. See Edwin Hall, *Sweynheym & Pannartz and the Origins of Printing in Italy* (McMinnville, Or.: Bird & Bull Press, 1991), though a more accessible and up-to-date monograph on the pair is a major *desideratum*.
11. *Catalogue des livres de la bibliothèque de feu m. le duc de la Vallière*, tome I, lot 2253.
12. Rylands 3455; Dibdin, *Bibliotheca Spenceriana*, i. 318–320; ISTC ic00503500; GW 6799.
13. *Catalogue des livres de la bibliothèque de feu m. le duc de la Vallière*, tome I, lot 2311.
14. Getty MS Ludwig XV 7 (83.MR.177); National Gallery, London, NG5.
15. Guillaume-François de Bure, *Supplement a la Bibliographie instructive, ou Catalogue des livres du cabinet de feu M. Louis Jean Gaignat*, tome premier (Paris: Chez Guillaume François de Bure le jeune, 1769), lots 1462, 1463, and 1475. For prices I have referred to the annotated copy at Bibliothèque Nationale de France 30307467.
16. Rylands 3520; BL Add MS 76017, fol. 153r-v; ISTC if00231000; GW 10092.
17. See Robert Proctor, *The Printing of Greek in the Fifteenth Century* (Oxford: Printed for the Bibliographical Society, 1900) who also discusses the fragments of Greek printing which had appeared in the 1460s, and, for a more current view of the field, Geri Della Rocca de Candal, "Printing in Greek Before Aldus Manutius", in *Printing R-Evolution and Society, 1450–1500*, ed. Cristina Dondi (Venice: Edizioni Ca' Foscari, 2020), 278–297.
18. Dennis E. Rhodes, "The Career of Thomas Ferrandus of Brescia", *Bulletin of the John Rylands Library* 67 (1984): 544.
19. Rylands 3325; Dibdin, *Bibliotheca Spenceriana*, ii. 53; ISTC ih00300800; GW 12900.
20. Ellic Howe, *A List of London Bookbinders, 1648–1815* (London: The Bibliographical Society, 1950), 53.
21. BL Add MS 76299, fols. 204–204[a].
22. Howe, 97; Dibdin, Thomas Frognall Dibdin, *The Bibliographical Decameron*, 3 vols. (London, 1817), ii. 520.
23. BL Add MS 76299, fol. 312 (the book in question was Spencer's copy of the 1471 Sweynheym and Pannartz Cicero).
24. Hering's first invoice to Spencer was paid 8 February 1797 (BL Add MS 76300, fols. 487–488).
25. Howe, 46–47; Dibdin, *Bibliographical Decameron*, ii. 525.
26. *ODNB*, s.n.
27. Dibdin, *Bibliotheca Spenceriana*, ii. 53.
28. *Bibliotheca Pinelliana: A Catalogue of the Magnificent and Celebrated Library of Maffei Pinelli, Late of Venice…Sold by Auction, on Monday, March 2, 1789, and the Twenty-Two Following Days…* (s.l.: s.n., 1789), 365, lot 9163.
29. Rylands 3246; Dibdin, *Bibliotheca Spenceriana*, ii. 55–62; ISTC ih00300000; GW 12895.
30. Mirjam M. Foot, *The Henry Davis Gift: A Collection of Bookbindings*, 3 vols. (London: The British Library, 1978–2010), i. 96–114.
31. Sylvester Harding, *Rogerus Payne* (London: Thomas Payne, 1 March 1800).

32. *Bibliotheca Spenceriana*, ii. 55–62.
33. Kristian Jensen, *Revolution and the Antiquarian Book: Reshaping the Past, 1780–1815* (Cambridge: Cambridge University Press, 2011), 155–157.
34. Dibdin, *Bibliotheca Spenceriana*, i. 258–261; ISTC ia00959000; GW 2334.
35. *Bibliotheca Spenceriana*, i. 261.
36. Nicolas Barker, "The Rape of the Rylands", *The Book Collector* (Summer 1988): 169–184 at 169.
37. Barker, "Rape of the Rylands", 180.
38. Barker, "Rape of the Rylands", 175.
39. Elizabeth L. Eisenstein, *The Printing Revolution in Early Modern Europe* (Cambridge: Cambridge University Press, 1983), 13–17.
40. I do not mean to suggest that all book collectors of the period were solely obsessed with incunabula. Most could hardly afford to be, and even those with deep enough pockets were not necessarily riding the iron rails of Spencer's particular obsession. Nor do I mean to suggest that this obsession was a product of Spencer's generation; as David McKitterick and others have shown, it had existed for at least a hundred years before, gradually gaining ground as one of the principal axes along which the European elite might choose to collect (see McKitterick, *Invention of Rare Books, passim*). That said, Spencer and many of his contemporaries *did* care about these earliest printed books to the exclusion of much else and that particular tradition of bibliomania has persisted, at least in some quarters, ever since.
41. Benjamin, "Unpacking My Library", 69.

CHAPTER 4

1. Déclaration des droits de l'homme et du citoyen, 26 August 1789.
2. *Archives Parlementaires de 1787 à 1860,* 1e série, Tome XI (Paris: Librairie Administrative de Paul Dupon, 1877), 648–649.
3. Costanza Ichino Rossi, "Crevenna, Pietro Antonio", *Dizionario Biografico degli Italiani,* https://www.treccani.it/enciclopedia/pietro-antonio-crevenna_(Dizionario-Biografico).
4. *Catalogue Raisonné De La Collection De Livres De M. Pierre Antoine Crevenna*, 6 vols. ([Amsterdam]: s.n., 1776).
5. *Catalogue des livres de la bibliothèque de M. Pierre-Antoine Bolongaro-Crevenna*, 5 vols. (Amsterdam: Chez de J. Changuion, & P. den Hengst, 1789), i. sig. π2r.
6. BL Add MS 76016, Reviczky-Spencer, 29 September 1789.
7. BL Add MS 76016, Reviczky-Spencer, 25 November 1789.
8. The full series of Althorp papers is BL Add MS 75301–78155. For details of their acquisition by the British Library and present status, I am grateful to Zoe Stansell of the library's Manuscripts Reference Service, e-mail communication, 30 May 2025.
9. BL Add MS 76016, Reviczky-Spencer, 31 July 1790. The *Philippics* were printed in Rome by Ulrich Han and are now Rylands 3154.
10. *Crevenna Catalogue*, i. II.
11. *Crevenna Catalogue*, i. 255, nr. 1279 (*Sefer Mitzvot*), iv. 61, nr. 6009 (*Historia de infantulo*); Thomas Frognall Dibdin, *Bibliotheca Spenceriana; or a Descriptive Catalogue of the Books Printed in the Fifteenth Century, and of Many Valuable First Editions, in the Library of George John Earl Spencer, K.G.*, 4 vols. (London: Printed for the Author, by W. Bulmer and Co., 1814–1815), iii. 378–381, 428–430. The *Sefer Mitzvot* is Rylands 1101 and the *Historia*, Rylands 8496.

12. Chiara Di Giorgio, "Ocheda, Tommaso de", *Dizionario Biografico degli Italiani*, https://www.treccani.it/enciclopedia/tommaso-de-ocheda_(Dizionario-Biografico).
13. Anthony Hobson, "Frederick North, Fifth Earl of Guilford", *Transactions of the Cambridge Bibliographical Society* 15 (2014): 73–83.
14. BL Add MS 76015, Ocheda-Spencer, 4 January 1790.
15. BL Add MS 76015, Ocheda-Spencer, 4 January 1790.
16. BL Add MS 76015, Ocheda-Spencer, 27 February 1790.
17. See Ida Giovanna Rao, "Per la biografia di Angelo Maria d'Elci", *Archivo Storico Italiano* 149 (1991): 375–449, and Angela Dillon Bussi, *La Collezione di Angelo Maria d'Elci: incunabuli ed edizioni rare: catalogo* (Florence: Ministro per i beni culturali e ambientali, 1989).
18. BL Add MS 76016, Reviczky-Spencer, 20 August 1790.
19. BL Add MS 76016, Reviczky-Spencer, 23 October 1790.
20. BL Add MS 76016, Reviczky-Spencer, 9 November 1790.
21. BL Add MS 76016, Reviczky-Spencer, 22 December 1790.
22. BL Add MS 76016, Reviczky-Spencer, 2 March 1791.
23. BL Add MS 76016, Reviczky-Spencer, 2 March 1791.
24. BL Add MS 76016, Reviczky-Spencer, 22 December 1790. For the earlier copy, see Count Reviczky (pseud. "Periergus Deltophilus"), *Bibliotheca Graeca et Latina... editio altera* (Berlin: typis Joannis Friderici Unger, 1784), 176–177.
25. BL Add MS 76016, Reviczky-Spencer, 15 March 1791.
26. BL Add MS 76016, Reviczky-Spencer, 15 April 1791.
27. For Prince Eugene, see Otto Mazal, *Bibliotheca Eugeniana: Die Sammlungen des Prinzen Eugen von Savoyen* (Vienna: Österreichische Nationalbibliothek, 1986) and Derek McKay, *Eugenio di Savoia: Ritratto di un condottiero 1663–1736* (Turin: Società Editrice Internazionale, 1989).
28. Rylands 3463; Dibdin, *Bibliotheca Spenceriana*, ii. 391–394; ISTC it00006000; GW M44712.
29. For works by the Pico Master which closely match the Tacitus, see Lilian Armstrong "The Impact of Printing on Venice after 1469", *Studies of Renaissance Miniaturists in Venice*, 2 vols. (London: The Pindar Press, 2003), i. 408–409, and for the Pico Master's career, Armstrong, "The Pico Master: A Venetian Miniaturist of the Late Quattrocento", in *Studies*, i. 233–338.
30. BL Add MS 76016, Reviczky-Spencer, 23 July 1791.
31. BL Add MS 76016, Reviczky-Spencer, 23 July 1791.
32. BL Add MS 76016, Reviczky-Spencer, 26 September 1791.
33. BL Add MS 76016, Reviczky-Spencer, 29 October and 19 November 1791.
34. BL Add MS 76016, Reviczky-Spencer, 18 January 1792.
35. Rylands 7547; Dibdin, *Bibliotheca Spenceriana*, i. 305–307; ISTC ic00576000; GW 6922.
36. BNF Bibliothèque de l'Arsenal Ms-2681.
37. J. H. M. Salmon, "Protestant Jurists and Theologians in Early Modern France: The Family of Cappel", in *Renaissance and Revolt: Essays in the Intellectual and Social History of Early Modern France* (Cambridge: Cambridge University Press, 1987), chap. 2.
38. See Graziano Ruffini, *La chasse aux livres: Bibliografia e collezionismo nel viaggio in Italia di Étienne-Charles de Loménie de Brienne e François-Xavier-Laire (1789–1790)* (Florence: Firenze University Press, 2012).
39. François-Xavier Laire, *Index librorum ab inventa typographia ad annum 1500; chronologicè dispositus cum notis historiam typographico-litterariam illustrantibus*, 2 vols. (Sens: apud viduam et filium P. Harduini Tarbé, 1791).

40. BL Add MS 76016, Reviczky-Spencer, 18 January 1792.
41. BL Add MS 76016, Reviczky-Spencer, 17 March 1792.
42. Kristian Jensen, *Revolution and the Antiquarian Book: Reshaping the Past, 1780–1815* (Cambridge: Cambridge University Press, 2011), 11.
43. Rylands 7726; Laire, *Index librorum*, i. 51–54; *Bibliotheca Spenceriana*, ii. 401–407.
44. Rylands 3075; Laire, *Index librorum*, i. 12–13; *Bibliotheca Spenceriana*, i. 117–121.
45. BL Add MS 76016, Reviczky-Spencer, 24 November 1792.
46. BL Add MS 76016, Reviczky-Spencer, 24 November 1792.
47. BL Add MS 76016, Reviczky-Spencer, 22 December 1792.
48. BL Add MS 76016, Reviczky-Spencer, 18 January 1793.
49. BL Add MS 76016, Reviczky-Spencer, 16 March 1793.
50. BL Add MS 76016, Reviczky-Spencer, 16 March 1793. For Count Thott, a major player in the previous generation's book collecting sphere, see Anders Toftgaard, "A Private Library as a Material History of the Book: Otto Thott's Encylcopedic Library in Copenhagen", in *Private Libraries and Their Documentation, 1665–1830: Studying and Interpreting Sources*, ed. Rindert Jagersma et al. (Leiden: Brill, 2023), 48–76.
51. BL Add MS 76016, Reviczky-Spencer, 25 July 1793.
52. Sterbebuch, Am Hof, Wien, 1783–1796, 03–01, fols. 73v–74r, digitised at https://data.matricula-online.eu/de/oesterreich/wien/01-am-hof/03-01/?pg=76.

CHAPTER 5

1. BL Add MS 76299, fol. 246r, previously reproduced in Eric Marshall White, "Gutenberg Bibles on the Move in England, 1789–1834", *Transactions of the Cambridge Bibliographical Society* 15 (2012): 79–100 at 84.
2. *ODNB*, s.n.
3. Lætitia-Matilda Hawkins, *Memoirs, Anecdotes, Facts, and Opinions*, 2 vols. (London: Printed for Longman, Hurst, Rees, Orme, Brown, and Green; and C. & J. Rivington, 1824), i. 269.
4. David Fallon. 'Stuffd up with books': The Bookshops and Business of Thomas Payne and Son, 1740–1831. *History of Retailing and Consumption* 5 (2019): 228–245.
5. Paul Needham, "Johann Gutenberg and the Catholicon Press", *Papers of the Bibliographical Society of America* 76 (1982): 395–565.
6. Thomas Frognall Dibdin, *Bibliotheca Spenceriana; or a Descriptive Catalogue of the Books Printed in the Fifteenth Century, and of Many Valuable First Editions, in the Library of George John Earl Spencer, K.G.*, 4 vols. (London: Printed for the Author, by W. Bulmer and Co., 1814–1815), iii. 38, contains a discussion of the third and fourth copies (the fourth is now Rylands 3383) and *A Catalogue of Rare and Valuable Duplicates from the Library of... Earl Spencer* (London: Evans, 1821), p. 8, no. 60, identifies the fifth (apparently from the Cassano Serra library).
7. British Library IC.74.
8. Rylands 3072; Dibdin, *Bibliotheca Spenceriana*, i. 42–47; ISTC ib00625000; GW 4296.
9. *Bibliotheca Spenceriana*, i. 42–47.
10. Guillaume-François De Bure le Jeune, *Bibliographie instructive: ou traité de la connoissance des livres rares et singuliers*, 10 vols. (Paris: Chez Guillaume-François De Bure le Jeune, 1763–1782).
11. De Bure, *Bibliographie instructive*, i. 32–33. For the episode as a whole, see Eric Marshall White, *Editio Princeps: A History of the Gutenberg Bible* (Turnhout: Harvey Miller Publishers, 2017), 103–104.

12. White, *Editio Princeps*, 111; *Guillaume-François de Bure, Supplement a la Bibliographie instructive, ou Catalogue des livres du cabinet de feu M. Louis Jean Gaignat*, tome premier (Paris: Chez Guillaume François de Bure le jeune, 1769), lot 16. Price realised from the priced copy at BNF 30307467.
13. White, *Editio Princeps*, 125.
14. White, *Editio Princeps*, 131.
15. White, *Editio Princeps*, 144–145.
16. BL Add MS 76014, Maugérard-Spencer, 25 March 1797 and 22 March 1798.
17. *Supplément*, lots 16 (Gutenberg Bible) and 52 (Psalter). I follow here the 1767 exchange rate of 40 *livres* to £3 as given in Benjamin Webb, *The Complete Negociator* (London: Printed for C. Rivington, 1767).
18. Rylands 3069; Dibdin, *Bibliotheca Spenceriana*, i. 3–6; ISTC ib00526000; GW 4201.
19. Rylands 3069, ii. fol. 267r. See the commentary at White, *Editio Princeps*, 138.
20. White, *Editio Princeps*, 141.
21. Bibliothèque numérique de Lyon, SJ TH 104/11.
22. *Archives Parlementaires de 1787 à 1860*, 1e série, Tome XI (Paris: Librarie Administrative de Paul Dupon, 1877), 649.
23. Claude Muller, "La suppression des couvents des Dominicains et des Augustins de Colmar (1790–1791)", *Annuaire de la Societe d'histoire et d'archeologie de Colmar* 36 (1988): 39–48 at 44–45; *Réimpression de l'ancien moniteur* (Paris: au bureau central, 1841), viii. 568.
24. Muller, "La suppression des couvents", 46–47; *Assemblée Nationale, Corps Administratifs et nouvelle politiques et littéraires de l'Europe* no. 666 (June 1791): 3.
25. Jean-Baptiste Labiche, *Notice sur les dépôts littéraires et la révolution bibliographique de la fin du dernier siècle* (Paris: Typographie de A. Parent, 1880), 22.
26. See the overview by Raymond-Josué Seckel, "La Bibliothèque nationale et les dépôts littéraires", in *1789 Le patrimoine libéré: 200 trésors entrés à la Bibliothèque nationale de 1789 à 1799* (Paris: Bibliothèque nationale, 1989), 23–24, and *passim*.
27. Labiche, 12.
28. Anders Rydell, *The Book Thieves: The Nazi Looting of Europe's Libraries and the Race to Return a Literary Inheritance*, tr. Henning Koch (New York: Penguin, 2017).
29. Labiche, 18–19.
30. Seckel, 24.
31. Labiche, 23.
32. Labiche, 24–25.
33. Labiche, 68.
34. Labiche, 30.
35. Labiche, 36.
36. Labiche, 52–53, 72.
37. Kristian Jensen, *Revolution and the Antiquarian Book: Reshaping the Past, 1780–1815* (Cambridge: Cambridge University Press, 2011), chap. 1.

CHAPTER 6

1. Hester Lynch Piozzi, *Observations and Reflections Made in the Course of a Journey through France, Italy, and Germany* (Dublin: Printed for Messrs. H. Chamberlaine et al., 1789), 235–236.

2. Georgiana (Spencer) Cavendish, Duchess of Devonshire, *Sketch of a Descriptive Journey through Switzerland* (Bern: Printed for J. J. Burgdorfer, 1816), 86.
3. Amanda Foreman, *Georgiana, Duchess of Devonshire* (London: HarperCollins, 1999), 266–283.
4. BL Add MS 76007, Della Lena-Spencer, 29 August 1793.
5. BL Add MS 76007, Della Lena-Spencer, 29 August 1793.
6. *Prospetto del Palazzo della Lena ai Bagni di Lucca da Levante con le sue Adiacenze, la Torre, e Quercia verde, e vi si ascende sopra con 60. scalini comodi. A. S. A. La signora Principessa de Lubomirska, nata Pr.a Czartorirska, Protetrice delle Belle Arti. D. D. D. L'Abate Eusebio della Lena*, Kunsthistorisches Institut in Florenz—Max-Planck-Institut, flno402686x_p.
7. Francis Haskell, "Francesco Guardi as *vedutista* and Some of His Patrons", *Journal of the Warburg and Courtauld Institutes* 23 (1960): 256–276 at 261–262.
8. Between 1773 and 1784, see Max Freiherr von Gemmell-Flischbach, *Album des kaisel. königl. Theresianums (1746–1880)* (Wien: Verlag der Buchhandlung von Moritz Perles, 1880), 17.
9. Pompeo Molmenti, "Carteggi Casanoviani", *Archivo Storico Italiano*, 5 ser. 45 (1910): 3–60 at 47–48.
10. Massimo d'Azeglio, *Miei ricordi*, 2 vols. (Firenze: G. Barbèra, editore, 1867), i. 108.
11. Victor Segesvary, *The History of a Private Library in 18th Century Hungary: The Library of Pál and Gedeon Ráday* (The Hague: Mikes International, 2005), 80.
12. BL Add MS 76007, Della Lena-Spencer, 18 October 1793.
13. BL Add MS 76007, Della Lena-Spencer, 12 February 1794.
14. BL Add MS 76007, Della Lena-Spencer, 27 May 1796.
15. A classic study in English, implicitly comparing the French looting with contemporary Nazi pillage, is Dorothy Mackay Quinn, "The Art Confiscations of the Napoleonic Wars", *American Historical Review* 50 (1945): 437–460. See now, especially for Germany, Bénédicte Savoy, *Patrimoine annexé: Les biens culturels saisis par la France en Allemagne autour de 1800*, 2 vols. (Paris: Éditions de la Maison des sciences de l'homme, Centre allemand d'histoire de l'art, 2003).
16. Kristian Jensen, *Revolution and the Antiquarian Book: Reshaping the Past, 1780–1815* (Cambridge: Cambridge University Press, 2011), 54.
17. BL G.9030. See John Thomas Payne and Henry Foss, *Bibliotheca Grenvilliana; or Bibliographical Notices of Rare and Curious Books, Forming Part of the Library of the Right Hon. Thomas Grenville* (London: Printed by William Nicol, 1842), i. 408; Thomas Frognall Dibdin, *Reminiscences of a Literary Life* (London: John Major, 1836), 514.
18. Irma Merolle, "L'abate Matteo Luigi Canonici: Le sue raccolte d'arte e la sua biblioteca", *Archivum Historicum Societatis Iesu* 27 (1958): 5–58. Sneyd, though a homebody himself, was a close friend of the (in)famous manuscript hunter Robert Curzon and shared the latter's taste for medieval manuscripts; see Ian Fraser, *The Heir of Parham: Robert Curzon, 14th Baron Zouche* (Alburgh, Norfolk: The Paradigm Press, 1986), *passim*.
19. Desmond Gregory, *Napoleon's Italy* (London: Associated University Press, 2001), 198, fn. 21; Francis Haskell, "More about Sommariva", *Burlington Magazine* 114 (1972): 691–695.
20. BL Add MS 76007, Della Lena-Spencer, 4 September 1797 and 17 March 1798.
21. BL Add MS 76007, Della Lena-Spencer, 17 March 1798. Spencer declined Count Balbi's offer.

22. Rylands 17280; *Bibliotheca Spenceriana*, iv. 108–115.
23. BL Add MS 76007, Della Lena-Spencer, 22 February 1797.
24. Alfred W. Pollard, *Italian Book Illustrations, Chiefly of the Fifteenth Century* (London: Seeley and Co., 1894), 26. These attributions are doubted by Sean Roberts, "Inventing Engraving in Vasari's Florence", *Intellectual History Review* 24 (2014): 367–388.
25. BL Add MS 76007, Della Lena-Spencer, 22 February 1797.
26. BL Add MS 76007, Della Lena-Spencer, 8 April 1797.
27. Rylands 9389; Dibdin, *Bibliotheca Spenceriana*, iv. 128–131; ISTC ia00886000; GW 2204.
28. Dibdin, *Bibliotheca Spenceriana*, iv. 131.
29. BL Add MS 76007, Della Lena-Spencer, 4 September 1797.
30. Rylands 8677; Dibdin, *Bibliotheca Spenceriana*, ii. 149–153; ISTC il00332900; GW M19133. For some of the large claims made by modern scholars about the role of Lucretius in Renaissance culture, see Stephen Greenblatt, *The Swerve: How the Renaissance Began* (London: Bodley Head, 2011).
31. Musée Condé IV-H-012.
32. Outlined in the catalogue entry at https://www.bibliotheque-conde.fr/opac/catalog/bib record?id=1394452804929461040.
33. Mara Bonfioli, "Boni, Mauro", *Dizionario Biografico degli Italiani*, https://www.treccani.it/enciclopedia/mauro-boni_(Dizionario-Biografico)/.
34. A. Sagredo, Review of *Collezione di documenti relativi alla Storia, all'Archeologia, alla Numismatica, Archivio Storico Italiano*, 3e ser. 4 (1866): 154–158.
35. BL Add MS 76007, Della Lena-Spencer, 30 September 1798, and *Bibliotheca Spenceriana*, iii. 159–161 (Aquinas); BL Add MS 76007, Della Lena-Spencer, 20 February 1799, and *Bibliotheca Spenceriana*, iv. 131–133 (Petrarch).
36. Conrad Gill, ed., *The Naval Mutinies of 1797* (Manchester: Manchester University Press, 1913), 176–177.
37. *Private Papers of George, Second Earl Spencer, First Lord of the Admiralty, 1794–1801*, 4 vols., ed. Julian S. Corbett ([London]: Navy Records Society, 1913–1924), ii. 103–104, 154–155.

CHAPTER 7

1. This is, I confess, a fanciful reconstruction of Maugérard's working practice which we know in detail only through its results, but see his account of the visit to Prüm at J. B. Buzy, *Dom Maugérard: Histoire d'un bibliographe lorraine de l'ordre de Saint-Benoît, au XVIIIe siècle* (Chalons-sur-Marne: Imprimerie de T. Martin, 1882), 130–131, and for his activities in the Rhineland more generally, Bénédicte Savoy, *Patrimoine annexé: Les biens culturels saisis par la France en Allemagne autour de 1800*, 2 vols. (Paris: Éditions de la maison des sciences de l'homme, 2003), i. 87–113, and Bénédicte Savoy, "Codicologue, incunabuliste et rabatteur. La mission de Jean-Baptiste Maugérard dans les quatre départements du Rhin (1802–1805)", *Bulletin du Bibliophile* (1999): 313–344.Ludwig Traube and Rudolf Ehwald's Jean-Baptiste Maugérard: *Ein Beitrag zur Bibliothekgeschichte* (München: Verlag der K. Akademie, 1904) remains essential background. The characterisation of Maugérard as a "bloodhound" (Schweißhund) is that of the German librarian Hermann Degering (1866–1942) in "Geraubte Schätze: Kölnische Handschriften in Paris und Brüssel", *Beiträge zur Kölnischen Geschichte, Sprache, Eigenart* 2.7 (1915): 38–55 at 43.

2. Traube and Ehwald, *Maugérard*, 321–329.
3. BL Add MS 76014, Maugérard-Spencer, 12 January 1797.
4. BL Add MS 76014, Maugérard-Spencer, 28 January 1797.
5. BL Add MS 76014, Maugérard-Spencer, 25 March 1797.
6. BL Add MS 76014, Maugérard-Spencer, 2 May 1797.
7. BL Add MS 76014, Spencer-Maugérard, June 1797.
8. BL Add MS 76014, Spencer-Maugérard, June 1797.
9. BL Add MS 76014, Maugérard-Spencer, 24 June 1797.
10. BL Add MS 76014, Maugérard-Spencer, 20 February 1798; Carl Heinrich von Heinecken, *Idée générale d'une collection complète d'estampes* (Leipzig and Vienna: chez Jean Paul Kraus, 1771).
11. BL Add MS 76014, Spencer-Maugérard, draft dated 9 March 1798.
12. BL Add MS 76014, Maugérard-Spencer, April 1798.
13. BL Add MS 76014, Maugérard-Spencer, 20 February 1798. It was presumably Johannes Brugman's *Life* of the fifteenth-century ice-skating saint, Liduina of Schiedam, but the exact edition is unclear.
14. BL Add MS 76014, Maugérard-Spencer, 9 March "1797" [*recte* 1798] and April 1798.
15. BL Add MS 76014, Maugérard-Spencer 28 January 1797.
16. A recent modern study is Henrike Lähnemann, "Biblische Geschichte für den Druck. Die Vier Historien (Bamberg 1462)", *Geschichte erzählen. Strategien der Narrativierung von Vergangenheit im Mittelalter*, ed. Sarah Bowden et al. (Tübingen: Gunter Narr Verlag, 2020), 299–323.
17. See Sabine Häußerman, *Die Bamberger Pfisterdrucke Frühe Inkunabelillustration und Medienwandel* (Berlin: Die Bamberger Pfisterdrucke Frühe Inkunabelillustration und Medienwandel, 2008).
18. Matthias Jakob Adam Steiner, "Eine ganz neue Entdeckung, die den Freunden der ältern tuetschen Litteratur, hoffentlich nicht unangenehm, und für die älteste Buchdruckergeschichte Bambergs, nicht unbedeutend seyn wird", *Historisich-Litterarisch-Bibliographisches Magazin* 5 (1792): 1–38.
19. For Father Bonifacius himself, see Joachim Heinrich Jäck, *Pantheon der Litteraten und Künstler Bambergs* (Bamberg: im Komtpoir der Zeitung und Erlangen in der Palmischen Buchhaundlung, 1812–1815), 1072.
20. Placidus Sprenger, *Aelteste Buchdruckergeschichte von Bamberg* (Nürnberg: in der Grattenauerischen Buchhandlung, 1800), 17.
21. He refers to them in his first letter to Spencer (BL Add MS 76014, Maugérard-Spencer, 28 January 1797).
22. Armand-Gaston Camus, *Notice d'un livre imprimé à Bamberg en MCCCCLXII, lue à l'Institut national* (Paris: Baudouin, imprimeur de l'Institut national. An VII [1799]), 17.
23. BNF livres rares, A-1646. See Camus, *Notice d'un livre, passim.*
24. BL Add MS 76014, Maugérard-Spencer, 24 June 1797.
25. BL Add MS 76014, Maugérard-Spencer, 8 August 1797.
26. BL Add MS 76014, Maugérard-Spencer, 25 August 1797.
27. Rylands 9375; Dibdin, *Bibliotheca Spenceriana*, i. 94–100; ISTC ih00286500; GW 12591.
28. BL Add MS 76014, Spencer's draft response on Maugérard-Spencer, 3 September 1799.
29. BL Add MS 76014, Maugérard-Spencer, 30 September 1797 and 27 January 1798.
30. BL Add MS 76014, Maugérard-Spencer, April 1798.

31. BL Add MS 76014, Spencer's draft response, dated 2 August, on Maugérard-Spencer, 7 July 1798.
32. BL Add MS 76014, Spencer's draft response on Maugérard-Spencer, 17 April 1798.
33. BL Add MS 76014, Spencer's draft response on Maugérard-Spencer, 2 July 1800.
34. BL Add MS 76014, Maugérard-Spencer, 2 August 1800 and Spencer's draft response to the same.
35. Traube and Ehwald, 330, 333–334. Maugérard died at home in Metz on 15 July 1815 (*ibid.*, 334).

CHAPTER 8

1. The quotation is from Thomas Grenville, referring to the Austrian foreign minister Thugut (M. Duffy, *British War Policy: The Austrian Alliance, 1793–1801* [University of Oxford D.Phil. Thesis, 1971], 115).
2. See the account of their mission in Duffy, 109ff.
3. Duffy, 125.
4. BL Add MS 76299, fols. 388–389, 391, 398; Kristian Jensen, *Revolution and the Antiquarian Book: Reshaping the Past, 1780–1815* (Cambridge: Cambridge University Press, 2011), 208, n. 68. For Trattner, see Christoph Augustynowicz and Johannes Frimmel, eds., *Der Buchdrucker Maria Theresias: Johann Thomas Trattner (1719–1798) und sein Mediumimperium* (Wiesbaden: Harassowitz, 2019). From Blumauer, see Bärbel Becker-Cantarino, *Aloys Blumauer and the Literature of Austrian Enlightenment* (Bern and Frankfurt-am-Main: Laing, 1973).
5. BL Add MS 76299, fols. 405–406.
6. Jensen, 43–44, 208, n. 55.
7. BL Add MS 75964, Horn-Spencer, 15 October 1794.
8. Anne Fremantle, ed., *The Wynne Diaries*, 3 vols. (London: Oxford University Press, 1935–1940), ii. 9. Betsey and her family spent time at the house of Mr. Blair in Regensburg between 21 and 31 December 1794, and she noted with a certain childish censoriousness that "father Maurus is always there he is a good young man but a bad monk... [t]hose bad Clergy men much wrongs our religion but there is abuses in everything nothing can be perfect in this world" (*ibid.*, ii. 8–9).
9. His name is given both as "Horn" and "Horne" in contemporary sources, but I have preferred the former, which he consistently used himself.
10. The register of the monastery at Regensburg supplies his birth date and notes that his young brother James (later Father Erhard) was born three years later in Montrose (Father William Forbes-Leith, ed., *Records of the Scots Colleges at Douai, Rome, Madrid, Valladolid and Ratisbon* [Aberdeen: Printed for the New Spalding Club, 1906], 253–254). That Montrose was also his birthplace appears from the records of the Masonic lodge in Regensburg, of which he was a member (see Bernhard Beyer, "Ausschnitte aus der Geschichte der früheren Großen Mutterloge", Carl zu den 3 Schlüsseln "in Regensburg", *Das Freimaurer-Museum* 4 [1928]: 197). Horn himself says nothing of his antecedents, but used a seal bearing the arms of the Hornes of Westerhall, a minor Aberdeenshire gentry family; compare the well-preserved seal on BL Add MS 75964, Horn-Spencer, 11 May 1799 with Sir James Balfour Paul, *An Ordinary of Arms Contained in the Public Register of All Arms and Bearings in Scotland*, 2nd ed. (Edinburgh: William

Green and Sons, 1903), 143–144. Whether this represented real descent or a blend of social ambition and wishful thinking is unclear.

11. Alexander Horn, "Autobiografie", in Claus Oberhauser et al., *Diplomatie aus dem Untergrund: Die merkwürdige Karriere des Alexander (Maurus) Horn(e) (1762–1820)* (Vienna: Böhlau Verlag, 2022), 247; *Records of the Scots Colleges*, 253.
12. Horn, "Autobiografie", 247.
13. *Records of the Scots College*, 285.
14. Horn, "Autobiografie", 248.
15. See Norbert Leithold, *Graf Goertz: Der große Unbekannte* (Berlin: Osburg Verlag, 2010).
16. Horn, "Autobiografie", 249.
17. Horn, "Autobiografie", 249–250.
18. Friedrich Carl Gottlob Hirsching, *Versuch einer Beschreibung sehenswürdiger Bibliotheken Teutschlands nach alphabetischer Ordnung der Städte*, 4 vols. (Erlangen: bey Johann Jakob Palm, 1786–1791), iii/2. 653–654.
19. Georg Wilhelm Zapf, *Literarische Reisen durch einen Theil von Baiern, Franken, Schwaben und der Schweiz in den Jahren 1780. 1781. und 1782* (Augsburg, 1783), 20.
20. Hirsching, iii/2. 659.
21. From the census of manuscripts by Hirsching, iii/2. 655. Neither were present in the small rump of Regensburg manuscripts which eventually reached the National Library of Scotland, Acc. 11218/1-13.
22. Hirsching, iii/2. 660–661.
23. BL Add MS 75964, Horn-Spencer, 15 October 1794.
24. BL Add MS 75964, Horn-Spencer, 15 October 1794.
25. *Bemerkungen über Menschen und Sitten auf einer Reise durch Franken, Schwaben, Bayern und Oesterreich. Im Jahre 1792* (s.l.: s.n., 1794), 24–25.
26. BL Add MS 75964, Horn-Spencer, 7 April 1796.
27. BL Add MS 75964, Horn-Spencer, 15 July 1797. Spencer's copy is Rylands 3221.
28. BL Add MS 75964, Horn-Spencer, 13 October 1797.
29. BL Add MS 75964, Horn-Spencer, 15 October 1794.
30. BL Add MS 75964, Horn-Spencer, 13 October 1797.
31. BL Add MS 76014, Maugérard-Spencer, 21 October 1797.
32. BL Add MS 75964, Horn-Spencer, 27 February 1798.
33. BL Add MS 75964, Sigismund Hogl-Horn, 23 February [1798].
34. Johann Georg Schelhorn, "Anmerkung von der allerersten Ausgabe des lateinischen Psalters", in *Nüzliche und angeneme Abhandlungen aus der Kirchen-Bücher- und Gelerten-Geschichte von verschiedenen Verfassern zusammen getragen*, Vol. I, ed. Johann Bartholomäus Riederer (Altdorf: verlegts Joseph Ehrenreich Ammermüller, 1768), 1–12 at 3.
35. Carl Heinrich von Heinecken, *Idée générale d'une collection complette d'estampes* (Leipzig and Vienna: Chez Jean Paul Kraus, 1771).
36. BL Add MS 75964, Horn-Spencer, 16 April 1798 and 12 May 1798.
37. *Bibliotheca Spenceriana*, i. 117.
38. Rylands 9784; Dibdin, *Bibliotheca Spenceriana*, i. 107–117; ISTC ip01036000; GW M36179.
39. Royal Collection, RCIN 1071478. The royal copy, however, has some extremely unfortunate gold appliqué detailing on its boards, including George III's monogram, which detracts from the otherwise pleasing velvet.

CHAPTER 9

1. BL Add MS 75964, Horn-Spencer, 14 November 1799.
2. Kristian Jensen, *Revolution and the Antiquarian Book: Reshaping the Past, 1780–1815* (Cambridge: Cambridge University Press, 2011), 60–61.
3. BL Add MS 75964, Horn-Spencer, 6 September 1800.
4. BL Add MS 75964, Horn-Spencer, 12 January 1801 and 22 October 1801.
5. *Bibliotheca Spenceriana*, i. xlvi–li. The Schelhorn-Hohenlohe indulgence is now Rylands 17250.2.
6. Baron Frédéric de Reiffenberg, "Note sur un exemplaire des lettres d'indulgence du Pape Nicolas V, pro regno Cypri", *Mémoires de l'Académie royale de Belgique* 5 (1829): 3–12.
7. The story is told within the larger context of theft from libraries during this period in David McKitterick, *Readers in a Revolution: Bibliographical Change in the Nineteenth Century* (Cambridge: Cambridge University Press, 2022), 104. The first printed notice of the theft seems to be Auguste Bernard, *De l'origine et des débuts de l'imprimerie en Europe*, 2 vols. (Paris: L'imprimerie impériale, 1853), i. 172. The account of the request for repatriation was given by Charles Ruelens, conservator at the Bibliothèque Royale in Brussels, in a discussion concerning international laws regulating the recovery of stolen antiquities, printed at Max Rooses, ed., *Compte-rendu de la première session de la conférence du livre tenue à Anvers au mois d'Août 1890* (Anvers: Imprimerie J.-E. Buschmann, 1891), 121–122. The Louvain indulgence is now Rylands 17250.1.
8. Edoardo Barbieri, "Re-reading the dossier about the Venetian prototypographers Johann and Wendelin from Spira", *JLIS.it* 12 (2021): 21–28.
9. Martin Davies, "Making Sense of Pliny in the Quattrocento", *Renaissance Studies* 9 (1995): 240–257 at 241–242.
10. BL Add MS 76018, fol. 53r.
11. Rylands 3221; Dibdin, *Bibliotheca Spenceriana*, ii. 253–256; ISTC ip00786000; GW M34312. Horn appears to have sold it via—or at least in care of—James Edwards as Spencer paid Edwards £120 for this volume on 16 August 1800 (BL Add MS 76300, fol. 735v). See *Bibliotheca Spenceriana*, ii. 253–256.
12. BL Add MS 75964, Horn-Spencer, 6 September 1800.
13. BL Add MS 75964, Horn-Spencer, 26 October 1800.
14. For this aspect of Horn's career, see Claus Oberhauser et al., *Diplomatie aus dem Untergrund: Die merkwürdige Karriere des Alexander (Maurus) Horn(e) (1762–1820)* (Wien: Böhlau Verlag, 2022).
15. BL Add MS 75964, Horn-Spencer, 16 August 1798.
16. BL Add MS 75964, Horn-Spencer, 12 November 1800.
17. BL Add MS 75964, Horn-Spencer, 1 January 1801.
18. BL Add MS 75964, Horn-Spencer, 1 January 1801. For this copy, see generally Eric Marshall White, "New Provenances for Four Copies of the 36-Line Bible", *The Book Collector* 62.3 (2013): 403–436 at 419–422.
19. White, "New Provenances", 420.
20. Thomas McInally, *A Saltire in the German Lands: Scottish Benedictines in Germany, 1575–1862* (Aberdeen: Aberdeen University Press, 2016); Mark Dilworth, *The Scots in Franconia: A Century of Monastic Life* (Edinburgh and London: Scottish Academic Press, 1974).
21. McInally, *Saltire*, 196.
22. BL Add MS 75964, Horn-Spencer, 12 November 1800.

23. White, "New Provenances", 423–424. See BL Add MS 75965, Horn-Spencer, 12 February 1810.
24. *Bibliotheca Spenceriana*, iv. 573–574.
25. Rylands 15365; ISTC ib00527000; GW 4202.
26. Ferdinand Geldner, " Zum frühesten deutschen und italienischen Buchdruck (Mainz, Baiern, Foligno)", *Gutenberg-Jahrbuch* (1979): 18–38; Clifford W. Maas, "German Printers and the German Community in Renaissance Rome", *The Library*, 5th ser. 31 (1976): 118–126.
27. BL Add MS 75964, Horn-Spencer, 9 July 1798.
28. BL Add MS 75964, Horn-Spencer, 5 March 1800.
29. Spencer's annotation to BL Add MS 75964, Horn-Spencer, 6 September 1800, and *ibid.*, 12 January 1801.
30. BL Add MS 75964, Horn-Spencer, 23 January 1801.
31. BL Add MS 75964, Horn-Spencer, 28 February 1801.
32. BL Add MS 75965, Horn-Spencer, 13 February 1806.
33. BL Add MS 75965, Horn-Spencer, 14 March 1806.
34. BL Add MS 75965, Horn-Spencer, 25 August 1806.
35. Palm had a long afterlife as a romanticised German martyr, though this strain of German hagiography was brought to a swift and inglorious close after he was approvingly taken up in Hitler's *Mein Kampf*; see Michel Kerautret, "Un crime et une faute de Napoléon? Réflexions sur l'affaire Palm", *Francia* 36 (2009): 375–388.
36. Nürnberg Stadtbibliothek Inc. 2.4 (Torquemada) and Inc. 97.2° (Boccaccio).
37. Rylands 8658.
38. For this episode, see also White, "Gutenberg for Sale", 227–230, and Kelsey Jackson Williams, "The Dispersal of Monastic Libraries in the Early Nineteenth Century: Buxheim and Karakallou", *Library and Information History* 40 (2024): 144–158.
39. Paul Needham, "The Library of Hilprand Brandenburg", *Bibliothek und Wissenschaft* 29 (1996): 95–125, and "Thirteen More Books from the Library of Hilprand Brandenburg", *Einband Forschung* 4 (1999): 23–25.
40. Honemann, 168. William Whobrey, in his extensive study of the Buxheim collections, has identified 155 of these scattered across the world at https://buxheimlibrary.org/wp-content/uploads/2021/10/Hilprand-all-books-final-1.pdf.
41. Martin Gerbert, *Iter Alemannicum, accedit Italicum et Gallicum. Sequuntur glossaria theotisca ex codicibus manuscriptis a sæculo IX. usque XIII.* (St. Blasien, 1765), 164–170.
42. *Germania Sacra, NF 32: Die Bistümer der Kirchenprovinz Mainz: Das Bistum Konstanz 4. Das (Freiweltliche) Damenstift Buchau am Federsee* (Berlin and New York: Walter de Gruyter, 1994), 250. John Rylands Latin MS 366. See Moses Tyson, "Hand-List of Additions to the Collection of Latin Manuscripts in the John Rylands Library, 1908–1928", *Bulletin of the John Rylands Library* 12 (1928): 581–609 at 600 and the more detailed description, with a transcription of Anna's donative inscription, in [Franz Krismer], "Formschneiderkunst", in Christoph Gottlieb von Murr, *Journal zur Kunstgeschichte und zur allgemeinen Litteratur* 2 (1776): 104–105.
43. This claim is dependent both on the falsity of the 1418 date on a woodblock print of the Madonna and Child now in the Bibliothèque Royale in Brussels and the accuracy of the 1423 date on the St. Christopher itself, neither being beyond suspicion. See Peter Parshall and Rainer Schoch, *Origins of European Printmaking: Fifteenth-century Woodcuts and Their Public* (Yale: Yale University Press, 2005), 26.

44. Karl-Heinrich von Heinecken, *Idée générale d'une collection complette d'estampes* (Leipzig and Vienna: chez Jean Paul Kraus, 1771), 250–251. Discussed in Eric Marshall White, "Gutenberg for Sale: Alexander Horn as an Agent of the International Antiquarian Book Trade", in Oberhauser, ed., *Diplomatie*, 226.
45. See Krismer, "Formschneiderkunst", 75–179; Parshall and Schoch, *Origins of European Printmaking*, 5.
46. Horn assumed that Spencer was unaware of von Heinecken's account when he referenced it in a letter of 17 November 1804, but Horn often assumed a superiority of bibliographical knowledge which was not always justified (see BL Add MS 75965, Horn-Spencer, 17 November 1804).
47. Annotation to BL Add MS 76014, Maugérard-Spencer, 16 October 1797.
48. BL Add MS 75965, Horn-Spencer, 14 March 1806.
49. Karl Zeumer, ed., *Quellensammlung zur Geschichte der Deutschen Reichsverfassung in Mittelalter und Neuzeit*, 2nd ed. (Tübingen: Verlag von J. C. B. Mohr, 1913), 509–528.
50. The literature on secularisation is immense. One important starting point is Wolfgang Schieder and Manfred Koltes, *Säkularisation und Mediatisierung in den vier rheinischen Departements, 1803–1813: Edition des Datenmaterials der zu veräussernden Nationalgüter*, 5 vols. in 7 (Boppard am Rhein: H. Boldt, 1991). A good introduction is Jeffrey Garrett, "The Expropriation of Monastic Libraries in German-Speaking Europe, 1773–1817", in *How the Secularization of Religious Houses Transformed the Libraries of Europe, 16th–19th Centuries*, ed. Cristina Dondi, Dorit Raines, and Richard Sharpe (Turnhout: Brepols, 2022), 83–97.
51. BL Add MS 75965, Horn-Spencer, 5 March 1802.
52. Honemann, 173–174.
53. BL Add MS 75965, Horn-Spencer, 4 July 1803.
54. BL Add MS 75965, Horn-Spencer, 19 September 1803.
55. BL Add MS 75965, Horn-Spencer, 12 January 1804.
56. BL Add MS 75965, Horn-Spencer, 12 January 1804.
57. BL Add MS 75965, Horn-Spencer, 4 September 1804.
58. BL Add MS 75965, Horn-Spencer, 17 November 1804.
59. White, "Gutenberg for Sale", 229–230.
60. White, "Gutenberg for Sale", 229.
61. Dibdin, *Bibliotheca Spenceriana*, i. i.

CHAPTER 10

1. *ODNB*, s.n.; George E. Cokayne et al., *The Complete Peerage of England, Scotland, Ireland, Great Britain and the United Kingdom, Extant, Extinct, or Dormant*, 13 vols. in 14 (London: St. Catherine Press, 1910–1959), xii/1. 409–410.
2. *Catalogue of the Valuable Library of the Late Right Honourable Lord Stuart de Rothesay, Including Many Illuminated and Important Manuscripts...: Which Will be Sold by Auction by Messrs. S. Leigh Sotheby & John Wilkinson, Auctioneers... the 31st Day of May, 1855, and Fourteen Following Days* ([London], 1855).
3. BL Add MS 76006, d'Elci—Spencer, 5 October 1802.
4. Rylands 18952; ESTC S123359. The English Short Title Catalogue (ESTC) is a bit like the ISTC and GW which we have already encountered but covers all books printed in England or in English up to the year 1800. It has a long and complex history and is

presently hosted by the Consortium of European Research Libraries (https://www.cerl.org/services/estc).

5. For Stuart's appearance I have drawn on the later but still youthful portrait by Baron François Gérard (painted *c.* 1828), Victoria and Albert Museum P.27–1987.
6. Giovanni Rao, "Pannocchieschi d'Elci, Angelo Maria", *Dizionario Biografico degli Italiani*, https://www.treccani.it/enciclopedia/pannocchieschi-d-elci-angelo-maria_(Dizionario-Biografico)/. The *DBI* places his emigration to Vienna in December 1798, but a letter of James Payne dated 28 September 1800 describes him as "just arriv'd" and notes that "his books are packed up in boxes at the Customhouse" (qtd. at Kristian Jensen, *Revolution and the Antiquarian Book: Reshaping the Past, 1780–1815* [Cambridge: Cambridge University Press, 2011], 249).
7. BL Add MS 76006, d'Elci-Spencer, 5 October 1802.
8. BL Add MS 76300, fols. 824–825.
9. BL Add MS 76006, d'Elci-Spencer, 5 October 1802.
10. BL Add MS 76006, d'Elci-Spencer, 2 December 1802.
11. BL Add MS 76006, d'Elci-Spencer, 9 December 1802.
12. BL Add MS 76006, d'Elci-Spencer, 1 February 1803.
13. BL Add MS 76300, fols. 824–825.
14. The point has been made before by Jensen, 125. For Payne, see David Fallon, "'Stuff'd up with books': The Bookshops and Business of Thomas Payne and Son, 1740–1831", *History of Retailing and Consumption* 5 (2019): 228–245. He was less fortunate than most book agents and died in a French prison, having been arrested in the course of a bibliophilic expedition. His partner Mackinlay killed himself while temporarily insane; theirs was a generally ill-starred business venture (John Nichols, *Literary Anecdotes of the Eighteenth Century*, 6 vols. (London: Printed for the Author, 1812–1816), iii. 310).
15. Rylands 12279; Thomas Frognall Dibdin, *Bibliotheca Spenceriana; or a Descriptive Catalogue of the Books Printed in the Fifteenth Century, and of Many Valuable First Editions, in the Library of George John Earl Spencer, K.G.*, 4 vols. (London: Printed for the Author, by W. Bulmer and Co., 1814–1815), ii. 367; ISTC is00700600; GW M4329910.
16. BL Add MS 76006, d'Elci-Spencer, 16 May 1803.
17. BL Add MS 76006, d'Elci-Spencer, 20 August 1803.
18. *Bibliotheca Pinelliana*, lot 9822 or 9823 (two copies of the same edition); Count Reviczky, *Bibliotheca Graeca et Latina... editio altera* (Berlin: typis Joannis Friderici Unger, 1784), *Second supplement*, 25.
19. *Bibliotheca Pinelliana*, lot 9953 (it cost Reviczky £10); Reviczky, *Second supplement*, 26.
20. *Bibliotheca Spenceriana*, ii. 287.
21. BL Add MS 76006, d'Elci-Spencer, 25 July 1804.
22. BL Add MS 76006, d'Elci-Spencer, 20 October 1804. For Taccone and d'Elci, see Vincenzo Trombetta, ed., *Collezionismo e bibliofilia a Napoli tra Sette e Ottocento: un ritratto epistolare* (Macerata: Bibliohaus, 2020), 49–79.
23. BL Add MS 76006, d'Elci-Spencer, 7 November 1804.
24. BL Add MS 76006, d'Elci-Spencer, 7 February 1805.
25. BL Add MS 76006, d'Elci-Spencer, 24 July 1805.
26. ISTC it00366200 (de Argentina Tibullus), ip01014000 (de Comitibus Propertius).
27. ISTC it00366600.
28. Biblioteca Medicea Laurenziana D'Elci 303.
29. BL Add MSS 76299–76301.

30. BL Add MS 76300, fols. 521–525.
31. BL Add MS 76300, fol. 579.
32. BL Add MS 76300, fol. 552.
33. BL Add MS 76300, fols. 850–851 (Payne & Mackinlay, 12 May 1804).
34. BL Add MS 76300, fols. 853–855.
35. Charles Spencer, *The Spencer Family* (London: Viking, 1999), 171.
36. Spencer, *The Spencer Family*, 170.
37. Charles Spencer, *Althorp: The Story of an English House* (London: Viking, 1998), 60–69; Sir Denis le Marchant, *Memoir of John Charles, Viscount Althop, Third Earl Spencer* (London: Richard Bentley and Son, 1876), 83–84.
38. BL Add MS 76301, fols. 981–1401.
39. *Bibliotheca Brandiana: A Catalogue of the Unique, Scarce, Rare, Curious, and Numerous Collection of Works... Being the Entire Library of the Late Rev. John Brand... Which Will be Sold by Auction... By Mr. Stewart... on Wednesday, May 6, 1807, and Thirty-Six Following Days...* (s.l.: s.n., 1807), 332, lot 8296. I have used the priced copy at Harvard B1609.9. Spencer paid by a draft on Hoare's, 25 June 1807 (BL Add MS 76301, fol. 1032).
40. BL Add MS 76301, fol. 1041.

CHAPTER II

1. Thomas Frognall Dibdin, *Bibliomania; or Book Madness: A Bibliographical Romance, in Six Parts* (London: Printed for the Author, 1811), 4–5.
2. Dibdin, *Bibliomania*, 650–651.
3. Rylands Library MS 71, Spencer-Dibdin, 9 September 1802.
4. The book in question was the *Abbreviamentum statutorum* (London: Lettou and Machlinia, *c.* 1482), now Rylands 15394.1.
5. BL Add MS 76008, Dibdin-Spencer, 17 November 1810.
6. John Rylands Library MS 71, Spencer-Dibdin, 17 November 1810.
7. John Rylands Library MS 71, Spencer-Dibdin, 10 December 1810.
8. BL Add MS 76008, Dibdin-Spencer, undated but docketed as received 27 July 1811.
9. BL Add MS 76008, Dibdin-Spencer, 1 October 1811.
10. BL Add MS 7008, Dibdin-Spencer, 28 October 1811.
11. Rylands MS 71, Spencer-Dibdin, 3 November 1811.
12. BL Add MS 7008, Dibdin-Spencer, 6 November 1811.
13. *Letters from Sarah, Lady Lyttleton, 1797–1870* (London: Spottiswoode & Co., 1873), 92.
14. *Complete Peerage*, xi. 224–227.
15. *A Catalogue of the Library of the Late John Duke of Roxburghe, Arranged by G. and W. Nicol... Which will be Sold by Auction... by Robert H. Evans, Bookseller, Pall-Mall...* (London: Printed by W. Bulmer and Co., 1812). For prices and buyers I have used the annotated copy at Bodleian Mus. Bibl. III. 8°. 675.
16. From Gillray's engraving of 1803 and the more flattering, but probably less accurate, mezzotint of William Whiston Barney after Richard Cosway (1803–1808), both National Portrait Gallery.
17. From the pen and ink portrait by John Harris (*c.* 1830), National Portrait Gallery. Heber seems to have looked much the same throughout his adult life.
18. Arnold Hunt, "A Study in Bibliomania: Charles Henry Hartshorne and Richard Heber", *The Book Collector* 42 (1993): 25–43, 185–212.
19. From the portrait by John Hoppner, Salford Museum & Art Gallery.

20. Boyd Alexander, *England's Wealthiest Son: William Beckford* (London: Centaur Press, 1962).
21. Thomas Frognall Dibdin, *The Bibliographical Decameron*, 3 vols. (London, 1817), iii. 52.
22. Dibdin, *Bibliographical Decameron*, iii. 53–54.
23. See Lotte Hellinga, *William Caxton and Early Printing in England* (London: British Library, 2010) and the partially outdated but still important William Blades, *The Life and Typography of William Caxton, England's First Printer*, 2 vols. (London: Published by Joseph Lilly, 1861–1863).
24. Dibdin, *Bibliographical Decameron*, iii. 55.
25. Dibdin, *Bibliographical Decameron*, iii. 68–69.
26. Dibdin, *Bibliographical Decameron*, iii. 60.
27. *White Knights Library: Catalogue of that Distinguished and Celebrated Library*... (London, 1819), no. 3799. This is *A Catalogue of the Library of the Late John Duke of Roxburghe... Which will be Sold by Auction*... (London, 1812), Bodleian Mus. Bibl. III. 8° 675. It is now in the Pierpont Morgan Library, MS M. 16.
28. *Roxburghe Sale Catalogue*, no. 6377 (it reappears in the *White Knights Catalogue*, no. 1726).
29. Dibdin (*Bibliographical Decameron*, iii. 64) particularly remarks on the poor weather and the consequent darkness of the auction room.
30. For a postboy reading the *Decameron*, see Thomas Frognall Dibdin, *A Bibliographical, Antiquarian, and Picturesque Tour in France and Germany*, 3 vols. (London, 1821), i. 139.
31. Dibdin, *Bibliographical Decameron*, iii. 62.
32. *Roxburghe Sale Catalogue*, 173.
33. Thomas Frognall Dibdin, *Bibliotheca Spenceriana*, 4 vols. (London, 1814–15), iv. 73.
34. Dibdin, *Bibliographical Decameron*, iii. 63.
35. Dibdin, *Bibliographical Decameron*, iii. 64.
36. For the course of the bidding I have followed the circumstantial account given in Dibdin, *Bibliographical Decameron*, iii. 64–67.
37. This modern sum is calculated as a factor of the change in income value between 1812 and the present, but see the "Note on Prices".
38. Dibdin, *Bibliographical Decameron*, iii. 69–70.
39. Rylands 15003.1 (*Liber festivalis*) and 15004 (*Chastysing*). For an introduction to de Worde, see Norman F. Blake, "Wynkyn de Worde: A Review of His Life and Work", in *Études de linguistique et de la littérature en l'honneur d'André Crépin*, ed. Danielle Buschinger and Wolfgang Spiewok (Greifswald: Reineke Verlag, 1993), 21–40.
40. *Roxburghe Catalogue*, lot 6360.
41. Rylands 15027; *Bibliotheca Spenceriana*, iv. 270–280; ISTC ib00690400; GW 4402.
42. *ODNB*, s.n.
43. Pynson, a Norman immigrant, had set up shop in London by 1502 and pursued a highly successful career as the principal London printer until his death in 1529/30. See *ODNB*, s.n. and Pamela Ayers Neville, *Richard Pynson, King's Printer (1506–1529): Printing and Propaganda in Early Tudor England* (Warburg Institute, University of London PhD Thesis, 1990).
44. Thomas Frognall Dibdin, *Reminiscences of a Literary Life*, 2 vols. (London: John Major, 1836), i. 488. The original of this letter is not to be found in John Rylands MS 71.
45. See De Ricci, *Census of Caxtons*, 1 (*Game of Chess*), 73 (History of Jason), 88 (Reynard the Fox).

46. BL Add MS 75008, Dibdin-Spencer, 19 September 1813.
47. In 1935 the promissory note and other ephemera were contained in a copy of the *Nosegay* belonging to Colonel C. H. Grey of Cranbrook, Kent, which was then examined by W. A. Jackson but is now untraced. See William Alexander Jackson, "The 'Lincoln Nosegay' Books", in *Records of a Bibliographer: Selected Papers of William Alexander Jackson* (Cambridge, Mass.: The Belknap Press of Harvard University Press, 1967), 149–155 at 150.
48. John Rylands Library MS 71, Spencer-Dibdin, 31 August 1814.
49. Thomas Frognall Dibdin, *Here begyneth a littel tome and hathe to name the Lincolne Nosegay* [London: Printed by W. Bulmer, 1814], 5. Now John Rylands 17316.1–2.
50. Beriah Botfield, *Notes on the Cathedral Libraries of England* (London: William Pickering, 1849), 272.
51. Botfield, *Notes*, 280.
52. Botfield, *Notes*, 281–282.

CHAPTER 12

1. C. E. Challis, ed., *A New History of the Royal Mint* (Cambridge: Cambridge University Press, 1992), 409 and *passim*; Henry Field, *Memoirs of the Botanic Garden at Chelsea*... (London: Printed by Gilbert and Rivington, 1878), 76, 88, 95. For his connection to the Stanesby family of instrument makers, see Eric Halfpenny, "Further Light on the Stanesby Family", *Galpin Society Journal* 13 (1960): 59–69.
2. National Archives PROB 11/1350/272, fol. 322v–323r.
3. Thomas Frognall Dibdin, *The Bibliographical Decameron*, 3 vols. (London, 1817), iii. 83.
4. *ODNB*, *sub* Thomas Johnes; Seymour De Ricci, *English Collectors of Books & Manuscripts (1530–1930) and Their Marks of Ownership* (Cambridge: At the University Press, 1930), 74.
5. R. J. Moore-Colyer, "Thomas Johnes of Hafod (1748–1816): Translator and Bibliophile", *Welsh History Review* 15 (1990): 399–415; James A. Dearden, "Thomas Johnes and the Hafod Press, 1803–10", *The Book Collector* (Autumn 1973): 315–336; Robert J. Gemmett, "'The Old Palace of Tertian Fevers': The Fonthill Sale of 1807", *Journal of the History of Collections* 22 (2010): 223–234.
6. Dibdin, *Bibliographical Decameron*, iii. 83.
7. BL Add MS 76008, Dibdin-Spencer, 23 January 1813.
8. BL Add MS 76008, Dibdin-Spencer, 26 January 1813.
9. Quoted in BL Add MS 76008, Dibdin-Spencer, 30 January 1813.
10. BL Add MS 76008, Dibdin-Spencer, 30 January 1813.
11. BL Add MS 76008, Dibdin-Spencer, "Wednesday" [3 February 1813] and 9 February 1813.
12. Dibdin's postscript reads, "The matter now, I presume, requires no concealment—at least, from those in your Lordship's family" (BL Add MS 76008, Dibdin-Spencer, "Wednesday" [3 February 1813]).
13. Dibdin, *Bibliographical Decameron*, iii. 84.
14. Dibdin, *Bibliographical Decameron*, iii. 84.
15. BL Add MS 76008, Dibdin-Spencer, 9 February 1813.
16. *Bibliotheca Stanleiana: A Splendid Selection of Rare and Fine Books, From the Distinguished Library of Colonel Stanley... Sold by Auction by R. H. Evans... On Friday the 30th of April, and Seven Following Days* (s.l.: s.n., 1813). I have referred to the priced copy at Houghton Library B 1682.13.2. See also Dibdin, *Bibliographical Decameron*, iii. 78–82.

17. *Bibliotheca Stanleiana*, 30, item 479.
18. *Catalogue of a Portion of the Valuable Library of the Late Stanesby Alchorne, Esq.... Sold by Auction, on Saturday the 22nd of May, by R. H. Evans...* (s.l.: s.n., 1813).
19. De Ricci, *English Collectors*, 74; Dibdin, *Bibliographical Decameron*, iii. 86–88.
20. Dibdin, *Bibliographical Decameron*, iii. 88.
21. Rylands 15388; *Bibliotheca Spenceriana*, iv. 310–312; ISTC ib00813000; GW 4576.
22. De Ricci, *Census*, 11–14, reported thirty-one copies or fragments of copies; it was no *Blanchardyn and Eglantyne*.
23. Rylands 15412; ESTC S106627.
24. Thomas Frognall Dibdin, *Reminiscences of a Literary Life*, 2 vols. (London: John Major, 1836), 484, 493; Rylands MS 71, Spencer-Dibdin, 5 August 1812.
25. BL Add MS 76008, Dibdin-Spencer, 22 November 1813.
26. Dibdin, *Reminiscences*, 527–528.
27. BL Add MS 76009, Dibdin-Spencer, 16 June 1815.
28. BL Add MS 76009, Dibdin-Spencer, 11 November 1815.
29. Rylands MS 71, Spencer-Dibdin, 10 December 1815.
30. BL Add MS 76009, Dibdin-Spencer, 8 September 1817.
31. BL Add MS 76009, Dibdin-Spencer, 5 December 1817. The text of the prospectus is reprinted in Dibdin, *Reminiscences*, 568–569.
32. Dibdin, *Reminiscences*, 586.
33. Dibdin, *Reminiscences*, 589–592.
34. BL Add MS 76011, Dibdin-Spencer, 28 August 1825.
35. BL Add MS 76010, Dibdin-Spencer, 11 December 1821.
36. BL Add MS 76010, Spencer-Dibdin, 13 December 1821.
37. BL Add MS 76011, Spencer-Dibdin, 10 May 1823.
38. Thomas Frognall Dibdin, *A Descriptive Catalogue of the Books Printed in the Fifteenth Century, Lately Forming Part of the Library of the Duke di Cassano Serra, and Now the Property of George John Earl Spencer* (London: Printed for the Author by William Nicol, 1823), x.
39. Rylands MS 74.

CHAPTER 13

1. BL Add MS 75965, Horn-Spencer, 4 August 1815.
2. BL Add MS 76007, Della Lena-Spencer, 25 March 1817.
3. Rylands 18022.1; Thomas Frognall Dibdin, *Aedes Althorpianae; or an Account of the Mansion, Books, and Pictures at Althorp; the Residence of George John Earl Spencer, K.G.*, 2 vols. (London: Printed by W. Nicol, 1822), ii. 279.
4. BL Add MS 76006, d'Elci-Spencer, 7 June 1818.
5. Ida Giovanna Rao, "Per la biografia di Angelo Maria d'Elci", *Archivisio Storico Italiano* 149 (1991): 375–449 at 416; *Catalogo dei Libri dal Conte Angiolo Maria d'Elci donati alla Imperiale e Real Libreria Mediceo-Laurenziana* (Florence: Tipografia All'Insegna di Dante, 1826).
6. Rylands 15370, degli Alessandri-Spencer, 6 April 1827, tipped in before the half-title.
7. Ludwig Albert, Freiherr von Gumppenberg, *Geschichte der Familie von Gumppenberg* (Würzburg: Druch von Friedrich Ernst Thein, 1856), 438.
8. Claus Oberhauser et al., *Diplomatie aus dem Untergrund: Die merkwürdige Karriere des Alexander (Maurus) Horn(e) (1762–1820)* (Vienna: Böhlau Verlag, 2022), 129–130, 267.

9. Oberhauser, 275–276.
10. Freiherr von Gumppenberg, *Geschichte,* 476. It is amusing to note that in the pompous official history of the family, Horn has been elevated to the nobility as "Freiherrn von Horn" (*ibid.*, 476).
11. BL Add MS 75965, Horn-Spencer, 20 June 1816.
12. BL Add MS 75965, Horn-Spencer, 20 June 1816.
13. BL Add MS 75965, Horn-Spencer, 20 June 1816.
14. Spencer's annotation to BL Add MS 75965, Horn-Spencer, 20 June 1816.
15. BL Add MS 75965, Horn-Spencer, 14 July 1816.
16. BL Add MS 75965, Horn-Spencer, 3 November 1816.
17. BL Add MS 75965, Horn-Spencer, 14 July 1816.
18. Rylands 17251; *Aedes Althorpianae*, ii. 273–278; ISTC it00534800; GW M48257.
19. Klaus Walter Littger, "Die Säkularisation der Eichstätter Bibliotheken", *Sammelblatt des Historischen Vereins Eichstätt* 87 (1994): 149–165.
20. BL Add MS 75965, Horn-Ocheda, 25 March 1819.
21. Oberhauser, *Horn(e)*, 245–246.
22. Mark Dilworth, "Two Necrologies of Scottish Benedictine Abbeys in Germany", *Innes Review* 9 (1958): 190.
23. *ODNB*, s.n.
24. Antoine-Claude Valery, *Voyages historiques et littéraires en Italie*, 3 vols. (Paris: Chez Le Normant, 1832), iii. 62–63.
25. *Letters from Sarah, Lady Lyttleton, 1797–1870* (London: Spottiswoode & Co., 1873), facing 93.
26. Thomas Frognall Dibdin, *Reminiscences of a Literary Life*, 2 vols. (London: John Major, 1836), ii. 593.
27. Valery, *Voyages*, ii. 62–63.
28. BL Add MS 76010, Dibdin-Spencer, 22 October 1818.
29. BL Add MS 76010, Dibdin-Spencer, Brighton, 3 November 1818.
30. *A Catalogue of the Valuable Library of James Edwards, Esq., Containing a Splendid Assemblage of Early Printed Books, Chiefly upon Vellum... which will be sold by auction, on Wednesday April 5, 1815 and the Five Following Days...* (London: Printed by W. Bulmer and Co., 1815), 44–45, lot 830. I have referred to the priced copy in the Getty Research Institute Library 1815 April 5 LoEvE. According to the description given there, Edwards had purchased it from the Duchess of Portland in 1786 (she had inherited it from her father, the great eighteenth-century collector Edward Harley, Earl of Oxford).
31. Mary Soames, *The Profligate Duke: George Spencer-Churchill, Fifth Duke of Marlborough, and His Duchess* (London: Collins, 1987), 148.
32. Soames, *Profligate Duke*, 157.
33. Soames, *Profligate Duke*, 162–166.
34. *White Knights Library: Catalogue of that Distinguished and Celebrated Library...* (London: Printed by W. Bulmer and Co. Cleveland-row, St. James's, 1819), lot 4012. I have referred to the priced copy at Pennsylvania State University Library 018.2 M344w.
35. *White Knights Library*, lot 3752.
36. *White Knights Libary*, lot 765.
37. Rylands 17659; Dibdin, *Bibliotheca Spenceriana*, iv. 75–80; ISTC ib00725300; GW 4441.

CHAPTER 14

1. BL Add MS 76009, Dibdin-Spencer, Caen, 12 May 1818.
2. BL Add MS 76009, Dibdin-Spencer, 21 and 26 April 1817; *Bibliotheca Rosicrusiana: A Catalogue of the Library of an Eminent Bibliographer... Sold by Auction, by Mr. Evans, at his house, no. 26, Pall-Mall, on Thursday, June 26, and Two Following Day* (s.l.: s.n., 1817).
3. Eventually published as Dibdin, *A Bibliographical, Antiquarian, and Picturesque Tour in France and Germany*, 3 vols. (London: Printed for the Author, by W. Bulmer and W. Nicol, Shakespeare Press, 1821). Here I quote from the second, expanded edition (London: Published by Robert Jennings, and John Major, 1829).
4. Thomas Frognall Dibdin, *Reminiscences of a Literary Life*, 2 vols. (London: John Major, 1836), ii. 653.
5. *ODNB*, s.n.
6. Dibdin, *Reminiscences*, ii. 654–660.
7. BL Add MS 76009, Dibdin-Spencer, Paris, 11 June 1818.
8. Ryland 9116; *Bibliotheca Spenceriana*, ii. 459–462; it appears in a long bill from Edwards for purchases made between May 1796 and December 1798, now BL Add MS 76300, fols. 582–585 (the Virgil being at 584).
9. British Library C.6.c.3; Bibliotheca Medicea Laurenziana D'Elci 470; Glasgow UL Hunterian Be.2.7.
10. Dibdin, *Tour*, iii. 18.
11. Dibdin, *Tour*, iii. 18–19.
12. Dibdin, *Tour*, iii. 16; BL Add MS 760010, Dibdin-Spencer, Stuttgart, 3 August 1818.
13. BL Add MS 760010, Dibdin-Spencer, Stuttgart, 3 August 1818.
14. Dibdin, *Tour*, iii. 19.
15. The sum in pounds is given by Dibdin at BL Add MS 760010, Dibdin-Spencer, Stuttgart, 3 August 1818.
16. Dibdin, *Tour*, iii. 17.
17. For the whole of this account I have drawn both on Dibdin's early, and probably more reliable narrative, contained in BL Add MS 760010, Dibdin-Spencer, Stuttgart, 3 August 1818, and the more florid and expanded account at Dibdin, *Tour*, iii. 45–49.
18. Dibdin, *Tour*, iii. 49.
19. BL Add MS 760010, Dibdin-Spencer, Stuttgart, 3 August 1818; Dibdin, *Tour*, iii. 49.
20. BL Add MS 760010, Dibdin-Spencer, Vienna, 2 September 1818.
21. BL Add MS 760010, Dibdin-Spencer, Vienna, 2 September 1818.
22. BL Add MS 760010, Dibdin-Spencer, Nuremberg, 28 September 1818.
23. BL Add MS 760010, Dibdin-Spencer, Mannheim, 7 October 1818.
24. Dibdin, *Tour*, iii. 50.
25. This account is primarily from BL Add MS 760010, Dibdin-Spencer, Mannheim, 7 October 1818, with additional input from the printed version at Dibdin, *Tour*, iii. 50.
26. Dibdin, *Tour*, iii. 50.
27. BL Add MS 75964, Horn-Spencer, 9 July 1798.
28. BL Add MS 75965, Horn-Spencer, 22 October 1802 and 18 April 1803.
29. Dibdin, *Tour*, iii. 151.
30. Bettina Wagner, "'Duplum Bibliothecae regiae Monacensis': The Munich Court Library and Its Book Auctions in the Nineteenth Century", *Papers of the Bibliographical Society of America* 111 (2017): 345–377 at 354–355.

31. The account here is drawn largely from BL Add MS 760010, Dibdin-Spencer, Munich, 14 August 1818, with some input from Dibdin, *Tour*, iii. 149–153.
32. Dibdin, *Tour*, iii. 152.
33. Rylands 19202; *Aedes Althorpianae*, ii. 307–308; ISTC ih00391000; GW 13396.
34. Thomas Frognall Dibdin, *Aedes Althorpianae; or an Account of the Mansion, Books, and Pictures at Althorp; the Residence of George John Earl Spencer, K.G.*, 2 vols. (London: Printed by W. Nicol, 1822), ii. 308.
35. *Allgemeine Deutsche Biographie*, 56 vols. (Leipzig: Verlag von Duncker & Humblot, 1875–1912), viii. 377.
36. This account derives from Dibdin, *Tour*, iii. 196–201.
37. BL Add MS 760010, Dibdin-Spencer, Vienna, 12 September 1818.
38. A list in Father Gärtner's neat hand is enclosed in BL Add MS 760010, Dibdin-Spencer, Vienna, 12 September 1818.
39. See Piero Scapecchi, "Reissinger, Sixtus", *Dizionario Biografico degli Italiani*, https://www.treccani.it/enciclopedia/sisto-reissinger_(Dizionario-Biografico)/, and Mariano Fava and Giovanni Bresciano, *La stampa a Napoli nel XV secolo* (Leipzig: R. Haupt, 1911–1913), i. 10–27, ii. 1–36.
40. Rylands 17761; *Aedes Althorpianae*, ii. 166; ISTC il00084000; GW M17204.
41. BL Add MS 760010, Dibdin-Spencer, Vienna, 12 September 1818.
42. Dibdin, *Tour*, iii. 394–400.
43. Dibdin, *Tour*, iii. 399–400.
44. Dibdin, *Tour*, iii. 398.
45. Vinzenz Oskar Ludwig, *Die Klosterneuburger Inkunabeln* (Vienna: W. Braumüller, 1920); https://www.stift-klosterneuburg.at/en/monastery-and-order/vocations/science/library/.
46. BL Add MS 76010, Dibdin-Spencer, Brighton, 3 November 1818.

CHAPTER 15

1. For Arnaldus, see Mariano Fava and Giovanni Bresciano, *La stampa a Napoli nel XV secolo* (Leipzig: R. Haupt, 1911–1913), i.47–56, and Bernard Stenuit, "Éditions incunables d'Horace: Arnold de Bruxelles et la princeps", *Les Études Classiques* 78 (2010): 231–240.
2. See the bill for books purchased in Vienna, dated 22 August 1794, which includes the first two volumes of the *Annales*, BL Add MS 76299, fol. 388.
3. Georg Wolfgang Panzer, *Annales typographici ab artis inventae origine ad annvm MD*, 11 vols. (Nuremberg: Impensis Joannis Eberhardi Zeh, Bibliopolae, 1793–1797), ii. 155.
4. BL Add MS 75964, Horn-Spencer, 11 May 1801.
5. BL Add MS 75964, Horn-Spencer, 6 July 1801.
6. BL Add MS 75965, Horn-Spencer, 15 July 1802.
7. Luca Covino, "Serra di Cassano, Luigi", *Dizionario Biografico degli Italiani*, https://www.treccani.it/enciclopedia/serra-di-cassano-luigi_%28Dizionario-Biografico%29/and Vincenzo Trombetta, *Storia e cultura delle biblioteche Napoletane: Librerie private, istituzioni francesi e borboniche, strutture postunitarie* (Naples: Vivarium, 2002), 262–267.
8. Vincenzo Trombetta, "La politica delle soppressioni e le nuove biblioteche a Napoli tra illuminismo regalista e restaurazione (1676–1815)", in *How the Secularization of Religious Houses Transformed the Libraries of Europe, 16th–19th Centuries*, ed. Cristina Dondi, Dorit Raines, and Richard Sharpe (Turnhout: Brepols, 2022), 195–217.
9. Rylands 13826 (Diogenes Laertius), 18960 (Zacchia).

10. Rylands 19687.
11. Quoted in Vincenzo Trombetta, ed., *Collezionismo e bibliofilia a Napoli tra sette e ottocento: un ritratto epistolare* (Macerata: Biblohaus, 2020), 29.
12. Rylands 18321.
13. It does not appear in his printed library catalogue of 1807 but was certainly known to be in his hands by 1815. See *Catalogo dell'edizioni del sec. XV, esistenti nella biblioteca del Duca di Cassano Serra* (Naples: s.n., 1807).
14. BL Add MS 76010, Dibdin-Spencer, 24 February 1820.
15. BL Add MS 75965, Horn-Spencer, 12 March 1815.
16. BL Add MS 75965, Horn-Spencer, 29 April 1815.
17. BL Add MS 75965, Horn-Spencer, 20 June 1816.
18. Biblioteca nazionale Vittorio Emanuele III, Naples, S.Q.3. C 51.
19. BL Add MS 76006, d'Elci-Spencer, 8 December 1819.
20. BL Add MS 76010, Dibdin-Spencer, 10 January 1820. We may both note and (possibly) forgive Dibdin for combining the Riessinger Terence and Han Juvenal into a single, imaginary book here.
21. BL Add MS 41854, Spencer-Grenville, 18 January 1820, fol. 288r.
22. BL Add MS 76006, Dibdin-Spencer, 27 February 1820.
23. Trombetta, *Storia e cultura*, 264–265.
24. BL Add MS 76010, Dibdin-Spencer, 24 February 1820.
25. Trombetta, *Storia e cultura*, 265.
26. Following the exchange calculation of 604 grains or 6.04 *ducati* to one pound sterling dated January 1820 and given in P. Kelly, *The Universal Cambist and Commercial Instructor*, 2nd ed., 2 vols. (London: Printed for the Author, 1821), ii. 80.
27. The estimate comes from comparing *A catalogue of rare and valuable duplicates from the library of the Rt. Hon. Earl Spencer, K.G. : including a considerable portion of the library of the Duke di Cassano... which will be sold by auction, by Mr. Evans, at his house, no. 93, Pall-Mall, on Friday March 2, and four following days* ([London: R. H. Evans, 1821]), which contained 463 lots (I have used the priced copy at Bodleian Library Mus. Bibl. III. 8° 87*), with Thomas Frognall Dibdin, *A Descriptive Catalogue of the Books Printed in the Fifteenth Century, Lately Forming Part of the Library of the Duke di Cassano Serra, and Now the Property of George John Earl Spencer* (London: Printed for the Author by William Nicol, 1823) which contained—the exact number is muddied by Dibdin's disorganisation—slightly more than 185 items.
28. BL Add MS 76010, Dibdin-Spencer, 27 February 1820.
29. BL Add MS 41854, Spencer-Grenville, fols. 289–290.
30. "French Papers", *The Times*, Thursday, 6 April 1820.
31. BL Add MS 76010, Dibdin-Spencer, 21 April 1820. Appleyard's correspondence is at BL Add MSS 76000–76004 and documents his increasingly central role in administering Spencer's library during the earl's old age.
32. BL Add MS 76000, Appleyard-Spencer, 15 April 1820.
33. BL Add MS 76010, Dibdin-Spencer, 21 and 23 April 1820.
34. BL Add MS 76010, Dibdin-Spencer, 29 July 1820.
35. BL Add MS 76010, Dibdin-Spencer, 29 July 1820.
36. BL Add MS 76010, Dibdin-Spencer, 2 December 1820.
37. BL Add MS 76010, Dibdin-Spencer, 28 December 1820.
38. *Catalogue of rare and valuable duplicates*, advertisement.
39. *Catalogue of rare and valuable duplicates*, lot 48.

40. *Catalogue of rare and valuable duplicates,* lots 41 (1462 Bible), 211 (Ovid), and 331 (Virgil).
41. *Catalogue of rare and valuable duplicates,* lot 172.
42. *Catalogue of rare and valuable duplicates,* lots 117 (*Fasciculus temporum*), 168 (Juvenal), 237 (Pliny).
43. Rylands 19045; *Cassano Serra Library*, 55; ISTC ih00439500; GW 13450.
44. *Cassano Serra Library*, 59.
45. Rylands 3190; *Cassano Serra Library*, 63–65; ISTC ij00625500; GW M15756.
46. *Catalogo*, 22.
47. *Cassano Serra Library*, 65.
48. Rylands 18028; *Cassano Serra Library*, 116–118; ISTC it00063800; GW M45431.
49. *Raccolta Ceramelli Papiani,* Archivio di Stato di Firenze, https://archiviodistatofirenze.cultura.gov.it/ceramellipapiani/index.php?page=Famiglia&id=3727.
50. Catherine Carey, "Modeling Collecting Behavior: The Role of Set Completion", *Journal of Economic Psychology* 29 (2008): 336–347.
51. Cassano Serra himself never got over the sale of his library and died, a broken man, in Naples on 21 October 1825 (see Covino, "Serra di Cassano, Luigi").

CHAPTER 16

1. *The Times*, Wednesday, 12 November 1834, which gives a quarter to three, but Appleyard, who was with him at his death, reported 2.25 p.m. (Thomas Frognall Dibdin, *Reminiscences of a Literary Life; With Anecdotes of Books, and of Book Collectors,* 2 vols. (London: John Major, 1836), i. 451).
2. "Earl Spencer, K.G.", *The Gentleman's Magazine* NS 3 (1835): 89–93 and 92–93.
3. "Capt. the Hon. Sir R. C. Spencer", *The Gentleman's Magazine* 101 (1831): 82–85. Captain Spencer was a promising naval officer and had died on shipboard near Alexandria of "an inflammation of the bowels". For Lavinia's death, see *Complete Peerage*, xii/1. 155.
4. *The Times,* Wednesday, 12 November 1834.
5. "No. XXIV. The Right Hon. George John Spencer, Earl Spencer", *Annual Biography and Obituary* 19 (1835): 298–307 at 305.
6. "Earl Spencer, K.G.", 92.
7. Dibdin, *Reminiscences*, i. 453.
8. BL Add MS 76013, Spencer-Dibdin, 20 March 1833 (draft).
9. *ODNB*, s.n.
10. For his various plans, see, for example, BL Add MS 76000, Appleyard-Spencer, 11 February 1820 and 18 September 1821. For the sheaf catalogues, see Larissa C. Brookes, *The Sheaf Catalogs of George John Spencer* (San José State University MLIS Thesis, 2009).
11. Rylands 23015.
12. "Earl Spencer, K.G.", 91.
13. *The Gentleman's Magazine* (1855): 445.
14. *ODNB*, s.n.
15. For Enriqueta Rylands, see Elizabeth C. Gow, *Enriqueta Rylands: The Public and Private Collecting of a Nonconformist Bibliophile, 1889–1908* (University of Manchester PhD Thesis, 2023).
16. *The Times*, 17 June 1892.
17. Gow, *Rylands*, 62–63.
18. "Earl Spencer, K.G.", 91.

19. For those, which I have given less attention to here, see especially the run of book bills in BL Add MS 76299–76301. Spencer regularly, one might with justification say obsessively, ordered new or recent books, often hundreds at a time, from the major London dealers.
20. This point has been made before by Kristian Jensen in his *Revolution and the Antiquarian Book: Reshaping the Past, 1780–1815* (Cambridge: Cambridge University Press, 2011) as well as in the volume edited by Cristina Dondi, Dorit Raines, and Richard Sharpe, *How the Secularization of Religious Houses Transformed the Libraries of Europe, 16th–19th Centuries*, ed. (Turnhout: Brepols, 2022).
21. Georg Wilhelm Zapf, *Ueber eine alte und höchst seltene Ausgabe von der Joannis de Turrecremata explanatio in psalterium und einige andere typographische Seltenheiten* (Nürnberg: im Verlag der Johann Leonhard Sixt Lechnerschen Buchhandlung, 1803), 10–11.
22. Heinrich Joachim Jäck, *Denkschrift für das Jubelfest der Buchdruckerkunst zu Bamberg: am 24. Juni 1840* (Erlangen: im Verlage von Ferdinand Enke, 1840), 53.
23. See their websites at https://stiftadmont.at/en/about-the-abbey-library/and https://www.stift-klosterneuburg.at/en/monastery-and-order/vocations/science/library/ for more details.
24. Seymour de Ricci gave the classic overview of these libraries and their fates in *English Collectors of Books & Manuscripts (1530–1930) and their Marks of Ownership* (Cambridge: At the University Press, 1930).
25. For the donation of Grenville's books to the British Library, see Karen Limper-Herz, *"A Monument of the Love of Letters": The Right Honourable Thomas Grenville and His Library* (University of London PhD Thesis, 2012).
26. The restitution debate is continually evolving (see https://www.returningheritage.com/ for recent updates) but is currently focused primarily either on acts of colonial violence against indigenous peoples or acts of ethnic and political violence committed by Europe's Fascist regimes. Restitution of Napoleonic-era looted artefacts remains a marginal area (with the Parthenon Marbles being the great exception). I have addressed some of these same problems in more compressed form in Kelsey Jackson Williams, "The Dispersal of Monastic Libraries in the Early Nineteenth Century: Buxheim and Karakallou", *Library and Information History* 40 (2024): 144–158.

Index

For the benefit of digital users, indexed terms that span two pages (e.g., 52–53) may, on occasion, appear on only one of those pages.